THE FOUR SEASONS COOKBOOK

 THE FOUR SEASONS

 Photography by Arie deZanger | Designed by Albert Squilla

COOKBOOK By Charlotte Adams | Special Consultant: James Beard

Ridge Press Book | Crescent Books | New York

Autumn

The Season 16

Appetizers 19 | Soups 26

Fish & Seafood 34

Chicken & Duck 42

Beef, Veal, Lamb & Pork 46 | Game 58

Vegetables 62 | Salads 65

Desserts 67

The Wines of Autumn by James Beard 79

Winter

The Season 83

Appetizers 84 | Soups 90

Fish & Seafood 97

Chicken & Duck 101

Beef, Veal, Lamb & Pork 105 | Game 120

Vegetables 124 | Salads 134

Desserts 135

The Wines of Winter by James Beard 143

Spring

The Season 147

Appetizers 148 | Soups 152

Fish & Seafood 159

Chicken & Pigeon 169

Beef, Veal & Lamb 174

Vegetables 192 | Salads 198

Desserts 200

The Wines of Spring by James Beard 205

Summer

The Season 209

Appetizers 210 | Soups 215

Fish & Seafood 223

Chicken & Duck 233

Beef, Veal & Lamb 237

Vegetables 247 | Salads 254

Desserts 258

The Wines of Summer by James Beard 271

Some Fundamentals

Wines for Cooking 274

Herbs & Spices 275 | Stocks 276

Soup Garnitures 279

Sauces 280 | Sweet Sauces 291

Pastries & Batters 292 | Dessert Basics 297

Basic Soufflés 300

Glossary of Cooking Terms 301

Equivalent Weights & Measures 305

Sources of Ingredients 306

Index 308

Foreword

This is a highly unusual cookbook for the reason that it reflects twelve years in the history of one of the truly fine restaurants ever to grace the city of New York. Furthermore, the recipes are the work of a rare assemblage of chefs. The home cook is fortunate to have these specialties brought within reach. Like the restaurant's menu, the recipes are based on the changes of the seasons and on the idea that certain foods are best enjoyed in their own time. Each recipe has had ample testing over the years, both in the restaurant kitchen and before the public. Each has proved to be workable and good, and has been in continuous demand. This collection, then, represents the most popular and the best of The Four Seasons' offerings. Some of the recipes are variations on classic themes; many are originals. They include easy recipes and those requiring patience and skill to achieve perfect results. All of them have been reduced to proportions and techniques suitable for the home kitchen. Once they are mastered, you can turn them out with the same flair for which The Four Seasons is noted.

This handsome restaurant, located in one of the city's finest contemporary buildings, began as the dream of one man—Joseph Baum—who wished to create a superlative eating place for New Yorkers. Such it has become. Although it has been called an American restaurant, a French restaurant, and even a Hungarian restaurant, it is basically without national ties. It embraces every nationality. Its cuisine owes allegiance only to the seasons and to the serving of food at its peak. As regular visitors to The Four Seasons know, the drama of the seasonal cycle is captured here not only in the change of menus, but also in the change of appointments, uniforms, plantings, and flowers.

It took immense organization to launch such a restaurant. Menus were planned for a year in advance of the opening by a team of food and cooking specialists joined, from time to time, by the writer. The discussions were lengthy and the ideas legion. Before the restaurant's kitchen was ready, testings and tastings took place in various kitchens around town. Since there were no national boundaries to consider, the repertory of recipes was virtually limitless. The cuisines of the world could be combed for the unusual and the homely, as well as for the classic and the lavish.

11

Meanwhile, prospecting began for sources of prime foods. A man was discovered in Oregon who raised tiny French carrots, because he had learned to like them in Europe, and as much of his crop as could be coaxed away from him was bought. Various vendors were signed up to supply an almost constant flow of wild mushrooms. The finest fruits were hunted down, and routine delivery of potted herbs was arranged.

The same care went into the selection of wines, which spanned the great vintages of the century. I doubt if any restaurant in this country or in Europe ever opened with as distinguished a wine list. In addition to the fine wines, there were small seasonal wines from many countries, and an astounding collection of brandies and white alcohols. For the first several years the restaurant was able to present a special seasonal wine list along with the current menu. The list is still quite impressive, although by now some of the very choice older wines have disappeared from the cellar, as they have from the world generally.

As the opening drew near, the pitch of activity heightened. The captains, together with all executive personnel, participated in classes to taste and evaluate every wine on the list, as well as the brandies and cognacs. Once the captains were equipped to discuss the wine list knowledgeably with patrons there was no need for sommeliers. The captains also were instructed in the art of table cookery, which has been a feature of The Four Seasons since its beginning. A specialist was engaged to teach the technique of omelette production. Each captain now has his own pan and performs the rite of the omelette at table for guests. Each is also expected to prepare dishes such as Crabmeat Casanova, a superb blending of crabmeat and seasonings; a version of Beef Stroganoff made in a few moments (as is the original recipe); and a glamorous combination of twin tournedos with chanterelles.

The opening of the restaurant finally arrived. The novelty of the pool dining room, the elegant simplicity of architect Philip Johnson's over-all design, the flowers, the appointments, the food, and the wine all made history. Since then The Four Seasons has become something of an institution for New Yorkers, and for visitors to the city, just as Joseph Baum dreamed it would.

Years of seasons have flowed by, and with each change the menu still is subjected to discussions and testings before it is offered to the public. Mainstays on the luncheon menu have been two great bourgeois dishes of France: Pot-au-Feu, consisting of beef, chicken, marrow bone, vegetables, and rich broth; and Poule-au-Pot, a simply poached chicken with vegetables. Both have been popular because of their honest flavors, and both are good choices for the home menu, since there is little or no last-minute preparation. Together with a good salad, cheese, and fruit, these make a perfect dinner or a Sunday lunch.

Those under the impression that The Four Seasons is too elaborate for people with plain tastes should note that it serves one of the most flavorful and most generous chopped steaks in New York, enhanced by a beautiful garnish of fresh vegetables. Other simple grilled meats are also stock items on the menu. The beef is specially chosen, and in spring the baby lamb provides a rare experience in good eating. Racks of lamb for two are eternally sought after, and so are the chops and steaks. My favorite steak is the entrecôte for two, a thick slice of the ribs cut and trimmed like a giant lamb chop. Also notable is the steak flavored at the last minute with Roquefort cheese and other seasonings, which give it piquancy and an exotic touch seldom found in such dishes. Grilled fish and other uncomplicated fish dishes have also abounded.

Lest we belabor simplicity, it must be confessed that The Four Seasons is also prepared to fly in choice items from France—ortolans, *poulet de Bresse, loup de mer* (a sea bass), sole, oysters, *haricots verts* —in addition to vegetables and fruits from other parts of the world.

One thing that has set the restaurant apart from others is its distinctive treatment of vegetables. It begins with the excellence of the vegetables themselves. The tenderest, the freshest, and the best have always found their way here. Each day patrons are invited to select their favorites from baskets of the market's choicest offerings, and the kitchen is banked with pressure cookers, so that the vegetables can be rushed from the basket to tables in a matter of minutes. Vegetables have been searched out that were never before served in a New York establishment—fiddlehead ferns, different types of greens, baby corn, and tiny eggplants—and they are prepared with endless inventiveness.

The pastry shop is another memorable part of The Four Seasons' history. Its first pâtissier set incredibly high standards. From this period date the first Four Seasons Fancy Cake and the first Chocolate Velvet, that delectable supermousse which combines eggs, butter, and chocolate to make the greatest chocolate dessert I have ever tasted.

When I think of desserts served at The Four Seasons I think of the enchanting tiny petit-fours concocted for certain dinners and, in season, the giant strawberries dipped in syrup to give them a crisp, transparent glaze, spectacular to look at and delicious to the bite. But I especially recall the sorbet that was chosen for a special dinner. Sorbet is best defined in English as water ice, and it is usually made with fruit flavors, although it can be done with liqueur and brandy flavorings, as well. The one created for this occasion was an extraordinary pineapple sorbet that was frozen at the last minute. It was made with chopped fresh pineapple and served in a firm but nicely pliable state. An overwhelming success, it initiated many subsequent servings of freshly made sorbet, perfumed in a variety of ways. This simple dessert is easily made at home, either in the freezer compartment of a refrigerator or in an ice-cream freezer.

The special dinners held at The Four Seasons make a separate chapter. A tough partridge ruined the first one, given for the *Commanderie de Bordeaux*, but this was forgotten in the parade of successes that followed, crowned by one of the annual dinners of another famed wine society, the *Confrérie du Tastevin*. The restaurant was closed to the public for the day. Planning had begun four to five months prior to that. The dinner featured processions carrying great *pièces montées* before each course. *Pièces montées* are the highly decorated, almost architectural "set pieces" of food, which became an art in the seventeenth and eighteenth centuries and are still produced on gala occasions. These *pièces* went beyond tradition. They were fantasies on the theme, built up to perhaps twenty times life size, using both real and constructed foods. Although none would have tasted much better than glue and sawdust, they were dramatic to the eye, which is exactly why they were created. The menu was fairly unostentatious as such affairs go. With the champagne at the reception wonderfully light cheese puffs were passed, along with a delicious blend of sturgeon and caviar, with a touch of cucumber, on black bread. The guests were ushered into the dining room and sat down to a rich turkey consommé that had cooked for five days—the result of reducing turkey after turkey after turkey until a pungent, savory, amber concentrate was produced, requiring no seasoning. Then great *loups de mer* were brought forth, each one stuffed with a mousse of the same fish, served with a delicate sauce. These were preceded by the presentation of a giant *loup* most elaborately fashioned on a stand about five feet high. Handsome pyramids of beef followed, made in a special mold and given a Burgundian garnish of tiny onions and mushrooms. Next came pâté of quail *en croute*. The dinner was finished off with a dessert of lusciously ripe pears, poached, shrouded in a thin coat of chocolate and imbedded in a rich cream. I am convinced this dinner could not have been matched anywhere for magnificence.

Since the beginning of the restaurant there has been, inevitably, a progression of chefs and directors who contributed much. Chef incumbent is Maurice Chantreau, who has brought to the restaurant imagination as well as technical skill. Among his creations offered here is a marrow soufflé in a rich crust, a truly remarkable dish.

The Four Seasons has been matured and refined over a number of years by the contributions of many people who valued its concept and have enriched it with their individual talents. Their common gift has been in bringing out the essential goodness of the ingredients they use. The person who cooks from this book can learn much from their achievements.

This collection offers hundreds of opportunities to plan interesting menus. For example, from the spring recipes you could assemble a delicious cream of wild asparagus soup, shad roe in lemon butter, a cucumber salad, some cheese, and perhaps a dessert of fresh strawberries in cassis. Whatever the menu, try to keep it simple, certainly within your scope as a cook, and choose dishes that will give you a sense of pleasure and achievement. Finally, if you want to bring some of the magic of The Four Seasons into your own kitchen, aim for good food, no matter what its origin or nationality, keep an eye out for the best produce in the market, and follow the round of the seasons.

James A. Beard

Autumn

Autumn is the season of hearty colors and tantalizing perfumes. The brilliant orange of pumpkins, the green of winter squash, the fiery red of peppers mingle with the yellows, purples, and browns to comprise the natural palette of harvest fruits and vegetables. Sometimes it seems that these vivid colors were created as a setting for the multihued plumage of game birds—the pheasants, quail, and partridge in grain fields and woodlots—not to mention the glinting, iridescent feathers of the ducks now found in ponds and marshlands along the traditional flyways of North America.

Complementing color is aroma which, in turn, is integral to taste. The aromatic fruits and vegetables of fall are metamorphosed: pears become preserves, cherries are ground into topping for winter desserts, apples are pressed for tangy cider or converted to jelly or sauce. Great pungent cabbages are slashed into sauerkraut, cucumbers are pickled, and meaty brown nuts—almonds, walnuts, filberts—are harvested.

And finally there is the gathering of the grape and the barrels of red or gold juice which come from the pressing. Here is the beginning of a subtle and sophisticated process by which the resulting wine will be able to retain color, aroma, taste, and the glorious sun itself, from infancy to the ripe years of maturity. —JB

Appetizers

Crabmeat Imperial

1½ POUNDS CRABMEAT
1 TABLESPOON BUTTER
2 TABLESPOONS DICED GREEN PEPPER
2 TABLESPOONS DICED SWEET
RED PEPPER/
1½ CUPS MAYONNAISE (SEE SAUCES)
SALT & PEPPER TO TASTE
DASH TABASCO
1½ CUPS SAUCE MOUSSELINE
(SEE SAUCES)/
6 TABLESPOONS FINE BREAD CRUMBS

This fine hot first course is served in coquille shells, which can be actual scallop shells, available in many gourmet shops, or oven-proof dishes made in the shape of scallop shells.

Pick over crabmeat and remove all bony tissue. Melt butter and sauté the green and red peppers in it until soft, but not brown (approximately 10 minutes over medium heat). Mix with crabmeat, mayonnaise, and seasonings. Spoon mixture into 6 coquille shells. Spread sauce mousseline over crabmeat in shells and sprinkle a tablespoon of bread crumbs over each. Run under the broiler, 5 inches from heat, until glazed and golden brown. Serves 6.
NOTE: This mixture may also be used to fill crêpes.

Four Seasons Ramekins of Snails

2 CELERY HEARTS
4 TABLESPOONS BUTTER
6 TABLESPOONS DRY SHERRY
36–48 LARGE CANNED SNAILS
1½ CUPS HEAVY CREAM
4 TABLESPOONS GLACE DE VIANDE
(SEE STOCKS)/
SALT & FRESHLY GROUND
BLACK PEPPER/

In France "ramekins" are pastry cases, but in the United States the word refers to small pottery baking dishes, and that is what is used here. We suggest that you use canned snails, because live ones are hard to find in our markets and a great nuisance to prepare.

Separate the stalks of the celery hearts, wash them thoroughly, and discard any leaves. Mince very fine. Sauté the celery in the butter over low heat until it is almost tender. Then increase the heat and add the sherry. Heat well and add snails, cream, and glace de viande. Season to taste with a little salt and freshly ground pepper. Mix well and cook all together for a few moments over high heat until the sauce thickens slightly. Serve very hot in small ramekins with French bread or toast. Serves 6.

Terrine of Hare with Pistachios

2½ POUNDS BONED HARE
½ POUND BONED PORK
1 POUND FATBACK
¾ TEASPOON JUNIPER BERRIES
¾ TEASPOON WHITE PEPPER
1 TABLESPOON SALT
1 TEASPOON QUATRE ÉPICES
(SEE GLOSSARY)/
1 EGG
¼ CUP COGNAC
2 TABLESPOONS SHELLED
PISTACHIO NUTS/
⅛-INCH-THICK SHEETS OF
FATBACK FOR LINING MOLD/

A terrine is an earthenware dish in which meat, game, or fish is cooked. Often the dish has a rabbit's head on top of the cover. By extension the term is used to describe the contents of the dish. Often, as in the following recipe, two or more meats are combined to make a terrine. The use of cognac is also typical—and the resulting dish is rich and delicious. It can be served as a first course at dinner, or with a salad for lunch, or with cocktails before a meal.

Grind twice, through the finest blade of meat grinder, half the hare, the pork, the pound of fatback, and the juniper berries. Chop the remainder of the hare into small dice. Place diced hare in the bowl of a mixer together with the ground mixture and the remaining ingredients, except the sliced fatback, and mix well on medium speed. Let stand in refrigerator for 48 hours. Line terrine or mold with fatback, letting a little hang over the edges. Fill to the top with the mixture, pressing down firmly. Fold edges of fat in and place terrine in a pan of water in a 300-degree oven. Bake for 1½ hours. Cool and then chill for 24 hours and serve.

Chilled Stuffed Mussels

30 MUSSELS, CLEANED
½ CUP PINE NUTS
½ POUND BULGUR WHEAT
¼ POUND CURRANTS
1 POUND CHINESE CABBAGE
(BOK CHOY)/
¼ CUP CHOPPED GRAPE LEAVES
2 TABLESPOONS BUTTER
¼ CUP LEMON JUICE
¼ CUP HONEY

Clean the mussels well (see below). Steam in a little water, covered, until they open (about 10 minutes). Discard those which stay closed. Drain and cool. Soak pine nuts, wheat, and currants in hot water about 1 hour. Chop the cabbage and sauté in butter with the grape leaves for 10 minutes. Drain the wheat mixture well and mix with lemon juice, honey, spices, salt, and pepper. Let stand for 20 minutes and strain off any excess liquid. Remove mussels from shells. Put a bit of stuffing into one side of a shell, then a mussel, then more stuffing and top with the second side of

½ TEASPOON GROUND CLOVES
½ TEASPOON CINNAMON
PINCH OF CAYENNE
¼ TEASPOON SALT
¼ TEASPOON PEPPER

the shell. Serves 6.

NOTE: Mussels are likely to be exceedingly sandy and to require long and careful cleaning. This is a nuisance, but well worth the trouble. First, they should be picked over, and any which are open or which are very light in weight should be discarded. Scrub the rest with a stiff brush or with steel wool to remove all surface dirt. With a small sharp knife remove the "beard" which sticks out from between the two shells. Now soak the mussels in cold water for an hour, during which time they will give off at least some of the sand inside their shells. One more scrubbing in clean water will rid them almost entirely of the remaining sand. Because of their sandiness, all juices and sauces from cooking mussels are usually strained through cheesecloth.

Galantine of Pheasant

1 4-POUND PHEASANT
½ POUND FATBACK
½ POUND LEAN VEAL
½ POUND LEAN PORK
2 TABLESPOONS QUATRE ÉPICES
(SEE GLOSSARY)/
¼ CUP COGNAC
SALT & PEPPER TO TASTE
2 EGGS, BEATEN LIGHTLY
3 OUNCES BLACK TRUFFLES, SLICED
3 QUARTS CHICKEN STOCK
(SEE STOCKS)/

A galantine is a classic French dish made from boned poultry, meat, or fish. The word probably comes from *geline,* or *galine,* which in old French meant chicken, since the dish was originally made only with poultry.

Bone the pheasant (or have your butcher do it). Skin it in one flat piece, being very careful not to break the skin. Save the skin. Cut breast in small dice. Cut ⅓ of the fatback, ⅓ of the veal, and ⅓ of the pork in dice. Grind the rest of the fatback, veal, pork, and pheasant meat fine. Mix with the diced meat. Add quatre épices, cognac, salt, and pepper. Add eggs and mix well. Let stand for 2 hours in the refrigerator. Spread the pheasant skin, outside down, on cheesecloth. Spread on it half of the stuffing. Arrange the truffle slices down the middle. Spread the rest of the stuffing on top. Draw the edges of the skin together to form a sausage-like roll. Roll the galantine up in the cheesecloth. Tie it with string at both ends and in the middle. Poach the galantine in the chicken stock for 1½ hours. Cool in the cooking liquid. Remove the galantine and squeeze it between two towels to remove the extra liquid. The following day, slice the galantine and decorate platter with chopped Port Aspic (see Stocks). Serves 6.

Steak Tartare Canapés with Caviar

2 POUNDS FRESHLY GROUND OR
SCRAPED TOP ROUND/
4 TABLESPOONS CHOPPED CHIVES
SALT & FRESHLY GROUND BLACK
PEPPER TO TASTE/
4 RAW EGG YOLKS
40 1½-INCH BUTTERED
PUMPERNICKEL ROUNDS (A
1-POUND LOAF THINLY SLICED)/
4 OUNCES BLACK CAVIAR

Mix meat, chives, salt and pepper, and egg yolks. Mound on bread rounds. Top with caviar. Serve immediately. NOTE: An explanation of how to scrape steak can be found under Steak Tartare.

Smoked Native Trout, Lemon Mayonnaise

¼ CUP MAYONNAISE (SEE SAUCES)
½ TEASPOON DRY MUSTARD
2 TEASPOONS STEAK SAUCE
4 TABLESPOONS BROWN SAUCE
(SEE SAUCES)/
2 TEASPOONS LEMON JUICE
½ TEASPOON WHITE PEPPER
6 SMALL SMOKED TROUT
LEMON HALVES OR WEDGES

If you are lucky enough to have a trout fisherman in the family and a commercial smokehouse available to which he can take some of his catch, you can serve the best smoked trout in the world—and it is indeed an elegant thing to eat.

Mix mayonnaise, mustard, steak sauce, brown sauce, lemon juice, and white pepper. Divide this sauce into 6 small garnish dishes or clam shells. Place a dish of sauce and 1 trout on each of 6 serving plates. Serve with lemon halves or wedges. Serves 6.

Hot Mousse of Chicken Livers, Sauce Suprême

1 MEDIUM ONION, SLICED
2 TABLESPOONS BUTTER
5 SLICES WHITE BREAD
1½ CUPS HEAVY CREAM
1 POUND CHICKEN LIVERS
7 OUNCES FATBACK
SALT & PEPPER TO TASTE
FRESHLY GROUND NUTMEG TO TASTE
4 EGGS, SEPARATED
BUTTER
SAUCE SUPRÊME (SEE SAUCES)

This makes a rich first course, and if you serve it as such the rest of the menu should be simple and preferably without sauces.

Sauté the onion in the butter until soft. Mix the bread with ½ cup of the cream. Grind finely the onion, bread, chicken livers, and fatback. Add salt, pepper, and nutmeg. Place mixture in a mixing bowl sitting in a bowl of cracked ice. Add the egg yolks and the remaining cream and mix well. Whip the egg whites stiff and fold into the mixture. Butter a 1-quart mold and pour in the mousse. Bake, in a pan of water, for 30 minutes in a 400-degree oven. Unmold and cover with sauce suprême. Serves 8.

Green Spinach Crêpes

1½ POUNDS FRESH SPINACH, COOKED & DRAINED/
1 RECIPE CRÊPE BATTER (SEE PASTRIES & BATTERS)/
½ POUND MUSHROOMS
2 TABLESPOONS BUTTER
½ TEASPOON SALT
FRESHLY GROUND PEPPER TO TASTE
DASH CAYENNE
HEAVY CREAM
PARMESAN CHEESE

It is amusing to note that this dish was invented through a misunderstanding with our test chef. We had been discussing spinach crêpes, which meant to us crêpes stuffed with spinach and other good ingredients, and he volunteered to make some. The next day there appeared at our daily testing some handsome green crêpes, not stuffed at all. He had put the spinach *into* the crêpe batter, and when we proceeded to stuff them with what we'd had in mind, we had an even better-tasting and certainly better-looking dish than any spinach crêpe we'd known before.

Chop spinach finely. Squeeze juice of about ⅓ of the spinach into crêpe batter and mix well. Cook crêpes according to recipe. Peel mushrooms and chop fine, including stems. Sauté in the butter 5 minutes. Combine with remaining spinach. Season. Add just enough cream to bind ingredients together. Spread this mixture on ⅓ of each crêpe and roll up. Place in greased gratin dish, side by side, seam side down. Sprinkle lightly with grated Parmesan cheese. Run under broiler to brown lightly. Serves 6.

Quiche aux Endives

6 HEADS BELGIAN ENDIVE
2½ TABLESPOONS LEMON JUICE
¼ TEASPOON SALT
1 CUP BOILING WATER
RICH PASTRY FOR ONE-CRUST PIE
(SEE PASTRIES & BATTERS)/
6 SLICES BACON, FRIED
CRISP & CRUMBLED/
3 EGGS, WELL BEATEN
1 CUP LIGHT CREAM
1 CUP GRATED GRUYÈRE CHEESE
———————————————
PREHEAT OVEN TO 375 DEGREES

A quiche with a vegetable as its main ingredient is unusual and, in this instance, an inspiration. This quiche may be served as a first course or as a luncheon entrée.

Leave endives whole, cutting off the discolored part of roots or any brown spots on the outer leaves. Put in a saucepan, add lemon juice, salt, and boiling water. Simmer for 20 minutes. Drain thoroughly. Cut into ½-inch slices. Meantime, roll out pastry to fit an 8-inch pie pan. Flute edges. Put crumbled bacon on the bottom of the pie crust. Arrange endive in a layer on top of bacon. Blend eggs, cream, and grated cheese. Pour over endive. Bake in a 375-degree oven 35–40 minutes, or until filling is just set. Serve warm. Serves 6.

Lebanese Barquettes of Lamb

3 ONIONS, FINELY CHOPPED
½ CUP BUTTER
1 POUND FINELY CHOPPED
COOKED LAMB/
½ CUP WHITE RAISINS
¼ CUP DRIED CURRANTS
½ CUP PINE NUTS
2 TABLESPOONS TOMATO PASTE
2 CLOVES GARLIC, FINELY CHOPPED
½ CUP CHOPPED PARSLEY
12 BARQUETTES, SMALLEST SIZE
(SEE PASTRIES & BATTERS)/
4 TABLESPOONS CRISP FRIED ONIONS

This dish is an interesting combination of Middle Eastern and French cuisine (lamb and barquettes), plus an American touch (fried onions).

Sauté onions in butter until brown. Add lamb, raisins, currants, nuts, tomato paste, and garlic. Heat through. Add parsley at the very end and mix well. Put into barquettes. Sprinkle fried onions on top.
NOTE: This filling is also good for crêpes or rissoles (puffpastry turnovers).

Talmouse with Sweetbreads and Brains

½ POUND CALF BRAINS
½ POUND SWEETBREADS
1 TABLESPOON WHITE VINEGAR
2 TEASPOONS SALT
1 TABLESPOON LEMON JUICE
DASH SALT & FRESHLY GROUND PEPPER
1 TABLESPOON BUTTER
¼ CUP SAUCE BÉCHAMEL
(SEE SAUCES)/
½ RECIPE PUFF PASTRY
(SEE PASTRIES & BATTERS)/
PREHEAT OVEN TO 375 DEGREES

In our opinion, any hors d'oeuvre made with puff pastry is bound to be delicious—and certainly elegant. A talmouse is one of the earliest-known French appetizers and may be filled with anything that suits your fancy.

Wash brains and sweetbreads in cold water. Soak both in cold water for at least 30 minutes, then carefully remove membrane from brains. Place brains in a saucepan and cover with cold water. Add vinegar and 1 teaspoon of salt and cook slowly for 20 minutes. Cool in the cooking liquid. Trim the sweetbreads. Place in a saucepan and cover with cold water. Add 1 teaspoon salt and the lemon juice. Bring to a simmer and cook for 15 minutes. Place under cold running water to cool. When the brains and sweetbreads are cool, cut them into ¼-inch cubes. Sprinkle with salt and pepper. Melt butter and sauté brains and sweetbreads in it for 5 minutes. Add Béchamel and mix well. Roll out puff pastry 1/16-inch thick and cut it into 2-inch squares. Place a bit of the sauce mixture in the center of each square and bring the four points together over the filling. Put a very small piece of the pastry— square, strip, or round—on top to cover the points. Bake in a 375-degree oven 15 minutes. Makes about 48 talmouses.

Oyster and Mushroom Tartlets

¼ POUND MUSHROOM CAPS,
PEELED & SLICED THIN/
6 TABLESPOONS BUTTER
1 TABLESPOON FRESH LEMON JUICE
SALT & PEPPER TO TASTE
1½ CUPS HEAVY CREAM
18 LARGE OYSTERS
6 TART SHELLS OF RICH PASTRY

The cultivated mushrooms which we find in our markets most of the year are known to the French as *champignons de couche*. When shopping for them, select mushrooms that are smooth, unblemished, and fresh looking. The freshest are closed on the under side of the cap, so that you cannot see the gills. Fresh mushrooms will keep well for several days tightly sealed in a plastic bag in the refrigerator.

*Appetizers (clockwise around champagne, starting
at upper right): Terrine of Hare with Pistachios (page 20),
Steak Tartare Canapés with Caviar (page 22),
Lebanese Barquettes of Lamb (page 24), Talmouse with
Sweetbreads & Brains (page 25).*

(SEE PASTRIES & BATTERS)/
¼ CUP SAUCE BÉCHAMEL
(SEE SAUCES)/
¼ CUP SAUCE HOLLANDAISE
(SEE SAUCES)/

Sauté mushrooms in butter for 3 minutes. Add lemon juice and salt and pepper to taste. Add cream and cook until reduced by ⅔. Add oysters and cook for 2 minutes. With slotted spoon, remove oysters and mushrooms and divide evenly among the tart shells. Add Béchamel and Hollandaise to sauce remaining in the pan. Stir together and pour over oysters and mushrooms to fill up shells. Run under the broiler for a minute or two until glazed and lightly brown. Serves 6.

Eggs Maintenon

6 SLICES WHITE BREAD
6 TABLESPOONS BUTTER
¾ CUP SAUCE SOUBISE
(SEE SAUCES)/
6 POACHED EGGS, DRAINED
FRESHLY GRATED PARMESAN CHEESE

Sauté bread in butter on both sides, until golden brown. Spoon a little of the hot sauce Soubise over each slice. Put an egg on each slice and cover with remaining sauce. Sprinkle with Parmesan and glaze under the broiler for a minute. Serve for luncheon or brunch. Serves 6.

Soups

Apricot Soup with Sour Cream (Cold)

1 POUND DRIED APRICOTS
½ CUP DRY WHITE WINE
LEMON JUICE TO TASTE
1 CUP HEAVY CREAM
SOUR CREAM

This is a tart and, we think, delicious soup which would be excellent as the first course of a game dinner.

Soak apricots in warm water to cover for 1 hour. Whirl apricots in the blender with the water in which they soaked until puréed. Strain and add wine. Add lemon juice to taste and stir in cream. Chill. Serve with garnish of sour cream. Serves 6.

Caraway Squash Bisque (Cold)

1 SMALL ONION, SLICED
1 STALK CELERY, CHOPPED
1 CARROT, CHOPPED
¼ CUP BUTTER
2 YELLOW CROOK-NECKED SQUASH,
EACH ABOUT ¾ POUND/
1 MEDIUM POTATO
1½ QUARTS BEEF STOCK
(SEE STOCKS)/
2 TEASPOONS CARAWAY SEEDS
¾ CUP HEAVY CREAM
SALT & PEPPER TO TASTE

There are many people who love cold soup at any season of the year and this one is particularly appropriate to fall. It has a rather hearty base to which the beef stock adds distinct authority.

Sauté onion, celery, and carrot in butter until soft but not browned. Peel squash and potato. Cut into ½-inch dice. Add to stock, with sautéed vegetables and caraway seeds. Cook until squash is very tender, about ½ hour. Strain. Force vegetables through sieve into stock or whirl in the blender with the stock. Mix in cream and season. Chill. Serves 6.

Green Tomato Gazpacho

1 CLOVE GARLIC, PEELED
5 GREEN TOMATOES, PEELED
2 EGGS
¼ BUNCH WATERCRESS
3 SPRIGS PARSLEY
¼ CUP WINE VINEGAR
¾ CUP TOMATO JUICE
½ TEASPOON SALT
⅛ TEASPOON CAYENNE
2 SPRIGS TARRAGON
¼ CUP OLIVE OIL

At one of our tastings we were sampling a proper Spanish gazpacho, which is a lovely, cooling summer soup, and a perfect luncheon in itself. But somehow our test soup seemed a little flat, and while we were discussing how to improve it, Paul Kovi, director of The Four Seasons, suggested making a gazpacho with green tomatoes. This was done, and proved to be a marvelous variation of the standard. Such sudden inspirations, though not always as successful as this one, are worth pursuing to add interest and variety to your menus. We offer this recipe here particularly for those home gardeners who have green tomatoes left at the end of the growing season.

Whirl all ingredients except oil in blender until smooth. Strain and chill. Add oil, mix well, and serve. Serves 6.

NOTE: Gazpacho may be garnished with croutons which have been sautéed in garlic and oil.

31

Consommé of Game with Quenelles

2 PHEASANTS, AS OLD AND
LARGE AS POSSIBLE/
1 4-POUND VENISON BONE
15 CUPS CHICKEN STOCK (SEE STOCKS)
1 LARGE ONION
3 CARROTS
3 LEEKS
1 STALK CELERY
SALT TO TASTE
2 EGG WHITES (FOR CLARIFYING)

If members of your family are hunters, no doubt in pheasant season they bring home some old birds. The consommé which follows offers a splendid way to turn these birds into a palatable dish. The way to determine age in a pheasant is first by the feet; the longer the claws, the older the pheasant. Second, if the breastbone is tender and separates at the joint, the bird is young. As a pheasant ages, the breastbone grows together and becomes inflexible.

Blanch pheasant for a few minutes in boiling water. Remove from water, and place in the chicken stock with the venison bone. Add the remaining ingredients. Cook, uncovered, for 2 hours. Strain. Clarify (see Stocks).

Quenelles:
1 POUND RAW PHEASANT MEAT,
GROUND FINE/
¼ TEASPOON WHITE PEPPER
1 TEASPOON SALT
⅛ TEASPOON FRESHLY
GROUND NUTMEG/
1 EGG WHITE
¾ CUP HEAVY CREAM

Place all ingredients except cream in a bowl over ice. Mix well. Add the cream very slowly, beating it with a wooden spoon until mixture is fluffy. Force through a sieve, cover, and let rest for 1 hour. To form quenelles, use 2 teaspoons first dipped in cold water: Fill one spoon with mixture, transfer the paste from one spoon to the other until it forms into a long, rounded oval. Poach in the simmering consommé for 5 minutes. Serve in the consommé. Serves 10.

Lentil Soup with Sausages

1 POUND LENTILS (ABOUT 3½ CUPS)
1 LARGE POTATO
1 MEDIUM ONION
1 BAY LEAF
2 TABLESPOONS SALT (OR TO TASTE)
2 QUARTS WATER

This is a delicious lentil soup, most unusual because it contains cream. You may be sure that because of that ingredient it becomes a cut above what most of us think of as typical lentil soup—in fact, arrives in the category of soups to serve when you wish to entertain in style. Chipolatas are small Italian sausages. They are excellent

1 PINT MILK
1 PINT LIGHT CREAM
12 CHIPOLATA SAUSAGES
2 TABLESPOONS OIL

with lentils, or with oysters as an appetizer.

Soak lentils in cold water overnight. Drain. Put into a pot with potato, onion, bay leaf, salt, and water. Cook, covered, for 2 to 3 hours, or until lentils are very tender. Put through a sieve to make a purée or whirl in the blender. Add milk and cream. The soup should be creamy. Slice the sausages and sauté in a skillet with the oil for a few minutes. Add to the soup. Let the soup boil gently for 5 minutes. Serves 6.

Cream of Lettuce Soup

1 HEAD BOSTON LETTUCE
5 CUPS CHICKEN OR BEEF STOCK
(SEE STOCKS)/
1 SMALL ONION, SLICED
1 STALK CELERY, CHOPPED
¼ CUP BUTTER
2 TABLESPOONS FLOUR
½ CUP HEAVY CREAM
SALT & PEPPER TO TASTE

Wash, core, and quarter lettuce. Shred very fine. Boil in 1 cup of the stock for 5 minutes. Remove from heat. Sauté onion and celery in butter until soft, but not browned. Add flour and mix well. Add remaining stock. Bring to a boil, and boil 15 minutes, uncovered. Strain. Add lettuce and stock in which it was cooked. Reheat. Add cream and mix well. Season. May be served hot or chilled. Serves 6.

Lobster Bisque

¼ CUP OIL
1 LARGE CARROT, CHOPPED
½ MEDIUM ONION, SLICED
1 SMALL STALK FRESH THYME
1 BAY LEAF
2 RIPE TOMATOES, COARSELY CHOPPED
2 POUNDS RAW LOBSTER MEAT,
CUT INTO SMALL PIECES/
2 TABLESPOONS COGNAC, WARMED

A bisque is basically a purée that involves some sort of seafood—lobster, shrimp, crayfish—and is served as a thick soup. (Many years ago in France the term was used for soups using meat and other bases, and you will find that some of our soups meet this broader definition.) Lobster Bisque is very rich and makes a perfect start for a formal dinner party. In planning the rest of the menu, however, care should be taken to avoid rich sauces, and the dessert should be simple, though elegant.

¼ CUP DRY WHITE WINE
3 CUPS FISH STOCK (SEE STOCKS)
¾ CUP RICE
SALT TO TASTE
1 TEASPOON PEPPER
½ CUP HEAVY CREAM
DASH TABASCO

Heat oil in a large casserole. Add vegetables, herbs, and lobster. Shake the pan constantly until the skin of the lobster turns red. Add the cognac and flame it. Add the wine. Simmer 5 minutes. Remove lobster and keep warm. Add the fish stock, rice, salt, and pepper. Cook over low heat for 45 minutes. Press the mixture through a sieve, or whirl in the blender. Put the bisque on the heat again, add cream, and stir. Cook a few minutes more. Correct seasoning with Tabasco and more salt, if necessary. To serve, pour into a large bowl or tureen and add the pieces of lobster meat. Serves 6.

Fish & Seafood

Baked Stuffed Sea Bass, Port Wine Sauce

6 1-POUND SEA BASS
SALT & PEPPER TO TASTE
1 CUP PLUS 2 TABLESPOONS
MOUSSE OF TROUT (PAGE 149)/
2 TABLESPOONS BUTTER
2 TABLESPOONS LEMON JUICE
3 TABLESPOONS MINCED SHALLOTS
½ CUP RED PORT WINE
1 CUP HEAVY CREAM
¼ CUP WHITE WINE SAUCE
(SEE SAUCES)/

You may think this is a rather complicated dish. Actually, each of the processes is simple in itself—making the mousse of trout and the white wine sauce, and putting the whole dish together. Although you need only a quarter cup of the white wine sauce, don't be tempted to omit it; it is essential to the final glorious dish. Since sea bass range in weight from a half a pound to five pounds, you may have to buy some slightly larger or smaller than the recipe requires. In this recipe you may use a little more or a little less of the mousse of trout and the various sauce ingredients without harming the final result in any way.

Have your fish market bone the fish. Rinse under cold water and dry with paper towels. Sprinkle inside with salt and pepper. Put 3 tablespoons mousse of trout into each fish. Sprinkle with pepper. Put butter, lemon juice, and shallots into a flame-proof dish. Put fish on top and add port wine. Cook in a 400-degree oven 20 minutes. Remove from oven and put fish on a serving platter. Keep warm. Reduce the cooking liquid by ⅔. Add cream. Reduce by ½. Add white wine sauce. Cook a few minutes longer. Correct seasoning. Strain the sauce over the fish. Serves 6. *(See illustration, page 30.)*

Bluefish à la Grenobloise

1 6–7 POUND BLUEFISH
SALT & PEPPER TO TASTE
FLOUR
¼ CUP CLARIFIED BUTTER
(SEE SAUCES)/
3 SLICES BREAD (CRUST
REMOVED), DICED/
½ CUP BUTTER
6 TABLESPOONS CAPERS
6 TABLESPOONS PEELED,
DICED LEMONS/
3 TABLESPOONS CHOPPED
FRESH PARSLEY/

If there's anything better than plain broiled bluefish, this is it. An exceedingly simple dish to prepare, it allows the bluefish to be the star performer.

Clean and fillet the fish (or have your fish market do it). Salt and pepper each fillet and sprinkle with flour. Put into a pan with the clarified butter. Cook slowly for 5 minutes on each side, until nicely browned. Remove fillets and arrange them on a serving platter. Keep warm. Meantime, fry the bread cubes in 3 tablespoons of the butter until golden brown on all sides. Put remaining butter in the pan in which the fish was cooked. Add capers and diced lemons, cook for 3 minutes, and pour the resulting sauce over the fillets. Sprinkle with fried bread cubes and parsley. Serves 6.

Lobster à la Nage

18 QUARTS SALTED WATER
FEW STALKS FENNEL
3 BAY LEAVES
4 CARROTS, CUT UP
2 LARGE ONIONS, QUARTERED

Poaching is one of the simple ways to cook lobster, and it produces a sound and simple dish to eat. You will find as well that poached lobster is frequently used in other dishes; if that is your intention, simply omit the sauce suggested here. This is a recipe of generous proportions.

1 TABLESPOON PEPPERCORNS
3 CUPS WHITE VINEGAR
6 2-POUND LIVE LOBSTERS
4 CUPS WHITE WINE SAUCE
(SEE SAUCES)/
6 TABLESPOONS JULIENNE OF CARROT
6 TABLESPOONS JULIENNE OF
GREEN BEANS/

If you cannot accommodate all the ingredients in one pot, divide them among several.

In a large pot place salted water, fennel, bay leaves, carrots, onion, peppercorns, and vinegar. Bring to a boil. Add lobsters and simmer for 8 to 10 minutes. Meantime, simmer white wine sauce with julienne of carrots and beans. When lobsters are done, split them and remove stomach and intestinal vein. Serve with sauce and vegetable mixture. Serves 6.

Gratin of Lobster
(Or Shrimp or Crayfish)

3 2-POUND LOBSTERS (OR 2 POUNDS
SHRIMP, OR 4 POUNDS CRAYFISH)/
COURT-BOUILLON TO COVER
(SEE STOCKS)/
⅓ CUP CLARIFIED BUTTER (SEE SAUCES)
¼ CUP COGNAC, WARMED
2 CUPS SAUCE NANTUA (SEE SAUCES)
SALT & PEPPER TO TASTE
1 TEASPOON LEMON JUICE

Whichever of the shellfish mentioned in this recipe you choose to use, you may be sure that the resulting dish will be rich and absolutely wonderful. In case you are not familiar with crayfish, which the French call *écrevisses,* and we sometimes also call crawfish, you should know that they are a freshwater crustacean, small and succulently delicious. They grow almost entirely in the West and parts of the Midwest, but sometimes can be found in eastern markets and should be seized upon with fervor if you see them.

Poach lobsters 8–10 minutes (or shrimp 3–5 minutes, until they turn pink; or crayfish 5 minutes) in court-bouillon. Remove meat from shells. Cut lobster in small dice. (If shrimp are used, cut them in half, lengthwise. Leave the crayfish whole.) Put the butter in a skillet or saucepan. Add lobster (or shrimp or crayfish). Sauté 5 minutes. Flambé with cognac. Reduce to dry. Add sauce Nantua and mix carefully. Correct the seasoning with salt and pepper. Add lemon juice. Pour into a gratin dish and run under the broiler to brown. Serves 6.

Baked Carp

6 TABLESPOONS BUTTER
2 LARGE ONIONS, SLICED IN RINGS
2 GREEN PEPPERS, SLICED IN RINGS
2 MEDIUM TOMATOES,
SEEDED & SLICED/
2 CUPS FISH STOCK (SEE STOCKS)
1 TEASPOON SALT
1 TEASPOON PAPRIKA
8 CUPS SLICED RAW POTATOES
4 POUNDS CARP FILLETS,
SLICED IN PIECES 1-INCH WIDE/
6 SLICES BACON
1 PINT SOUR CREAM
¼ CUP FLOUR

Carp are obtainable the year around, but are considered to be at their best when taken from cold waters. The peak season, therefore, is from November to April. This is a firm-fleshed, lean-meated fish of great delicacy when prepared properly. The recipe below has Hungarian overtones and is exceedingly good.

Spread baking dish with butter. Place onions, peppers, and tomatoes in dish, pour in fish stock, and sprinkle with salt and paprika. Spread potatoes on top. Cut 2 lengthwise slits in each slice of carp. Slice several pieces of bacon in thirds (the short way) and insert them into the slits in the fish. Place carp in baking dish. Spread remaining bacon around it. Place in a 375-degree oven for 15 minutes, uncovered. Mix sour cream with flour and pour over fish. Cook for an additional 10 minutes, uncovered. Serves 6.

Frogs' Legs Provençale

24 PAIRS MEDIUM FROGS' LEGS
MILK FOR DIPPING
FLOUR FOR COATING
SALT & WHITE PEPPER TO TASTE
¾ CUP OIL
¾ CUP PEELED TOMATOES
¾ TEASPOON MINCED GARLIC
2 TABLESPOONS MINCED PARSLEY

Dip frogs' legs in milk. Dredge them in flour seasoned with salt and white pepper. Heat oil in a skillet, add frogs' legs and cook 3 or 4 minutes until light brown on both sides. Remove to platter and keep warm. Add tomatoes, garlic, and parsley to skillet and cook for 10 minutes. Pour over frogs' legs. Serves 6.

Scotch Crêpes Four Seasons

6 TABLESPOONS CHOPPED ONIONS
2 TABLESPOONS BUTTER
1 CUP PLUS 2 TABLESPOONS
(5 OUNCES) CHOPPED
SMOKED SALMON/

This dish derives its name from the smoked Scotch salmon whose beautiful flavor makes it one of The Four Seasons' more popular items. It is easy to make at home, is a perfect luncheon entrée or first course for dinner.

37

1½ CUPS SOUR CREAM
12 CRÊPES
(SEE PASTRIES & BATTERS)/
2 CUPS LIGHT SAUCE BÉCHAMEL
(SEE SAUCES)/
2 TABLESPOONS BREAD CRUMBS

Cook onions in butter until soft but not browned. Mix with the salmon and sour cream. Spoon the mixture onto ⅓ of each crêpe and roll up. Place the crêpes, seam side down, in a baking dish. Cover with the Béchamel and sprinkle with the bread crumbs. Run under broiler to brown. Serves 6.

Turbot Braised in Champagne

1 8–10-POUND TURBOT
SALT & PEPPER TO TASTE
½ RECIPE MOUSSE OF LOBSTER
(SEE MOUSSE OF TROUT, PAGE 149)/
¼ CUP BUTTER
6 TABLESPOONS MINCED SHALLOTS
2 POUNDS MUSHROOMS, STEMMED,
PEELED & SLICED/
1 QUART CHAMPAGNE
2 CUPS WHITE WINE SAUCE
(SEE SAUCES)/
1 QUART HEAVY CREAM
12 SLICES BLACK TRUFFLE
RED CAVIAR BEIGNETS (SEE BELOW)
SCALLOPS IN SHELLS (SEE BELOW)

For those ambitious and adventurous cooks who tackle this recipe, there awaits that great feeling of achievement which is the cook's most rewarding sensation. It is a spectacular dish for your most elegant party and one of the best things we have ever eaten. Turbot is hard to come by at best, and totally unavailable in some parts of the United States. Nevertheless, we decided to offer this recipe, if only for your reading delectation. Perhaps you will try the Red Caviar Beignets and the Scallops in Shell and use them as garnitures for some simpler fish dish.

Have your fish market clean the turbot and cut it lengthwise, removing the bone, and making a large pocket. Sprinkle the inside with salt and pepper. Fill the pocket with the lobster mousse and sew up the opening. Sprinkle outside of fish with salt and pepper. In the bottom of a large baking pan, put butter, minced shallots, and mushrooms. Carefully place the turbot on top. Pour in the champagne. Place in a 350-degree oven and bake 45 minutes. Remove from the oven and carefully put the turbot on a large silver tray (a square one makes the best presentation). Keep warm. Reduce the cooking liquid by half. Add the white wine sauce and reduce by half again. Add the cream and cook the sauce for 5 minutes more. Strain

38

the sauce into a bowl. Remove the mushrooms from the strainer and place them around the fish. Take off the black skin of the turbot. Arrange two lines of truffle slices down the sides of the turbot. On the sides and ends of the tray make a garniture of red caviar beignets and scallops in shells. Serves 6 to 8.

Red Caviar Beignets

3 TABLESPOONS RED CAVIAR
½ CUP BEIGNET BATTER
(SEE PASTRIES & BATTERS)/

Dip a teaspoonful of caviar at a time into the batter. Fry in 375-degree deep fat until light brown and crisp. Makes 9 beignets.

Scallops in Shell

½ POUND BAY SCALLOPS
1 TABLESPOON BUTTER
SALT & PEPPER TO TASTE
1 TEASPOON LEMON JUICE
1 TABLESPOON WHIPPED CREAM
1½ TABLESPOONS SAUCE
HOLLANDAISE (SEE SAUCES)/

Heat the butter and sauté the scallops in it briefly. Sprinkle with salt and pepper. Add lemon juice. Put a few scallops in each of 8 little scallop shells. Mix whipped cream and Hollandaise (this is a sauce mousseline) and spread over scallops in each shell. Run under the broiler for 2 minutes.

Poached Salmon with Sauce Hollandaise

3 POUNDS SALMON
COLD COURT-BOUILLON (SEE STOCKS)
SAUCE HOLLANDAISE (SEE SAUCES)

Nothing could be easier to cook, and richer or more satisfying to eat than poached salmon. Success is assured for even the most amateur of amateurs, if the recipe is followed carefully.

Wrap the piece of salmon in cheesecloth and let long ends of the cheesecloth hang over the edges of the poaching pan so you can lift the fish out easily when it is done. Add unheated court-bouillon. Bring to a boil. Lower heat and simmer for 25 minutes. Remove fish to a serving platter and take off cheesecloth. Serve at room temperature or chilled with Hollandaise. Serves 6.
NOTE: If you wish to present the salmon whole, substitute a 6-pound fish dressed. It will serve 8–10.

41

Alaskan Salmon Trout

3 2-POUND SALMON TROUT
¼ CUP MILK
FLOUR FOR DIPPING
SALT & PEPPER TO TASTE
½ CUP BUTTER
¼ CUP OIL
6 TABLESPOONS LEMON JUICE
3 TABLESPOONS MINCED
FRESH PARSLEY/
12 SLICES SKINNED &
SEEDED LEMON/

Have your fish market fillet the trout. Wash fillets under cold water and dry with paper towels. Dip in milk, then in flour. Sprinkle with salt and pepper. Put 3 tablespoons of the butter and all of the oil into a large skillet and heat. Add the fillets and cook until very nicely browned on each side (4–5 minutes). Do not overcook. Put the fillets on a serving dish and sprinkle the lemon juice over them. Discard the fat from the skillet. Add remaining butter and brown it. Pour over the fillets. Sprinkle with parsley. Place slices of lemon on the fillets as decoration. Serves 6.

Chicken & Duck

Farmhouse Duckling au Poivre

1 6-POUND DUCKLING
6 TABLESPOONS COARSELY CRUSHED
BLACK PEPPER/
2 OUNCES COGNAC
1 PINT VEAL STOCK (SEE STOCKS)
½ PINT CREAM
1 TEASPOON GLACE DE VIANDE
(SEE STOCKS)/

This is one of the most popular dishes served at The Four Seasons. Try it, and you'll see why.

Place duckling on a rack in a roasting pan. Roast in 325-degree oven 1¼ hours, pricking the skin frequently. Remove from the oven and press pepper into the skin of the duckling. Return to the oven for 15 minutes more. Pour off all the fat from the pan. Pour the cognac over the duckling and flame. Remove the duckling from the pan. Add the veal stock, cream, and glace de viande, and heat well. Strain the sauce and serve separately. Serves 4.

Basque Chicken

¾ CUP BUTTER
3 2½ POUND CHICKENS, SPLIT

The onion, tomatoes, and olives make this dish characteristic of the Basque country. It is quick and easy to prepare,

1 MEDIUM ONION, CHOPPED
¾ CUP OLIVE OIL
6 TOMATOES, PEELED & CUT
INTO EIGHTHS/
¾ CUP DRY WHITE WINE
¾ CUP MIXED LARGE GREEN & BLACK
OLIVES, PITTED & SLICED/
1 CUP SLIVERED ALMONDS
SALT & PEPPER TO TASTE

and the almonds add an unexpected and welcome note.

Melt butter in a large, shallow, flame-proof baking dish. Arrange chicken in dish, skin side down. Bake, uncovered, for 30 minutes in a 375-degree oven. Turn and bake 15 minutes longer, or until golden brown and tender. Remove chicken and keep warm. Cook onion in the oil until golden. Stir in tomatoes, wine, and olives. Simmer 10 minutes. Add ¾ cup of the almonds. Pour over the chicken and heat in oven 5 to 7 minutes. Season and sprinkle with remaining almonds. Serves 6.

Breast of Chicken Paprikás in Champagne

3 CHICKEN BREASTS, HALVED,
BONED & SKINNED/
3 TABLESPOONS PAPRIKA
SALT & PEPPER TO TASTE
2 TABLESPOONS CHOPPED SHALLOTS
¼ CUP BUTTER
1 PINT CHAMPAGNE
1½ PINTS HEAVY CREAM

A suprême of chicken is half of a boned and skinned breast. When it has a sauce as rich as the one suggested here (and it usually does), you will find that one suprême is about as much as any one person will want to eat.

Sprinkle chicken breasts (suprêmes) with paprika, salt, and pepper. Put in a flame-proof casserole with shallots, butter, and champagne. Poach in a 350-degree oven, covered, for 10 minutes. Take casserole from oven, remove suprêmes to serving plate. Keep warm. Reduce the cooking liquid by ⅔. Add heavy cream and reduce until thickened. Strain over suprêmes and serve immediately. Serves 6.

Suprême of Chicken with Oysters in Cream

6 CHICKEN BREASTS, HALVED,
BONED & SKINNED/
SALT & PEPPER

Sprinkle chicken breasts (suprêmes) lightly with salt and pepper. Place in large flame-proof casserole with butter, shallots, and wine. Cover and cook for 10 minutes in a

1/4 CUP CLARIFIED BUTTER
(SEE SAUCES)/
2 TABLESPOONS MINCED SHALLOTS
1/2 CUP DRY WHITE WINE
24 OYSTERS, WITH THEIR LIQUOR
1/2 CUP HEAVY CREAM
2 TABLESPOONS LEMON JUICE
4 DROPS TABASCO

350-degree oven. Remove suprêmes to serving dish. Keep warm. Add oysters (with their liquor) to casserole. Reduce liquid for 5 minutes. Add cream and heat for an additional 5 minutes. Season with lemon juice and Tabasco. Add oysters to serving dish and pour sauce over. Serves 6.
NOTE: Nutted Wild Rice is wonderful served with this dish.

Quenelles of Chicken Breast with Creamed Mushrooms

1 POUND CHICKEN-BREAST MEAT,
BONED & SKINNED/
SALT & PEPPER TO TASTE
1/2 TEASPOON NUTMEG
2 EGG WHITES
3 CUPS HEAVY CREAM
1/4 CUP CLARIFIED BUTTER
(SEE SAUCES)/
1 1/2 CUPS MINCED MUSHROOMS
1/2 CUP FLOUR
1 QUART BOILING CHICKEN STOCK
(SEE STOCKS)/
1 TEASPOON LEMON JUICE

A quenelle is a sort of dumpling composed of forcemeat—fish or meat minced to the finest degree possible and bound together with a thickening agent, in this case, egg whites and heavy cream. The binding process is hastened by placing the bowl containing the meat in a larger bowl filled with cracked ice and leaving it there during the addition of the egg whites and cream. As always, when making quenelles, test one first and if it falls apart add another egg white to the mixture.

Put chicken meat 3 times through the finest blade of the grinder into a bowl. Place bowl in a larger bowl filled with cracked ice. Add salt, pepper, nutmeg, and egg whites. Beat the mixture very thoroughly. Slowly add 2 cups of cream, beating constantly. Let stand for 1 hour in the refrigerator. With 2 tablespoons shape the quenelles and poach them in simmering salted water for 15 minutes. Do not boil. Put the butter in a casserole with mushrooms and flour. Beat with a wire whisk. Add the chicken stock and mix well. Cook for 20 minutes until reduced by 1/3. Add remaining cream and cook 5 minutes more. Strain. Correct the seasoning and add lemon juice. When quenelles are done, drain them and put in a baking dish. Cover with sauce. Put the dish in a 375-degree oven for 15 minutes. The quenelles should double in size. Serves 6.

NOTE: The dish may be garnished with truffles, mushrooms, or wild rice.

Breast of Guinea Hen
with Dariole of Noodles, Sauce Smitane

3 2-POUND GUINEA HENS
SALT & PEPPER TO TASTE
2 TABLESPOONS MINCED SHALLOTS
¼ CUP CLARIFIED BUTTER
(SEE SAUCES)/
½ CUP MADEIRA WINE
1 POUND THIN NOODLES
3 EGGS
⅓ CUP HEAVY CREAM

Full-grown guinea hens are inclined to be tough, so it is logical to use only the breasts to make the dish which follows. (Besides, the rest of the bird has very little meat on it.) If you doubt your ability to remove the breasts, have your butcher do it. A dariole was originally a small pastry for which a cylindrical mold was used. The term is now applied generally to the mold itself, and, as you will see, the dishes that can be made in it are not limited to pastries. Noodles baked in dariole molds, then unmolded onto a platter where they surround a meat dish, are most decorative, and in this case complement the guinea hen beautifully. If you have no dariole molds and can't find any, use large custard cups or individual baking dishes from which you can easily unmold the finished product.

Remove breasts from the hens. Remove the skin. Sprinkle the breasts with salt and pepper. Place in an oven-proof casserole with shallots, butter, and Madeira. Cover and poach in a 350-degree oven for 18 minutes. Remove casserole from oven, cover, and keep breasts warm. Meanwhile, cook the noodles for 15 minutes in salted boiling water. Drain. Break eggs in a bowl, add cream and salt, and pepper to taste. Mix well and add the noodles. Mix well again. Butter 6 individual dariole (cylindrical) molds and fill with noodles. Cover and place in a pan of water. Cook for 12 minutes in a 350-degree oven. Place breasts on an oval platter. Unmold the darioles around the platter. Pour Sauce Smitane (see below) over the breasts. Serve very hot. Serves 6.

Sauce Smitane

¼ cup clarified butter
(see sauces)/
2 medium onions, minced
⅔ cup white wine
1 cup sour cream
salt & pepper to taste
2 tablespoons lemon juice

Put the butter, onion, and wine in a saucepan and reduce until dry. Add sour cream, cook slowly for 8 minutes. Do not let it boil. Season with salt and pepper. Add lemon juice. Strain sauce and serve very hot.

Beef, Veal, Lamb & Pork

Steak Occitane

3 tablespoons butter
3 tablespoons oil
1 tablespoon salt
6 8-ounce shell steaks
2 tablespoons cognac, warmed
½ cup dry white wine
3 tablespoons dijon mustard
½ cup brown sauce (see sauces)
½ cup heavy cream

On those occasions when you want to add a sauce to your perfectly cooked steak, we strongly recommend that you try this one. It is superb and adds a totally new dimension to America's favorite food. The steaks, you will note, are sautéed, rather than broiled.

Heat butter and oil in a skillet. Salt steaks. Sauté over fairly high heat (5 minutes on each side for rare, 7 minutes for medium, and 10 minutes for well done), adding more butter and oil if necessary. Pour warm cognac over steak, flambé, and shake skillet until flames die. Remove steaks to serving platter. Keep warm. Pour out fat. Pour wine into skillet and reduce until almost dry. Add mustard and brown sauce. Reduce by ⅓. Add cream and heat through. Strain sauce over steak and serve. Serves 6.

Filet Mignon Poivre, Flambé

6 6-OUNCE FILETS MIGNONS
3 TABLESPOONS CRACKED
BLACK PEPPER/
¾ CUP MELTED BUTTER
DASH SALT
6 TEASPOONS DRY ENGLISH MUSTARD
¾ CUP CALVADOS, WARMED
¾ CUP HEAVY CREAM
1½ CUPS BROWN SAUCE (SEE SAUCES)

Press the cracked pepper into the filets with the heel of your hand. Sauté steaks in half of the melted butter until brown on both sides and done to your taste. Remove steak. Place remaining butter in same skillet. Add salt and mustard and stir. When butter is hot, add steak. Flame with Calvados and remove from pan. Add cream and the brown sauce. Return steak to sauce. Do not allow to boil. Serves 6. *(See illustration, page 39.)*

Double Steak Stuffed with Oysters

6 12-OUNCE SHELL STEAKS
SALT & PEPPER TO TASTE
36 TINY RAW OYSTERS
¼ CUP CLARIFIED BUTTER
(SEE SAUCES)/
¼ CUP OIL
1 TABLESPOON MINCED SHALLOTS
¼ CUP DRY WHITE WINE
½ CUP THIN BROWN SAUCE
(SEE SAUCES)/

At one of our daily tastings for this book it was remarked that a steak smothered with sautéed oysters lacked a suitably appetizing appearance. That is the way steak with Galway oysters, for instance, is always served in Ireland, and a good dish it is, too, though hardly handsome. One of the tasters suggested cooking the oysters inside the steak and the result follows. May we say that a twelve-ounce steak (it has to be that size to allow for the pocket), plus oysters, is far too much for any woman and even some men. We would suggest that for your lady guests you consider cutting each steak in half to make two servings.

Cut a pocket in each steak. Sprinkle with salt and pepper. Put 6 oysters in the pocket of each steak. Secure with small skewers. Put the steaks in a large skillet with butter and oil. Cook slowly for 6 minutes on each side. Remove the steaks to a platter. Keep warm. Add shallots and wine to the skillet and reduce to dry. Add the brown sauce and cook a few minutes more. Strain over the steaks. Serves 6.

Steak with Anchovy Butter

6 TABLESPOONS BUTTER
3 TABLESPOONS OIL
1 TEASPOON SALT
6 8-OUNCE SHELL STEAKS
10 ANCHOVY FILLETS,
CHOPPED COARSELY/

The combination of anchovies in butter poured over steak is certainly not a standard dish, but if you like anchovies, we think you will love it. These steaks are well accompanied by baked potatoes and Spinach Elizabeth.

Heat 3 tablespoons butter and the oil in a skillet. Salt steaks and sauté over fairly high heat (5 minutes on each side for rare, 7 minutes for medium, and 10 minutes for well done), adding more oil and butter, if necessary. Remove steaks to serving platter. Pour out fat from the pan. Add 3 tablespoons butter and anchovies. Mix together and heat for 2 minutes. Pour over steaks and serve. Serves 6.

Rare Fillets of Beef Stroganoff

12 ½-INCH-THICK SLICES
OF BEEF FILLET/
¼ CUP CLARIFIED BUTTER
(SEE SAUCES)/
2 TEASPOONS PAPRIKA
SALT TO TASTE
1 CUP BEEF STOCK
(SEE STOCKS)/
2 TEASPOONS LEMON JUICE
¼ CUP DRY SHERRY

The authentic Russian Stroganoff was made with very thin strips of fillet of beef. Cutting the beef in half-inch slices, as this recipe requires, helps to keep it rare, which is how it should be in any case.

Put fillet slices and butter into a cold pan and bring to high heat to brown the beef fast. Add paprika and salt. Remove from heat (so paprika will not burn) and turn the meat well in the mixture. Return to heat and add beef stock, lemon juice, sherry, and cognac. Remove meat and

¼ cup cognac
½ cup sour cream

keep warm. Reduce sauce to about ¾ cup. Remove pan from heat and add sour cream. Stir well. Reheat a little, but not too much or the sauce will curdle. Turn meat in the sauce and serve at once. May be served with rice, or noodles. Serves 6.

Saddle of Veal Orloff

14-pound saddle (loin) of veal
½ cup oil
3 tablespoons butter
salt & pepper to taste
2 large carrots, sliced
1 stalk celery, sliced
2 pounds pork skin, diced
3 ripe tomatoes,
peeled & chopped/
3 cups dry white wine
3 cups brown stock (see stocks)
2 cups brown sauce (see sauces)
2 bay leaves
1 4-inch stalk thyme (or
¼ teaspoon dried)/
1 quart sauce soubise
(see sauces)/
2 ounces black truffle, sliced

A saddle of veal comprises the entire back of the animal; as a retail cut it would be known as a double loin. The dish for which it is used here is a classic one, and its preparation is somewhat time-consuming. The only process which is at all difficult is the cutting out of the two fillets after the saddle is cooked. However this is something a good carver should be able to do with ease. Escoffier suggests serving cucumbers cooked in cream with Veal Orloff. Parfaits of Spinach or Mange-touts are also appropriate.

Have your meat market trim the saddle and tie it for roasting; bones should be cut short. Put the oil and butter in a roasting pan. Add the saddle, standing on the short bones. Salt and pepper it, and place in a 400-degree oven to brown. Add vegetables, pork skin, and tomatoes, and brown them at same temperature. Add wine, brown stock, brown sauce, bay leaves, and thyme. Lower oven heat to 325 degrees and cook saddle for 2 hours, basting frequently. Remove saddle from oven and let it rest for 10 minutes. Carefully cut out the 2 fillets (loin meat). Cut each fillet into 10 slices. Replace loin slices neatly in the saddle. Between each 2 slices pour a tablespoon of sauce Soubise and insert a slice of truffle. Pour remaining sauce Soubise over the meat and put the saddle under the broiler until lightly browned. Strain the sauce from the cooking of the saddle and serve it separately. Serves 10.

Ragoût of Veal Niçoise

4 POUNDS BONELESS VEAL
FROM THE LEG/
¼ CUP OIL
1 MEDIUM ONION, CHOPPED
3 CLOVES GARLIC, CHOPPED
1 4-INCH STALK ROSEMARY (OR
¼ TEASPOON DRIED)/
1 4-INCH STALK THYME (OR
¼ TEASPOON DRIED)/
1 BAY LEAF
5 TOMATOES, PEELED,
SEEDED & CHOPPED/
1 CUP DRY WHITE WINE
½ CUP VEAL STOCK (SEE STOCKS)
12 SMALL ONIONS
SALT & PEPPER TO TASTE
½ POUND BLACK OLIVES,
PITTED & HALVED/
MINCED PARSLEY

This is a typical dish of Nice, with its garlic, tomatoes, and black olives. It is easy to prepare and can be held, covered, if dinner has to be delayed. Just reheat it at serving time, adding the olives at that point.

Cut the veal in 1½-inch dice. Heat oil in a flame-proof casserole. Brown meat in the oil. Add chopped onion, cook for 3 minutes. Add garlic, rosemary, thyme, bay leaf, and tomato. Cook 5 minutes. Add wine, veal stock, onions, salt, and pepper. Cook slowly for 45 minutes. Five minutes before serving, add the black olives. Just before serving, sprinkle with parsley. Serves 6. *(See illustration, page 40.)*

Sautéed Veal Chops Zingara

6 10-OUNCE VEAL CHOPS
¼ CUP FLOUR
SALT & PEPPER TO TASTE
¼ CUP OIL
¼ CUP BUTTER
¼ CUP DRY WHITE WINE
1 CUP BROWN SAUCE (SEE SAUCES)
1 TEASPOON CHOPPED FRESH
TARRAGON (OR ½ TEASPOON DRIED)/
¾ CUP JULIENNE-SLICED COOKED HAM
¾ CUP JULIENNE-SLICED
SMOKED TONGUE/
2 CUPS JULIENNE-SLICED MUSHROOMS
2 LARGE BLACK TRUFFLES,
JULIENNE-SLICED/

Dip chops in flour. Sprinkle with salt and pepper. Heat oil and butter in a large, heavy skillet. Sauté chops slowly for 6 or 7 minutes on each side. Remove chops to serving plate and keep warm. Pour off grease in skillet. Replace skillet over heat and pour in wine. With a wooden spoon scrape up all the brown bits sticking to pan. Stir and scrape for a few minutes more and add the brown sauce and tarragon. Mix well. Add remaining ingredients, stir in sauce until heated and pour over chops. Serves 6.

Veal Kidneys with Rosemary

1 POUND GREEN BEANS
6 VEAL KIDNEYS
SALT & PEPPER TO TASTE
3 TABLESPOONS OIL
6 4-INCH STALKS FRESH ROSEMARY
(OR 1½ TEASPOONS DRIED)/
¾ CUP SAUCE BÉCHAMEL
(SEE SAUCES)/
3 TABLESPOONS BREAD CRUMBS
½ CUP HOT SAUCE BORDELAISE
(SEE SAUCES)/

Cut ends from beans. If they are small ones you may be able to use them whole. Otherwise cut them about 1½ inches in length. Cook 12–15 minutes in boiling, salted water, or until just tender and still slightly crisp. Drain. Split the kidneys, but do not cut them in two. Sprinkle the cut side with salt and pepper and brush them all over with oil. Put a stalk of fresh rosemary (or a dash of dried) in the center of each. Broil 5 minutes on each side. When done, arrange kidneys on a broiler-proof serving platter. Remove the rosemary and place a bouquet of green beans in the center of each kidney. Top each with 2 tablespoons of Béchamel and sprinkle with bread crumbs. Run under the broiler again to brown. Pour hot sauce Bordelaise around the kidneys and serve. Serves 6.

NOTE: Asparagus Chinoise may be substituted for green beans in this recipe.

Carré of Lamb Bretonne

1 POUND DRY WHITE BEANS
1 CARROT
1 BAY LEAF
1 MEDIUM ONION, PEELED &
STUCK WITH 4 WHOLE CLOVES/
DICED SKIN FROM PORK BELLY
(BELOW)/
1 TABLESPOON SALT
½ CUP OIL
2 TRIMMED RACKS OF LAMB
(6 CHOPS EACH)/
SALT & PEPPER TO TASTE
1 MEDIUM ONION, CHOPPED
2 CLOVES GARLIC, MINCED
4 RIPE MEDIUM TOMATOES, SKINNED,

A carré of lamb is the trimmed rack (loin). Each carré usually has six chops. When you see the word "Bretonne" in the title of a dish you may be sure that it will appear with a garnish of dry white beans, cooked in the manner of Brittany. Lamb has a great affinity for dried beans of various types, as this dish well illustrates.

Soak the beans in cold water for 24 hours. Drain. Place in a pot with 3 quarts boiling water, carrot, bay leaf, the onion stuck with cloves, and the pork belly skin. Cook at a low boil for 1½ hours. At the end of an hour, add the tablespoon of salt (if you add it at the start of the cooking the beans will become hard). Meanwhile, put ¼ cup of the oil in a baking pan. Add the carrés and sprinkle them with salt and pepper. Roast in a 375-degree oven 30 minutes.

SEEDED & COARSELY CHOPPED/
1 TABLESPOON TOMATO PURÉE
4 OUNCES PORK BELLY, DICED

Put the remaining oil in a casserole with the chopped onion and cook over medium heat. After 5 minutes add garlic and stir with a spoon. Add the tomatoes, purée of tomato, and diced pork belly. Stir for a few minutes longer and add a cup of the cooking water from the beans. Correct seasoning with salt and pepper. Cook for 10 minutes. When the beans are done, drain them and put them into the tomato mixture. Heat a few minutes and place in a serving bowl. Put the carrés on a platter and cut each one into 6 chops. Arrange chops on the beans and serve very hot. Serves 6.

Double Rack of Smoked Pork

4-POUND RACK OF SMOKED PORK

Mirepoix: 1 CARROT, CHOPPED
1 STALK CELERY, CHOPPED
1 BAY LEAF
1 MEDIUM ONION, CHOPPED
1 STALK THYME

¼ CUP PORK FAT
½ CUP PORT WINE
½ CUP THIN BROWN SAUCE
(SEE SAUCES)/
SUGAR FOR SPRINKLING

Smoked pork will not be found in every meat market, but should be obtainable at specialty butcher shops, particularly in German neighborhoods.

Put pork in a baking pan with mirepoix and fat. Brown on top of range. Add wine and brown sauce. Cook in a 350-degree oven for 40 minutes. Sprinkle meat with sugar from time to time. Remove from oven and put on a platter. Strain sauce over the top. Serves 6.

NOTE: Red Cabbage au Caramel and Apple Beignets are both good with this dish.

Loin of Pork Stuffed with Apples

4 POUNDS BONED LOIN OF PORK
3 SMALL APPLES, PEELED,
CORED & SLICED/
SALT TO TASTE

Have your butcher bone the loin of pork—a tenderloin, actually, and a delectable bit of tender meat it is. Pork and apples were, of course, made for each other. And the final, perfect touch is added by the glazed chestnuts.

4 OUNCES PORK FAT, CUBED

———————

Mirepoix: 1 CARROT, CHOPPED
1 MEDIUM ONION, CHOPPED
1 BAY LEAF
1 STALK THYME
1 STALK CELERY, CHOPPED

———————

⅓ CUP DRY SHERRY
½ CUP BROWN SAUCE (SEE SAUCES)
1 POUND CHESTNUTS,
OR 1-POUND CAN WHOLE CHESTNUTS
(NATUR, NOT SWEETENED)/
3 TABLESPOONS HONEY

Once you've tried them you will always want to serve them with pork dishes.

Cut the loin lengthwise to make a pocket. Fill with the apple slices. Tie the loin with 3 rings of kitchen string. Sprinkle with salt. Cook the pork with the cubed fat and the mirepoix on top of the range in a roasting pan for 10 to 12 minutes to brown. Add sherry and brown sauce. Roast in a 350-degree oven 1 hour and 45 minutes. Remove roast to a platter. Strain the sauce and pour it around the meat. Glaze the chestnuts in the honey for a few minutes over low heat, stirring to be sure they are well coated. Serve on the side. Serves 6.

Deviled Pork Chops with Glazed Pears

¼ CUP OIL
¼ CUP CLARIFIED BUTTER
(SEE SAUCES)/
SALT & PEPPER TO TASTE
6 PORK CHOPS, CUT 1-INCH THICK
3 PEARS
2 CUPS WATER
½ CUP SUGAR
3 TABLESPOONS LEMON JUICE
¼ CUP HONEY
1 CUP HOT SAUCE DIABLE
(SEE SAUCES)/

Pork chops and pears are perhaps a new combination to you, as they were to us when we encountered this dish at a Four Seasons tasting. The Sauce Diable cuts the sweetness of the pears and together they complement the pork beautifully.

Heat oil and butter in a large skillet. Sprinkle chops with salt and pepper. Cook in the oil and butter over low heat for 25 minutes, turning frequently. Peel and core the pears. Put water, sugar, and lemon juice into a saucepan and boil 2 minutes. Add pears and cook until they are soft but not mushy (10–15 minutes). Cut each pear lengthwise. Put the honey in a pan and let it get warm. Add the pears and cook over low heat until honey is reduced and pears become shiny. Remove the chops to a serving platter. Pour Sauce Diable around them. Put half a pear on each chop and pour any remaining honey over the pears. Serves 6.

Game

Cutlet of Venison Grand Veneur

4 POUNDS LEG OF VENISON,
SLICED IN 12 PIECES/
MARINADE TO COVER (SEE STOCKS)
¼ CUP CLARIFIED BUTTER
(SEE SAUCES)
¼ CUP OIL
SALT TO TASTE
¼ CUP DRY WHITE WINE
1 TABLESPOON FRESHLY GROUND
BLACK PEPPER (OR MORE, TO TASTE)/
½ CUP OF THE MARINADE
½ CUP GAME SAUCE (SEE SAUCES)
2 TABLESPOONS BAR-LE-DUC
¼ CUP HEAVY CREAM

If your deer is young and you use the proper cut, there's nothing better than venison cooked rare. With older animals and tougher cuts long marinating and long cooking are necessary. The sauce served with this dish is a truly distinguished one for rare venison.

Marinate the venison slices 24 hours. Remove slices and pat dry with paper towels. Heat butter and oil in a skillet. Put in venison slices and brown for 3 minutes on each side. They should be rare. Put the slices on a serving dish. Season with salt. Keep warm. Pour the white wine into the skillet and add pepper. Reduce to dry. Add the ½ cup of marinade and reduce by ⅔. Add game sauce and simmer 10 minutes. Strain. Add Bar-le-Duc and cream, and cook 3 minutes. Strain over the venison. Serves 6.

NOTE: Serve with apples, sliced and sautéed in butter, or with Red Cabbage au Caramel.

Roast Mallard Duck with Olives

3 MALLARD DUCKS, CLEANED
1 CUP MELTED BUTTER
SALT & PEPPER TO TASTE
2 CUPS DRY WHITE WINE
1 CUP SMALL GREEN OLIVES

If possible, pay your butcher to draw and pick your ducks. The picking is really a frightful job; even seasoned hunters view it with dread. This recipe will produce rare ducks, which is the way we think they should be.

Tie the ducks and place on a trivet in a roasting pan. Brush the breasts with butter. Place in a 475-degree oven and roast 15 to 20 minutes, depending on the size of the ducks. Baste every 5 minutes with melted butter. Remove from oven and season with salt and pepper. Keep hot on a warm platter. De-grease the roasting pan and add wine and olives. Reduce by ⅓. Serve in a sauce boat. Serves 6.

Roast Pheasant

3 SMALL PHEASANTS
SALT & PEPPER TO TASTE
½ POUND (2 STICKS)
BUTTER, MELTED/

You could scarcely find an easier recipe, yet it will produce for you a very grand dish. With it you may serve Bread Sauce, Game Sauce, and currant jelly.

Clean and truss pheasants. Sprinkle with salt and pepper. Place on a rack in a roasting pan and cook in a 375-degree oven 45 minutes to 1 hour, or until tender, brushing frequently and generously with the melted butter. Serves 6. *(See illustration, pages 50–51.)*
NOTE: You may stuff the pheasants if you like. Also, they may be served on large croutons of bread, browned in the pan juices after the birds are cooked.

Salmis of Pheasant

6 BABY PHEASANTS
SALT
WHITE PEPPER
¾ CUP BUTTER
¾ CUP OIL
―――――――
Sauce: ½ CUP CHOPPED CARROTS
½ CUP CHOPPED ONIONS
2 BAY LEAVES
1 TEASPOON DRIED THYME
1 TABLESPOON BLACK PEPPER
1 BOTTLE RED WINE
2 CUPS GAME SAUCE (SEE SAUCES)
1 TRUFFLE, THINLY SLICED
1 TABLESPOON MELTED BUTTER
1½ CUPS THINLY SLICED MUSHROOMS
¼ CUP COGNAC, WARMED
1 TEASPOON LEMON JUICE
2 TABLESPOONS BUTTER

The Ring-necked Pheasant, introduced from China into the United States in the 1800's, is a highly adaptable bird and exciting game for shooters. To be good eating, a pheasant shot in the wild or raised on a game farm should be hung for a week. The bird may be frozen, but it is our opinion that a frozen pheasant is likely to be dry and stringy when cooked. There always has been considerable controversy regarding the type of wine to be used in a salmis. While white is the classic choice, The Four Seasons uses red because it gives better color to the sauce.

Sprinkle pheasants with salt and pepper. Put into a roasting pan with oil and butter. Roast in a 450-degree oven for 8 to 10 minutes. Pheasant should be rare. Place chopped carrots and onions, bay leaves, thyme, black pepper, and wine in a saucepan. Reduce by ⅔. Cut pheasants in half, lengthwise, then cut each breast into 2 pieces. Skin them. Chop the remainder of the pheasant, including the bones. Add the chopped trimmings to the reduced wine and vegetables. Add the game sauce. Simmer for 30 minutes. Meanwhile, place the truffle in a pan with the melted butter. Add the mushrooms. Place skinned breasts on top. Strain sauce over pheasant and simmer gently for 10 minutes. Skim off the fat. Remove the breasts to a serving dish and keep warm. Flame the cognac in a ladle and pour it over the sauce. When flames die, add the lemon juice and the 2 tablespoons of butter. Correct seasoning. Pour over pheasant. Serves 6.

NOTE: Dish may be decorated with croutons sautéed in butter and spread with pâté of pheasant liver, or mousse of goose liver.

Chukar Partridge in Cognac with Cabbage

3 POUNDS CABBAGE
½ POUND LARD
1 SMALL CARROT, SLICED
½ MEDIUM ONION, SLICED
1 POUND SKIN OF SLAB BACON, CHOPPED COARSELY/
1 BAY LEAF
1 2-INCH STALK THYME (OR ¼ TEASPOON DRIED)/
2 JUNIPER BERRIES
1 TABLESPOON SALT
1 TEASPOON PEPPER
3 PARTRIDGES
3 SLICES FATBACK
2 TABLESPOONS OIL
¼ CUP WHITE WINE
2 TABLESPOONS COGNAC

In the United States there is some confusion of nomenclature concerning partridge. In the South the bobwhite quail is dubbed "partridge," and in the North "partridge" often refers to the ruffed grouse. The chukar partridge originated in the Himalayas and was, after a good deal of difficulty, transplanted to California, Minnesota, Nevada, North Dakota, Washington, and Wyoming. To make really good eating, partridge must be hung for several days before it is cooked. It is not absolutely necessary that you have chukar partridge to make the fine dish which follows. All the various birds we call partridge have flesh of similar quality and will take to this treatment.

Wash and quarter cabbage. Blanch in water to cover for 15 minutes. Rinse cabbage with cold water. Chop coarsely. Heat lard in a heavy flame-proof casserole. Add carrot and onion. Brown. Add bacon skin, bay leaf, thyme, juniper berries, cabbage, salt, and pepper. Mix well and set casserole aside. Wrap each partridge with a slice of fatback. Tie with string. Put oil and wine in a roasting pan. Add partridges and place in a 450-degree oven for 8 minutes, or until brown. Remove from oven. Heat cognac, pour over partridges and ignite. Shake pan until flames die. Place partridges on top of cabbage in casserole. Cook, uncovered, in a 350-degree oven 45 minutes. Remove from oven. Divide cabbage among 3 oval molds, each approximately 6 inches long and 4 inches high. Press cabbage into molds as firmly as possible. Press a partridge, breast down, very firmly into each. Smooth cabbage that has come up the sides of mold over partridge. Place again in a 350-degree oven for 10 minutes. Turn molds out carefully onto a large serving platter. Each cabbage-covered partridge serves 2 people. Serves 6.

Brace of Quail, Purée of Chestnuts

12 QUAIL

SALT

6 TABLESPOONS CLARIFIED BUTTER (SEE SAUCES)/

6 TABLESPOONS OIL

4 CUPS CHESTNUT PURÉE (PAGE 130)

¾ CUP GAME SAUCE (SEE SAUCES)

Quail are small birds weighing up to six ounces. They have delicately flavored white meat which tends to be dry and needs plenty of butter or oil, as in the following recipe, or barding to keep it moist. The delicacy of the meat makes it important to season lightly, avoiding strong flavors. Presentation is important for any dish and this arrangement of the quail in little nests of puréed chestnuts is attractive and appetizing.

Salt the quail. Stick toothpicks through the drumsticks to hold each bird together while roasting. Pour butter and oil over the quail and bake in a 450-degree oven 12 to 15 minutes, until golden brown. Discard toothpicks. Have the purée piping hot. Put it through a pastry bag to make circles (or "nests") on the serving platter. Place 1 quail in the center of each circle, with legs toward the edge of the platter. Pour game sauce over quail only. Serves 6.

Artichoke Bottoms Gratinés

12 COOKED ARTICHOKE BOTTOMS
(PAGE 247)/
2 TABLESPOONS BUTTER
2 TABLESPOONS OIL
1 CUP THIN SAUCE BÉCHAMEL
(SEE SAUCES)/
¾ CUP GRATED GRUYÈRE CHEESE

Slice the artichoke bottoms into thick julienne strips and sauté them in a skillet with the butter and oil for 5 minutes. Do not brown. Place in a flame-proof dish. Pour the Béchamel over. Sprinkle with grated cheese and run under the broiler to brown. Serves 6.

Artichokes Stuffed with Foie Gras, Choron

12 COOKED ARTICHOKE BOTTOMS
(PAGE 247)/
5 TABLESPOONS CLARIFIED BUTTER
(SEE SAUCES)/
2 TABLESPOONS OIL
12 ½-INCH-THICK SLICES FOIE GRAS
¾ CUP SAUCE CHORON (SEE SAUCES)

Foie gras is the liver of goose specially fattened to make the liver rich and succulent. The finest comes from Alsace and southwestern France. A good foie gras is creamy white, tinged with pink, and very firm in texture. Tinned goose liver, imported from France, is sometimes rather hard to find. If you can't buy it, we suggest you use a pâté de foie gras (without truffles) for the following dish.

Sauté the artichoke bottoms in the butter and oil to heat but not brown (about 5 minutes). Remove to a flame-proof dish. Place a slice of foie gras on each. Place a tablespoon of sauce Choron on top. Run under the broiler to brown. Serves 6.

Red Cabbage au Caramel

2 POUNDS RED CABBAGE
⅔ CUP SUGAR
⅓ CUP WATER
¼ CUP RED WINE VINEGAR
WATER TO COVER
SALT TO TASTE
1 TABLESPOON KÜMMEL

If you like sweet-and-sour red cabbage you will find this a superlative recipe for it. The French touch of caramelizing the sugar for the sweetening is a great inspiration.

Slice the cabbage fine and blanch it for 15 minutes in boiling water. Drain. In a casserole with a cover, make a caramel of the sugar and the ⅓ cup of water (see "Caramelize" in Glossary). It should be very brown, but it must not burn. Add vinegar and cook 5 minutes. Add the cabbage and water to cover. Cover the casserole and cook in a 350-degree oven 60 minutes. Season with salt and add Kümmel. Serves 6.

Purée of Flageolets

½ POUND DRY FLAGEOLETS
1 LARGE POTATO
¼ CUP BOILING MILK
SALT, PEPPER & NUTMEG TO TASTE
¼ CUP BUTTER

If you've never tried a purée of dried legumes, the time has come. These purées are an unusual way to serve dried beans or peas and a splendid accompaniment to many meats; this one, using flageolets, is one of the best.

Soak flageolets in cold water for 24 hours. Drain. Cover flageolets and potato with boiling water and cook, covered, at a low boil 2–3 hours, or until flageolets are very tender. Drain. Put through a fine sieve or whirl in the blender. Mix well with milk. Season with salt, pepper, and nutmeg. Finish away from heat by stirring in butter gradually. Serves 6.

Sauerkraut with Champagne

2 POUNDS FRESH SAUERKRAUT
½ POUND FATBACK
1 LARGE ONION, CHOPPED
1 CUP CHAMPAGNE
1 TABLESPOON SUGAR
1 TEASPOON WHITE PEPPER

Buy fresh sauerkraut in the butcher shop. It is a delicious vegetable and is here carried into another world by combining it with the grandeur of champagne.

Wash sauerkraut in cold water and squeeze dry in towel. Place fatback in saucepan and heat just long enough to render 2 tablespoons of fat. Remove fatback. Add onion to melted fat and stir over medium heat long enough to soften without browning (about 10 minutes). Spread onion evenly over bottom of pan and place solid fatback on top. Add sauerkraut. Add champagne and enough water to cover by ½ inch. Add sugar and pepper. Cover and cook over low heat for 1 hour. Remove fatback. Serves 6.

63

Noodles Charlotte

3 EGGS
⅓ CUP HEAVY CREAM
SALT & PEPPER TO TASTE
1 POUND NOODLES,
COOKED & DRAINED/

Noodles should always be cooked *al dente*—"hard to the tooth"—so that you know you're biting into something. This takes eight to ten minutes in rapidly boiling salted water. The degree of doneness may be tested by pinching a noodle between two fingers, or by removing a noodle and biting through.

Beat eggs, cream, salt, and pepper well. Add noodles and gently mix in. Pour into an oven-proof, buttered round mold. Place in a pan of water and bake for 15 minutes in a 350-degree oven. Unmold on serving plate. Serves 6.

Tarhonya Noodles

1½ CUPS COARSE
TARHONYA NOODLES/
3 TABLESPOONS BUTTER
1 TEASPOON SALT
1½ TEASPOONS PAPRIKA
(OR TO TASTE)/
WATER TO COVER

Tarhonya noodles are Hungarian egg-barley noodles, quite different from any other type of pasta. They are made in two sizes. The fine size is used in soup and the coarse as an accompaniment to an entrée, as here. They are obtainable in stores selling Middle European foods.

Brown noodles in the butter in a flame-proof casserole, stirring to brown on all sides. Add salt, paprika, and water to cover. Cover casserole and cook in a 350-degree oven until all liquid is absorbed, and noodles are flaky, like well-cooked rice (about 1 hour). Serves 6.

Spätzle

1 CUP WATER
1 CUP MILK
2 CUPS FLOUR
2 EGGS
⅛ TEASPOON WHITE PEPPER

Spätzle are little dumplings which make a fine accompaniment to meats. They can be bought ready-made in stores selling Eastern European foods. Many such stores also offer spätzle makers, implements through which the dough is pressed out in the proper size and shape.

64

1¼ TEASPOON SALT
¼ CUP BUTTER, MELTED

Mix water and milk together. Add flour, eggs, pepper, and ¼ teaspoon salt. Beat together very well, until bubbles appear on the surface of the batter. Fill a large saucepan ¾ full of water, add remaining salt and bring to a boil. Place about 1 cup of batter in a 2-inch-wide strip on a chopping board. With a very dull knife or spatula quickly shave slices (as thin as possible) into boiling water. When spätzle rise to surface of water, remove with a slotted spoon and place in cold water. Drain. Repeat process until all batter is used. Mix spätzle with butter and serve. Serves 6.

NOTE: Cooked as above, spätzle are fine to serve with meats in sauce. When you prefer a crisp accompaniment, to broiled meat, for instance, try frying them in butter until golden.

Salads

Endive and Grapefruit Salad

1 POUND ENDIVE
2 LARGE GRAPEFRUIT, SECTIONED

You will notice that no dressing is suggested for this salad. It is really best in its pristine state. However, if you prefer, you may offer a sauce boat with a simple French Dressing (see Sauces) for those who wish it.

Alternate leaves of endive and grapefruit sections on a platter. Or arrange them like spokes of a wheel in a salad bowl. Serves 6. *(See illustration, page 69.)*

Leeks à la Grecque

6 LARGE LEEKS, CLEANED
2 MEDIUM TOMATOES,

Leeks belong to the lily family and are somewhat like scallions in appearance, though very much larger, and their

65

PEELED & SEEDED/
12 PITTED JUMBO BLACK OLIVES
½ MEDIUM ONION
¾ CUP LEMON JUICE
½ CUP OLIVE OIL
1 TEASPOON SALT
¼ TEASPOON PEPPER
1 TEASPOON SUGAR

taste, though authoritative, is not so sharp. They are essential in French cooking, for flavoring and as a main ingredient. To the French cook "à la Grecque" means something plentifully seasoned with lemon juice, in the manner of Greek cooking.

Clean leeks (see below). Blanch for 2 minutes and cool. Split from the top almost all the way through lengthwise, leaving about 1 inch attached. Chop tomatoes, olives, and onion into small dice. Mix lemon juice, oil, salt, pepper, and sugar. Mix with chopped vegetables. Place mixture on leeks and chill. Serves 6.

NOTE: Leeks are likely to be exceedingly gritty and must be carefully washed if they are going to make good eating. Cut off the root ends and all but an inch of the green tops. Soak leeks in cold water to cover for half an hour. Run water in the tops so that it goes down through the stalk to remove further grit. Shake upside down. Repeat the process to get the leeks as clean as possible.

Raw Mushroom Salad

24 MEDIUM-SIZED WHITE
MUSHROOMS, SLICED/
½ MEDIUM ONION, FINELY DICED
1 CUP PEELED, DICED CELERY
¼ CUP DICED RED RADISH
1 TABLESPOON CHOPPED PARSLEY
1 TABLESPOON CHOPPED TRUFFLE
4 TABLESPOONS OLIVE OIL
2 TABLESPOONS TARRAGON VINEGAR
SALT & PEPPER TO TASTE
BOSTON LETTUCE

Those who think that almost any dish is improved by the addition of mushrooms lament the fact that too few people are accustomed to using them raw. The flavor is quite different from that of cooked mushrooms, and equally great. The salad which follows can be prepared at the table, which is something guests seem to enjoy watching when it is done with flair. Have all the ingredients ready in separate dishes on a big tray, the oil and vinegar in cruets. Toss ingredients together with the dressing components. Then put them into another bowl already lined with lettuce.

Toss all ingredients, except lettuce, together. Line a bowl with lettuce and serve salad in it. Serves 6.

Alsatian Apple Tart

SWEET DOUGH TO LINE TART PAN
(SEE PASTRIES & BATTERS)/
¼ CUP CANNED ALMOND PASTE
½ CUP CRÈME PÂTISSIÈRE
(SEE DESSERT BASICS)/
3½ MEDIUM APPLES
3 EGGS
1 CUP MILK
2 TABLESPOONS SUGAR
1 TABLESPOON FLOUR
¼ TEASPOON VANILLA
APRICOT GLAZE
(SEE DESSERT BASICS)/

PREHEAT OVEN TO 350 DEGREES

Almond paste can be bought in cans in delicacy shops and departments. It is practically impossible to make at home. If tightly covered, almond paste keeps for months in the refrigerator.

Line an 8-inch tart pan with the sweet dough. Soften the almond paste with a little water and mix it with the crème pâtissière. Spread filling on the crust. Peel and core the apples and cut them in half. Make 2 or 3 slashes in each half (lengthwise) from one end to within ½ inch of the other end. Place 1 half apple, cut side down, in the center of the tart. Place the others around it with the unslashed ends toward the center to create a fan effect. Cook in a 350-degree oven about 30 minutes, or until the crust is almost set. Mix eggs, milk, sugar, flour, and vanilla, and press through a sieve or whirl in the blender. Pour over tart. Return to 400-degree oven for 10 minutes. Cool. Spread with apricot glaze. Serves 6.

Honey-glazed Early McIntosh, Applejack Cream

6 MCINTOSH APPLES
6 TABLESPOONS LIQUID HONEY
WHITE WINE
¾ CUP APPLESAUCE
3 TABLESPOONS APPLEJACK
1 CUP CRÈME PÂTISSIÈRE
(SEE DESSERT BASICS)/
½ CUP WHIPPED CREAM

PREHEAT OVEN TO 350 DEGREES

The use of applejack to flavor this dish gives it great zip and authority. It's a perfect fall dessert.

Wash apples and peel them from the top down about 1½ inches. Core them. Place in a baking dish and sprinkle each with honey. Pour in white wine to a depth of ½ inch. Bake in a 350-degree oven until apples are tender (about 30 minutes). Cool and chill. Mix the applesauce with 1 tablespoon of the applejack and fill the apple cavities with the mixture. Mix the crème pâtissière and whipped cream with the remaining applejack and pour over the apples to serve. Serves 6.

Fresh Pears in Meringue

3 FRESH PEARS
SIMPLE SYRUP (SEE DESSERT BASICS)
½ LEMON, SLICED
4 CUPS CRÈME ANGLAISE
(SEE SWEET SAUCES)/
1 CUP MERINGUE
(SEE PASTRIES & BATTERS)/

This is an unusual dessert which must be made ahead of time, thus saving work at the last minute. It is easy—and effective to present.

Peel and core pears. Cut in half. Poach in sugar syrup with lemon until soft enough for your taste. Drain well. Place some crème Anglaise in the bottom of each of 6 flame-proof individual casseroles. Place a pear half on top and cover with meringue. Run under the broiler to brown lightly. Cool. Chill. Serve cold. Serves 6.

Anise Fig Tart

SWEET DOUGH TO LINE AN
8-INCH TART PAN (SEE PASTRIES)
& BATTERS)/
1 CUP CRÈME PÂTISSIÈRE
(SEE DESSERT BASICS)/
1 OUNCE ANISETTE
10 FRESH FIGS
½ RECIPE FRANGIPANE (SEE
DESSERT BASICS)/
1 CUP MERINGUE (SEE PASTRIES
& BATTERS)/
_____
PREHEAT OVEN TO 350 DEGREES

Fresh figs are a rare and beautiful fruit, and eating one is always an exotic experience, even if you pick it from a tree in your own backyard. They are delicious eaten alone, or with prosciutto as an appetizer. Or try them in this recipe.

Line tart pan with sweet dough. Flavor crème pâtissière with ½ ounce anisette. Place in tart. Place one fig in the center and the rest around the outside edge of the tart. Flavor the frangipane with remaining anisette and spread over figs. Bake in a 350-degree oven 35 minutes. Cover top with meringue, return to oven, and bake until meringue is golden (about 15 minutes). Cool.

Hudson Valley Cake

7 MCINTOSH APPLES
1 CUP WHITE WINE
WATER
1 CUP SUGAR

This cake is named for a great apple-growing area in New York State. The form of angelica required is candied and sprinkled with dry sugar (otherwise it would be very sticky); it is used largely for decorating cakes, as in this

1. Mixing ingredients of meringue.

2. Spreading meringue on parchment paper.

3. Removing parchment from baked meringue.

7. Adding rest of amaretti to whipped cream.

8. Mixing.

9. Placing praline mixture on meringue.

13. Adding another meringue.

14. Trimming edges.

15. Covering with reserved praline mixture.

16. Patting almonds on sides.

17. Sprinkling with powdered sugar.

18. Dusting stencil with cocoa.

Torte Sorrano

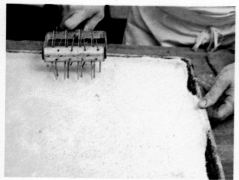

4. Pricking chilled puff pastry.

5. Mixing maraschino liqueur with whipped cream.

6. Crumbling amaretti. Two thirds will be mixed with praline paste & butter cream.

10. Spreading.

11. Placing baked puff pastry on top.

12. Spreading whipped cream on pastry.

19. Completed Torte Sorrano.

Pastry Chef Bruno Comin displays Torte Sorrano, one of his many original creations.
For recipe, see page 73.

RICH PASTRY
(SEE PASTRIES & BATTERS)/
PUFF PASTRY
(SEE PASTRIES & BATTERS)/
3 TABLESPOONS CRÈME PÂTISSIÈRE
(SEE DESSERT BASICS)/
½ TEASPOON RUM
APRICOT GLAZE
(SEE DESSERT BASICS)/
1 CUP SWEETENED WHIPPED CREAM
PIECES OF ANGELICA

PREHEAT OVEN TO 350 DEGREES

instance. The candied angelica stem is a pale green, which is why it can simulate the stem of an apple. Angelica comes from an herb which grows wild in the Alps, the Pyrenees, and Northern Europe. It is also cultivated, and remains very like the original wild variety. It may be bought in jars in delicacy stores and departments.

Peel and core the apples. Put into a deep dish with the white wine and enough water so that the apples are ¾ covered. Add sugar. Bake in a 350-degree oven until apples are cooked but not too soft (about 30 minutes). Drain and cool apples. Make a 9-inch round of rich pastry ¼-inch thick. Place a ring of puff pastry ¼-inch thick around the outside of the round of rich pastry. Let rest 1 hour. Prick the center of the bottom pastry with a fork to prevent bubbles. Bake in a 350-degree oven 15 minutes. Cool. Mix crème pâtissière and rum. Spread over the bottom of the pastry. Put 1 apple in the center and the rest around it (if your apples are very large you may use only 6 in all). Brush with apricot glaze. With a pastry tube, fill the centers of the apples and the spaces between them with whipped cream. Decorate with angelica to make "stems."

Torte Sorrano

10 EGG WHITES
2 CUPS SUGAR
¼ CUP CORNSTARCH
4 CUPS ALMOND FLOUR (SEE NOTE)
½ RECIPE FOR PUFF PASTRY
(SEE PASTRIES & BATTERS)/
1 CUP WHIPPED CREAM
2–3 TEASPOONS MARASCHINO LIQUEUR
½ CUP CANNED PRALINE PASTE

This is one of the most delicate, yet rich and delicious tortes we have ever tasted. It is one of the many creations of Bruno Comin, pastry chef of The Four Seasons.

Beat egg whites with sugar. When thick, add cornstarch. Mix in the almond flour gently with the hands. With a pastry bag or spatula make 2 equal squares of the almond meringue on a cooking parchment on a cookie sheet. Bake in a 200-degree oven 30 minutes. When you take meringue

2 CUPS BUTTER CREAM (SEE DESSERT BASICS), FLAVORED WITH 2 OUNCES UNSWEETENED CHOCOLATE MELTED AND COOLED/ 1 CUP COARSELY BROKEN ITALIAN MACAROONS (AMARETTI)/ ½ CUP SLICED TOASTED ALMONDS COCOA FOR DUSTING

PREHEAT OVEN TO 200 DEGREES FOR ERINGUE, 350 DEGREES FOR PUFF PASTRY

squares from the oven they will be soft. Turn squares over. Cool. Remove paper. Roll out puff pastry ⅛-inch thick in the same size and shape as the above squares. Place on greased baking sheet and chill. Prick pastry all over with a thick-tined fork. Bake in a 350-degree oven 55 minutes, or until puffed and brown. Mix maraschino liqueur with whipped cream. Mix praline paste with chocolate-flavored butter cream and ⅔ of the amaretti. Mix the rest of the amaretti into the whipped cream. On 1 square of the meringue spread chocolate praline cream, reserving enough to cover the whole cake thinly at the end. Place the puff pastry layer on top. Cover with the whipped cream, then with the second meringue layer. Trim edges. Cover the cake with the reserved praline cream. Pat almonds onto the sides. Dust top of cake with powdered sugar. Make a stencil out of paper or cardboard in any design that suits your fancy. Place gently on cake and dust cocoa through the slits to form the design. Remove stencil. *(See illustration, pages 70-71.)*

NOTE: If you can't buy almond flour, simply pulverize blanched almonds (about 1½ pounds) in the blender.

Chocolate Nut Crêpes

7 8-INCH DESSERT CRÊPES (SEE PASTRIES & BATTERS)/ 1½ CUPS SHELLED WALNUTS 2 SQUARES BITTER CHOCOLATE ¾ CUP COTTAGE CHEESE 2 EGGS, BEATEN 2 EGG YOLKS, BEATEN ¼ CUP FLOUR GRATED PEEL OF ½ LEMON ¾ CUP (APPROXIMATE) SUGAR

Grind walnuts. Grate chocolate. Put cottage cheese through a sieve and mix with the eggs, egg yolks, flour, lemon peel, and ¼ cup of the sugar. Mix raisins with crème pâtissière. Grease a cake pan 8 inches across and 4 inches deep with butter and put in a crêpe. Spread with walnuts and sprinkle with sugar. Add second crêpe and spread with half of the cheese mixture. Add third crêpe and sprinkle with grated chocolate and sugar. Add fourth crêpe and spread with apricot jam. Add fifth crêpe and sprinkle with raisin mixture. Add sixth crêpe and spread

¼ CUP SEEDLESS RAISINS
½ CUP CRÈME PÂTISSIÈRE
(SEE DESSERT BASICS)/
½ CUP APRICOT JAM
4 EGG WHITES
¼ CUP VANILLA SUGAR
(SEE DESSERT BASICS)/

PREHEAT OVEN TO 400 DEGREES

with remaining cottage-cheese mixture. Put the last crêpe on top. Bake in a 400-degree oven for 15 minutes. Meanwhile, beat egg whites until they hold soft points. Gradually add ¼ cup of the sugar and continue beating until whites hold stiff peaks. Remove cake from oven and turn heat up to 450-degrees. Put cake in the refrigerator to cool for about 10 minutes. (It will thus be easier to handle.) Turn cake from pan onto an oven-proof serving dish. Do this with great care, as the crêpes are inclined to slip about. Spread meringue over top and sides of cake. Return to oven and bake at 450-degrees until brown (about 10 minutes). Sprinkle with vanilla sugar. For serving, cut into wedges as you would a cake. Serve warm or chilled. Serves 6–8.

Riz à l'Impératrice

1 POUND RICE
3 QUARTS MILK
2½ CUPS SUGAR
DASH SALT
1 VANILLA BEAN
1 CUP (5 OUNCES) DICED,
GLACÉED FRUITS/
¼ CUP APRICOT JAM
½ CUP (1 STICK)
BUTTER, SOFTENED/
12 EGG YOLKS
4½ TABLESPOONS
(PACKAGES) GELATIN/
⅓ CUP HEAVY CREAM, WHIPPED
¼ CUP BAR-LE-DUC

PREHEAT OVEN TO 350 DEGREES

This not-to-be-missed dessert from classic French cookery is probably the most elegant rice pudding in the world. It is a Bavaroise (Bavarian cream), which would seem to indicate that it originated in Bavaria, although probably it was the invention of an expatriate French chef to honor a visiting empress. All Bavarian creams, of which there is a considerable variety, are based on a custard to which gelatin is added.

Cook the rice in 2 quarts boiling water for 5 minutes. Rinse with cold water. Put 2 quarts of the milk in a flame-proof casserole with 1¼ cups of the sugar, the salt, and the vanilla bean. Bring to a boil and add the rice. Put the casserole, covered, in a 350-degree oven for 30 minutes. Remove casserole from oven. The rice should be thick but not dry. Remove the vanilla bean. Carefully, with a fork,

75

mix the rice with the glacéed fruit and the apricot jam. Gently fold in the butter.

While the rice is cooking, prepare the Bavaroise. Bring the remaining quart of milk to a boil. Place egg yolks in a bowl. Mix them with remaining sugar and stir in the boiling milk. Add 4 packages of the gelatin. Mix well and cook until smooth, stirring frequently. Do *not* allow to boil. Cool. Add half the Bavaroise to rice mixture. Fold in the whipped cream. Dissolve the Bar-le-Duc with ½ package of gelatin. Strain into the bottom of a mold (must be at least 2½ quarts). Place in refrigerator for 15 minutes. Fill the mold with the rice mixture. Pour the remaining Bavaroise onto a large round platter and refrigerate mold and platter 4 hours or overnight. To serve, carefully unmold the rice mixture into the center of the platter. Serves 6 or more.

Chocolate Velvet Four Seasons

1 SPONGE CAKE, 11 X 16 INCHES
(SEE DESSERT BASICS)/
3 EGG YOLKS
1 TABLESPOON INSTANT COFFEE
¼ CUP KIRSCH
¼ CUP RUM
¼ CUP CRÈME DE CACAO
⅓ CUP (FIRMLY PACKED)
CANNED PRALINE PASTE/
6 TABLESPOONS MELTED BUTTER
1½ POUNDS SEMI-SWEET
CHOCOLATE, MELTED/
3 EGG WHITES

This confection has long been one of the most popular served at The Four Seasons and almost always appears on the pastry cart. It is mouth-wateringly rich.

Completely line a round 1-quart mold with basic sponge cake by cutting out a round to fit the bottom of the mold. Then, from the remaining cake cut 1 long or 2 short strips to cover the sides. Reserve any cake left to make into a top (see below). Mix egg yolks, coffee, kirsch, rum, crème de cacao, and praline paste. Beat until smooth. Heat butter to hot and add. Heat melted chocolate to hot and add. Add the pinch of salt to the egg whites and beat until they form soft peaks. Add sugar, a tablespoonful at a time, beating

PINCH OF SALT
¼ CUP CONFECTIONER'S SUGAR
2 CUPS HEAVY CREAM, WHIPPED
(UNSWEETENED)/

well after each addition. Continue beating 5 more minutes, or until very stiff. Fold whipped cream and beaten egg whites into original mixture. Pour into sponge-lined mold. Place in refrigerator for 2 hours or until filling is firm. Cover top with remaining sponge cake, fitting together any bits and pieces if there is not a single piece big enough. Loosen sides of mold with a sharp knife. Turn out upside down on a plate. Frost all over with semi-sweet chocolate icing.

Semi-Sweet Chocolate Icing

5 SQUARES SEMI-SWEET CHOCOLATE
1 CUP BOILING WATER

Melt chocolate. Mix chocolate and water, blending well. Frost cake all over and chill.

Coupe Filigree

48 STRAWBERRIES
½ CUP MELBA SAUCE
(SEE SWEET SAUCES)/
1 QUART (APPROXIMATE)
VANILLA ICE CREAM/
6 ICE CREAM SHELLS
(SEE PASTRIES & BATTERS)/
1 CUP WHIPPED CREAM
6 CARAMEL FILIGREES

The filigree is the unusual touch to this dish. We cannot emphasize enough how careful you must be in working with hot caramel. Even expert chefs arm themselves with potholders, mitts, towels, etc., to avoid burning their fingers. The end result is charming, however, and worth trying.

Chop half of the strawberries and mix with the Melba sauce. Place 5 tiny balls of ice cream in each of the shells. Pour the sauce over. Slice remaining strawberries in half, and decorate the ice cream with them. Decorate with whipped cream between the strawberries. Place a caramel filigree on top of each. Serves 6.

Caramel Filigree

2 CUPS SUGAR
½ CUP WATER

Boil the sugar and water together until the mixture is a light caramel color. Put the pan into another pan filled with ice until the mixture is no longer bubbling. Cool a little, but not so much that the mixture hardens. Put into a paper tube of waxed or heavy parchment paper, with a ¼-inch hole. Work with a potholder or gloves, because the mixture must be quite hot to make your filigrees. To make filigrees, you need a round metal surface the same size as the ice cream shells. A shallow tartlet mold or the bottom of a pot turned upside down may be used, but you must oil the surface before you make the filigree. First make a ring of syrup around bottom of mold or rim of pot. Then make weaving lines back and forth to complete filigree. Allow to harden, and lift off when cool.

Sugar-glazed Strawberries

2 CUPS SUGAR
⅔ CUP WATER
PERFECT STRAWBERRIES, NOT HULLED

Glacéed fruit is one of those after-dinner offerings generally classed as petit-fours. Make as many as you like.

Heat the sugar and water together in a saucepan, stirring constantly, until the syrup reaches the "crack" stage (270 degrees on a candy thermometer). Place saucepan in a pan of hot water to keep it warm. Holding strawberries by their stems, dip them into the syrup. Cover each one completely except for the stem. Place strawberries on an oiled surface to harden.

Kabuki Parfait

Place 4 tablespoons of coffee ice cream in each parfait glass. Add 2 tablespoons maple syrup. Continue layering the ice cream and syrup, ending with ice cream. Top each with a rosette of whipped cream, sprinkled lightly with brown sugar.

The Wines of Autumn

This is the bountiful season when oysters return to favor, dark-flavored game birds and wildfowl grace the table, and the markets are filled with the earth's last out-pouring of succulent vegetables and fruits. The breath of fall is chill, its light is amber, and appetite's keen edge is turned with hearty food and the heavier, more robust wines.

Cellars which have been little used during the hot months now give forth their finest vintages: the monumental Bordeaux, superbly aged Burgundies, sturdy Rhône Valley reds, as well as fine champagnes, luscious white Burgundies, and the sweet dessert wines of Sauternes. Fall is a time of holidays, tradition, and enjoyment of the best in food and wine. It is the harvest season.

Following are suggestions for complementing the foods of fall with wine, and a list of seasonal vintages.

CHILLED STUFFED MUSSELS: Mussels seem to flourish best in the late summer and fall, and these—deliciously stuffed and dressed—are eternally popular. They respond best to the contrast of a simple French Pinot Chardonnay from Ligny.

GALANTINE OF PHEASANT: The complexity and richness of a fine game galantine is beautifully matched with a red wine. An Auxey-Duresses, a little-known Burgundy, might well be the choice for it.

STEAK TARTARE CANAPÉS WITH CAVIAR: A favorite German hors d'oeuvre, it is most accommodating and exciting as a first course. Or it can be a main luncheon or supper course, with a salad and cheese to follow. It can take a chilled vodka, a Beaujolais, or even a chilled Chablis.

OYSTERS: Any fine, dry white wine—perhaps a Chablis Les Preuses or a Puligny-Montrachet Les Combettes—is excellent with oysters. So are dark bread and butter.

LEBANESE BARQUETTES OF LAMB: If you are serving a fine red—for example, a Carruades de Château Lafite-Rothschild, 1955—you might start with this rather different hot appetizer and continue through the rest of the dinner with the same wine.

ALASKAN SALMON TROUT: Rich and beautifully textured, this superb fish is similar to some of the European lake trout. Try it with the excellent Montrachet from the Marquis de Laguiche, a wine worthy of the best in food.

BREAST OF GUINEA HEN, SAUCE SMITANE: This way of preparing this pleasant and somewhat underrated bird—with Polish sour-cream sauce and noodles—is a delight. A Juliénas would be my choice for the hen and for the dinner itself.

FARMHOUSE DUCKLING AU POIVRE: A great Four Seasons specialty. Crisp and peppery, it needs a strong wine, but not necessarily a rare one. I would try the red Chassagne-Montrachet, a wine of singular interest and the only red of any consequence from the district.

DOUBLE STEAK STUFFED WITH TINY OYSTERS: This is a modern version of what used to be called a Carpetbag Steak, a dish much in vogue in San Francisco in the nineties. A strong, vigorous wine, such as a 1952 Château Montrose, from St. Estèphe, would be a good contrast to the subtle combination of meat and sea-

79

food flavors.

SADDLE OF VEAL ORLOFF: A festive dish of interesting contrasts for special occasions, Veal Orloff is certainly deserving of special drinking. The Chambolle-Musigny, 1959, of Robert Drouhin, might be the subtlest wine. Or, should you prefer a Bordeaux, a Château Margaux would be a gracious choice.

ROAST PHEASANT: Serve the best with this delectable bird: Château Latour, 1937, a gem of a wine, but extremely rare, or one of the more recent fine years —say, a 1952 or 1953—would be extravagant but satisfying.

ROAST MALLARD DUCK WITH OLIVES: The sharply defined taste of green olives which pervades this dish requires a full-bodied wine to cap it. A luxurious choice would be La Tâche, 1962, a rarity from the Domaine de la Romanée-Conti. Or you might settle for a fine Juliénas if you are not in a luxury mood.

CHOCOLATE VELVET: The velvet is a supermousse, as chocolatey as a dessert can be. A Château d'Yquem of a fine year—perhaps, 1959—would be a superb ending for a classic dinner.

White:

Montrachet, Marquis de Laguiche—One of the world's great white wines.
Musigny Blanc, 1967.
Puligny-Montrachet, Les Combettes, 1962.
Chablis, Les Preuses, 1966—For oysters and shellfish.
Rivaner—A delightful wine from Luxembourg.
Pinot Chardonnay, Ligny—A French bottling.
Pinot Chardonnay, Wente—A California bottling.

Red:

St. Estèphe, Château Montrose, 1952—A long-lived wine.
Graves, Château Bouscaut, 1953—A rather special wine at its peak.
Pauillac, Château Margaux, 1952—A rare treat for a game dinner.
Pauillac, Carruades de Château Lafite-Rothschild, 1955.
Pauillac, Château Latour, 1937—For a superlative duck dinner.
Chambolle-Musigny, Robert Drouhin, 1959—A wine of incredible finesse.
Auxey-Duresses, Côte de Beaune, 1962—A fine wine little known in the U.S.
Chapelle-Chambertin, Pierre Damoy, 1964—A fitting background for game.
Volnay, Les Champans, Marquis d'Angerville, 1964.
Chassagne-Montrachet, Ramonet—Red version of a famous white.
Beaujolais, Juliénas, 1969.
Beaujolais Villages, 1969.
Chinon, 1966—From the Loire Valley.

Champagne:

Pommery et Greno, brut, N.V.
Bollinger, brut, 1959.
Perrier-Jouët, 1964.

Italian Wines:

Frascati—Light and delicious with seafood.
Barolo—A robust red wine of great charm.

—JB

Winter

Perhaps more than any other season, winter evokes memories of childhood and of the protecting and sustaining gifts of warmth and food at holiday gatherings of the family. Gracious smells sent forth from the kitchen suffused the house, and the crackling fire on the hearth defied the enveloping, snow-clad cold. Images arise of enormous cauldrons of soup simmering on the stove, of stews maturing in their heavy casseroles, and of spice-laden cakes and tarts and well-textured puddings issuing in profusion from the oven—specialties of the season, all the more delicious for their familiar, once-a-year strangeness preserved in the sense-memory.

Other dishes were purely winter's bounty: great terrines and pâtés of game looking like mosaics when sliced and tasting of many flavors woven into a web of goodness; cocottes of beans with various meats and seasonings, bubblingly rich and filled with homely flavors; soups with winter roots, heightened with herbs. One remembers spiced rounds of beef, flaming puddings, and flaky game pies; fruits preserved, pickled, and frozen for the length of winter. One revels in rich baking, and in the benison of long draughts of good wine. What joyous feasting winter brings, what benign satisfaction! The senses purr with delight. It is a cozy feeling to partake of good living that triumphs over the cold! —JB

Couronne of Whole Brie

4 PACKAGES DRY YEAST
2 CUPS TEPID WATER
8 CUPS BREAD FLOUR
1½ TABLESPOONS SALT
3 TABLESPOONS SUGAR
3 TABLESPOONS BUTTER, SOFTENED
1 EGG, LIGHTLY BEATEN
12-INCH-DIAMETER BRIE CHEESE

PREHEAT OVEN TO 400 DEGREES

A *couronne* is a crown, and a crown of bread is exactly what you are making for your Brie, that king of cheeses. This is a handsome appetizer to serve at a huge cocktail party, and it allows guests to cut servings for themselves. George E. Lang, who served the first couronne for the Escoffier Society dinner, cuts it like a pie, serving cheese and bread together in a wedge. Take care to select a whole Brie that is ready for eating, and be sure to take it from the refrigerator a good three hours before you plan to serve it, so that it may reach room temperature and be delightfully soft when it is eaten. (This handsome crown may also be served in place of dessert, with or without fruit, on a buffet table.)

Prepare yeast according to package directions. Add water. Mix flour, salt, and sugar, and add to make a stiff dough. Add butter. Knead until dough is smooth and elastic (about 10 minutes). Place dough in a bowl. Dust lightly with flour. Cover with a tea towel and let rise in a warm, draft-free place until it has doubled in bulk. Punch down and knead again briefly. Place again in the bowl, cover, and let rise again until almost double in bulk. Grease a cookie sheet and place in the center of it an oven-proof object (such as a bowl, open side down), which has the same diameter as the Brie with which you're going to serve the couronne. Grease the bowl on the outside. Form the dough into two round sausages, each about 1 inch in diameter and long enough to encircle the bowl. Twist these together along their entire length and place around the bowl, blending the ends of the twist together, so that you have an unbroken circle. Brush with beaten egg and bake in a 400-degree oven for 30–35 minutes, or until golden brown. Cool. Serve the couronne with the Brie in the center.

NOTE: This same recipe makes 2 loaves of bread (baked

in 9 x 5 x 3-inch pans). After baking, remove from pans and cool on a rack.

NOTE: Bread flour is high-gluten flour, which gives a firm texture. It is not available in retail markets, but can sometimes be bought from a friendly bake shop. If you can't get it, use regular "all-purpose" flour.

Malossol Beluga Caviar
with Buckwheat, Potato, and Carrot Blinis

The word Malossol means "little salt" and it is used here to describe a fresh Beluga caviar, a most elegant and expensive appetizer and one which does great honor to guests. The Beluga sturgeon is one of many varieties found in the Caspian Sea, and its roe provides the largest and finest of all caviars. Partly because Malossol caviar is so lightly salted, it does not keep unless very carefully refrigerated and tightly covered. Since it is such a precious commodity, it rates the best care you can give it. The recipes for "blinis" which follow make delicious little accompaniments for caviar. These are not authentic Russian blinis, which are prepared with yeast, however they are less trouble to make and very good.

The presentation of caviar is most important. At The Four Seasons it is brought to the table in its original tin, surrounded by crushed ice and decorated with two fresh roses. Each diner is presented with a plate, upon which there are three tiny plates containing chopped egg whites, grated egg yolks, and chopped onion. A pitted half lemon is also on the serving plate. Using "caviar spoons," the captain then serves two spoonfuls to each person, thus: Scrape caviar gently off the top over onto the serving plate, using a second spoon to help ease it out in a perfect

85

rounded shape. (The caviar spoons used at The Four Seasons are copies of an antique silver one which is used for very special occasions. In size of bowl and length of handle they are about the same as iced-tea spoons.)

Potato Blinis

2 LARGE POTATOES, GRATED
1 TEASPOON GRATED ONION
½ TEASPOON SALT
¼ TEASPOON PEPPER
2 EGGS, WELL BEATEN
3 TABLESPOONS FLOUR
¼ CUP BUTTER

Place potato in towel and squeeze dry. Mix with all other ingredients except butter and beat very well. Cover and refrigerate for 2 hours. Heat half the butter in a 10-inch skillet and pour in half the batter. Cook until bottom is golden brown, turn and brown the other side. Turn out onto plate and repeat with remaining butter and batter. Cut each pancake into 2-inch circles with a cookie cutter or a small glass. Keep warm in low oven. Makes approximately 25 blinis.

NOTE: If you use a different size skillet, adjust the amount of butter accordingly.

Carrot Blinis

4 LARGE CARROTS, GRATED
1 MEDIUM POTATO, GRATED
½ TEASPOON SALT
¼ TEASPOON PEPPER
2 EGGS, WELL BEATEN
3 TABLESPOONS FLOUR
¼ CUP BUTTER

Combine all ingredients except butter very well. Cover and refrigerate for 2 hours. Proceed as in recipe above for Potato Blinis.

Buckwheat Blinis

2 CUPS BUCKWHEAT FLOUR
2 EGGS, WELL BEATEN
1 CUP MILK
DASH FRESHLY GRATED NUTMEG
¼ TEASPOON SALT
DASH PEPPER
¼ CUP BUTTER

Combine all ingredients except butter and beat well. Cover and refrigerate for 2 hours. Proceed as in recipe above for Potato Blinis.

Fillet of Smoked Eel, Sauce Verte

1½ POUNDS SMOKED EEL

6 LETTUCE LEAVES

6 TABLESPOONS FRESHLY GRATED
HORSERADISH /

3 LEMONS

6 TABLESPOONS CHOPPED ONION

GREEN MAYONNAISE (SEE SAUCES)

Smoked eel with the suggested condiments makes a delicious and appetite-provoking first course for a hearty meal.

Skin the eel and halve it lengthwise. Slice into 3-inch pieces. Place in center of serving platter. At one end of platter place lettuce leaves, with a tablespoon of horseradish in each. Halve lemons with sawtooth edge. Place at other end of platter and top each half with 1 tablespoon chopped onion. Serve with Green Mayonnaise. Serves 6.

Sturgeon and Caviar

6 VERY THIN SLICES PUMPERNICKEL
BREAD, BUTTERED /

12 THIN SLICES SMOKED STURGEON

6 TABLESPOONS CAVIAR

1 HARD-COOKED EGG YOLK, SIEVED

1 TABLESPOON MINCED PARSLEY

4 SMALL BUNCHES PARSLEY

1 MEDIUM CUCUMBER, PEELED AND
SLICED VERY THIN /

The following recipe is for a canapé to be served with cocktails. It is good-looking, especially if presented as suggested, and, while delectable, it is not so hearty as to destroy appetites for the dinner to follow.

Cut bread into oblongs 1½ by ½ inch. Cut the sturgeon into pieces the same shape but slightly smaller, and place on bread. Arrange around the edge of an oval platter. Spoon caviar carefully onto the center of each canapé. Spoon tiny amounts of the minced parsley and minced egg yolk at either end of the caviar. Alternate the egg and parsley from outside to inside ends on each piece, to form a pattern around the platter. Garnish each canapé with a cucumber slice, using the small slices from the ends of the cucumber. A slice can be made to stand upright by making a cut from the center to the edge and twisting the cut edges in opposite directions. Arrange a row of overlapping cucumber slices down the center of the platter. Place a bunch of parsley at each end of the platter and at each side of the row of cucumbers. Chill and serve.

87

Winter Farmhouse Terrine

1 POUND PORK FATBACK
10 OUNCES VEAL
10 OUNCES PORK
5 OUNCES COOKED HAM
2 WHOLE EGGS
¼ CUP HEAVY CREAM
¼ CUP ARMAGNAC OR COGNAC
1 TEASPOON SALTPETER
1 TABLESPOON SALT
1 TEASPOON WHITE PEPPER
½ POUND FATBACK, THINLY SLICED
3 OUNCES BLACK TRUFFLES

This is a rather simple, home-style pâté, but it makes a very fine first course or accompaniment to cocktails. It can even be the basis of a luncheon, accompanied by a salad and French bread. You will note that saltpeter is among the suggested ingredients. You may be able to buy saltpeter (potassium nitrate) in a drug store, though in most places it is not available at retail due to legal restrictions. If you can't get it, its omission will not be fatal. It is used to give red color to meat and adds nothing to taste. Sometimes—in fact, usually—one is instructed to cover a pâté while it is cooking. Chef Chantreau prefers not to, because he thinks the crust which forms when the pâté is left uncovered has a more appetizing appearance.

Take ⅔ of the unsliced fatback, together with the veal and the pork, and put through the finest blade of the grinder twice. Cut remaining fatback and the ham in small dice and mix well with the ground meats. Add eggs, cream, Armagnac, saltpeter, salt, and pepper. Mix very well. Let stand in refrigerator for 24 hours. Line a terrine with the thinly sliced fatback. Put in half of the meat mixture. Arrange the truffles down the middle of the terrine (the long way). Fill with the remaining meat mixture. Put the terrine in a pan of hot water and cook in a 350-degree oven 1½ hours. Cool. Put a heavy weight on top and let stand for 24 hours in the refrigerator before serving. Serve from the terrine or in slices on a platter. Serve with Port Aspic and pickles.

Stuffed Mussels

18 MUSSELS, CLEANED (PAGE 20)
2 TABLESPOONS LEMON JUICE

The title of this recipe is somewhat of a misnomer, since the mussels are really covered, rather than stuffed.

1 TABLESPOON CHOPPED SHALLOTS
1 POUND SWEET BUTTER
1 TEASPOON WHITE PEPPER
2 TABLESPOONS CHOPPED HAZELNUTS
1 TABLESPOON CHOPPED GARLIC
3 TABLESPOONS BREAD CRUMBS
1 TABLESPOON CHOPPED PARSLEY
1 TABLESPOON CHOPPED CHIVES

Steam mussels in a small amount of water with one tablespoon of the lemon juice and the shallots until shells open. Remove top shells. (Discard any mussels which remain closed.) Cool. Mix remaining ingredients very thoroughly; kneading with the hands does it best. Cover each mussel in its shell generously with the mixture. Run under the broiler to brown lightly. Serves 6.

Baked Oysters, Fines Herbes

¾ POUND BUTTER
9 SHALLOTS, GRATED
¼ CUP MINCED PARSLEY
¼ CUP MINCED TARRAGON
¼ CUP MINCED FRESH CHIVES
¼ CUP CRACKER CRUMBS
2 TEASPOONS LEMON JUICE
36 OYSTERS ON THE HALF SHELL

These oysters are simple, but delicious, and offer a way to vary the first course nicely. The object of putting them in beds of rock salt is, first, to keep them piping hot, as the salt retains heat, and, second, to keep them from tipping and losing their seasonings, as they would do if put into the pans without anything to hold them in place. Rock salt can be bought in hardware stores.

Make a paste of all ingredients except oysters. Put a teaspoonful of this on each oyster. Fill 6 pie pans with rock salt. Put into 500-degree oven for 10 minutes. Place 6 prepared oysters in each pan of rock salt. Run under broiler just long enough to plump the oysters and serve at once on the rock salt beds. Serves 6.

Fried Oysters in Horseradish Sauce

4 EGGS
½ CUP MILK
24 BLUEPOINT OYSTERS, ON
HALF SHELLS/
FLOUR IN WHICH TO DIP OYSTERS

Combine eggs with milk and beat well. Remove oysters from shells and dip in flour, in egg mixture, then in bread crumbs. Fry in 450-degree fat for 1 minute, until golden brown. Mix Béchamel with prepared horseradish and divide among shells. Place an oyster in each shell. Top with

2 CUPS BREAD CRUMBS
FAT FOR DEEP FRYING
1 CUP SAUCE BÉCHAMEL (SEE SAUCES)
2 TABLESPOONS PREPARED HORSERADISH
4 TABLESPOONS SHREDDED FRESH
HORSERADISH/

shredded fresh horseradish and brown under broiler for 1 minute. Serve very hot. Serves 6.

Marrow Soufflé in Crust

5 OUNCES MARROW, CUT IN DICE
2 CUPS WATER
1 TEASPOON SALT
1 TEASPOON LEMON JUICE
6 EGG YOLKS
1 QUART THICK SAUCE BÉCHAMEL
(SEE SAUCES)/
1 TEASPOON FRESHLY GRATED NUTMEG
3 TABLESPOONS CHOPPED CHIVES
SALT & PEPPER TO TASTE
7 EGG WHITES
6 CROUSTADES (SEE PASTRIES & BATTERS)
PREHEAT OVEN TO 350 DEGREES

Beef marrow has a delicate but lovely flavor. Have your butcher split the bones and remove marrow for you. Dice it, when ready to use, with a knife dipped in hot water to keep marrow from sticking to the blade.

Place the diced marrow in water to which the salt and lemon juice have been added and poach for 15 minutes. Drain and set aside. Mix egg yolks with Béchamel, add nutmeg and chives. Correct seasoning. Add marrow. Whip the egg whites until stiff and fold them gently into the yolk mixture. Fill the crusts ¾ full with the soufflé mixture. Put in a 350-degree oven for 20 minutes. Serve immediately. Serves 6.

Soups

Apple Vichyssoise

3 LARGE DELICIOUS APPLES
2 QUARTS CHICKEN STOCK
(SEE STOCKS)/
1 CUP HEAVY CREAM, CHILLED
SALT TO TASTE

Many times it's nice to start a hearty meal with a cold soup, even in the dead of winter. Here is an excellent example of this good idea.

Peel and core apples. Cut into small pieces and cook in

SUGAR TO TASTE
FRESH LEMON JUICE TO TASTE
½ APPLE, CUT IN VERY FINE
JULIENNE/

broth for about 20 minutes, or until tender. Force through sieve or whirl in blender. Cool and chill. Add cream and mix well. Add salt, sugar, and lemon juice. Make the julienne of apple at the last moment so it will not discolor. Sprinkle on top of soup and serve at once. Serves 6.

Cheddar Cheese Soup

3 TABLESPOONS MINCED ONION
3 TABLESPOONS GRATED CARROT
3 TABLESPOONS BUTTER
4 CUPS CHICKEN STOCK (SEE STOCKS)
½ TEASPOON DRY MUSTARD
½ TEASPOON PAPRIKA
¼ CUP MILK
2 TABLESPOONS CORNSTARCH
¼ POUND SHARP CHEDDAR CHEESE,
GRATED (1 CUP)/
SALT & PEPPER TO TASTE
2 TABLESPOONS CHOPPED PARSLEY

Sauté the onion and carrot in butter over low heat for 10 minutes. Add the chicken stock, mustard, and paprika, and simmer for 15 minutes. Combine the milk and cornstarch. Stir into the first mixture and cook for 5 minutes. Add the cheese and stir until it is melted. Season and serve with chopped parsley on top. Serves 6.

Cream of Knob Celery

2 POUNDS KNOB CELERY
SALT & PEPPER TO TASTE
2 CUPS SAUCE BÉCHAMEL (SEE SAUCES)
4 CUPS CHICKEN STOCK (SEE STOCKS)
½ CUP HEAVY CREAM
3 TABLESPOONS SWEET BUTTER

Celery knob is also known as celeriac and celery root (in French, *céleri-rave*). It is a variant of celery whose enlarged root is the delight of gourmets. Well-known and prized in Europe, it is not as much used here as it should be. The flavor is unusual and delicious.

Peel the celery knobs and cut them into cubes. Put into a saucepan, cover with boiling water, add salt and pepper, and cook until soft (about 20 minutes). Put through the finest blade of the grinder (or whirl in the blender). Add the Béchamel and simmer for 10 minutes. Add the chicken stock and heavy cream. Cook 5 minutes more. Strain. At the last minute before serving add the butter and mix well. Serves 6.

Onion Soup, Gratinée

9 LARGE ONIONS, SLICED
¾ CUP OIL
3 QUARTS BEEF STOCK (SEE STOCKS)
1 BAY LEAF
2 TABLESPOONS SALT
1 TEASPOON PEPPER
¾ CUP PORT WINE
6 SLICES FRENCH BREAD, TOASTED
¾ CUP FRESHLY GRATED
SWISS CHEESE/

Onion soup is as French as any dish there is. Pilgrims to Paris who have eaten it in Les Halles late at night, or early in the morning after a night on the town, always will connect it with that city. Here it is given a rather unusual touch of wine, which adds a certain elegance to a very down-to-earth dish.

Cook onions in the oil until brown. Pour off oil. Add the beef stock, bay leaf, salt, and pepper. Cook over low heat for 1½ hours. Remove from heat and add port. Pour into 6 flame-proof serving bowls. Float a slice of toast in each bowl. Sprinkle the cheese on top and brown for a few moments under the broiler. Serves 6.

Sweet Potato Vichyssoise

1 MEDIUM ONION, SLICED
1 STALK CELERY, SLICED
2 TABLESPOONS BUTTER
2 TABLESPOONS FLOUR
2 QUARTS BEEF STOCK (SEE STOCKS)
1½ POUNDS SWEET POTATOES,
PEELED & SLICED THIN/
SALT & PEPPER TO TASTE
1 CUP HEAVY CREAM, CHILLED

This dish was vastly improved by our test chef when he substituted beef stock for the chicken stock which had formerly been used, thus adding authority and character to a very seasonable cold soup.

Cook onion and celery in butter until soft but not brown. Mix in flour. Gradually add stock, mixing well. Add potatoes and cook until they are very soft, about 30 minutes. Force through sieve or whirl in blender. Season, cool, and chill. At last moment mix in heavy cream. Serves 6.

Soufflé Neptune

½ CUP DICED CRABMEAT
½ CUP DICED COOKED LOBSTER
2 TABLESPOONS BUTTER
1½ CUPS THICK SAUCE BÉCHAMEL
(SEE SAUCES)/
6 EGGS, SEPARATED
1 EGG WHITE
―――――――――――――
PREHEAT OVEN TO 375 DEGREES

Sauté crabmeat and lobster in a pan with the butter for 2–3 minutes. Stir in Béchamel. Add egg yolks, one by one, mixing well. Beat the egg whites stiff and fold gently into the above mixture. Butter an 8-cup mold and pour in the soufflé mixture. Bake in a 375-degree oven 40 minutes, or until puffed and brown. Serve with Anchovy Sauce. Serves 6.

Lobster Aromatique

6 TABLESPOONS CLARIFIED BUTTER
(SEE SAUCES)/
2 TABLESPOONS CHOPPED SHALLOTS
4½ CUPS SLICED LOBSTER MEAT
¼ CUP PERNOD, WARMED
1½ TEASPOONS SALT
¼ TEASPOON ENGLISH MUSTARD
¼ TEASPOON PAPRIKA
¼ TEASPOON CAYENNE
¼ TEASPOON CURRY POWDER
SQUEEZE OF LEMON JUICE
1 TABLESPOON MINCED CHIVES
1 TABLESPOON MINCED PARSLEY
1½ CUPS LOBSTER SAUCE
(SEE SAUCES)/
½ CUP WHIPPED CREAM

This dish is prepared and served tableside at The Four Seasons. It will make a pleasantly spectacular addition to your repertoire of chafing-dish cookery. You will probably need two chafing dishes to prepare it for six at your own table. A good tip from the captains who provide it for guests is that you use the professional way of squeezing juice from a half lemon; that is, stick a fork into the cut fruit, then squeeze, thereby avoiding spatter.

Heat butter in pan. Add shallots and sauté until soft, but do not brown. Add lobster. Mix well and allow to warm. Flame with Pernod, which will brown the shallots slightly. Mix salt with spices. Add to pan and mix well. Add lemon juice. Add chives, parsley, and lobster sauce, and mix well. Reduce 3–5 minutes. Take off heat and add whipped cream, mixing well. Serve at once. Serves 6.

Lobster Croustade

3 LIVE LOBSTERS, ABOUT
1½ POUNDS EACH/
12 MEDIUM MUSHROOMS
1 CUP CLARIFIED BUTTER

A croustade is a shell usually made from rich pastry or puff pastry, which is filled with whatever mixture one wishes. It can also be made from hollowed-out thick pieces of bread, which are deep fried before they are filled. They

(SEE SAUCES)/
3 TABLESPOONS LEMON JUICE
1½ TEASPOONS SALT
1 CUP SAUCE NANTUA (SEE SAUCES)
6 HEATED CROUSTADES
(SEE PASTRIES & BATTERS)/
6 MUSHROOMS
6 SLICES BLACK TRUFFLE

make an elegant presentation of such rich lobster dishes as the following.

Poach lobsters as described on page 35. Split lobster and clean. Remove all meat and cut up. Slice and coarsely chop the 12 mushrooms. Put into pan with butter, lemon juice, and salt. Sauté until dry. Mix with lobster meat. Put back on heat and add sauce Nantua. Mix well and heat through. Serve in croustades, set on napkins. Decorate with sautéed mushroom cap in the center of each topped by a truffle slice, and with the lobster legs along the side. Serves 6.

Lobster Quiche

1 LIVE LOBSTER, ABOUT 1½ POUNDS
2 TABLESPOONS BUTTER
2 TABLESPOONS COGNAC, WARMED
RICH PASTRY (SEE PASTRIES &
BATTERS) FOR 6 INDIVIDUAL SHELLS/
1 TABLESPOON CHOPPED PARSLEY
½ CUP GRATED GRUYÈRE CHEESE
1 PINT HEAVY CREAM
4 EGGS, BEATEN
SALT & PEPPER TO TASTE
DASH NUTMEG
───────────────────────
PREHEAT OVEN TO 350 DEGREES

The best way to make individual pastry shells is by using flan rings, which you place on a greased cookie sheet, then line completely with rich pastry, fluting the edge. Fill as directed and bake. It is simple to slide the quiches off the cookie sheet, removing the rings as you do so.

Poach lobster as described on page 35. Cut lobster meat into ½-inch squares and sauté 3 minutes in the butter. Pour warmed cognac into pan and ignite, shaking pan until flames die out. Place lobster into 6 pastry shells, 4 inches in diameter. Sprinkle with parsley and cheese. Mix cream, eggs, salt, pepper, and nutmeg. Pour over lobster. Cook in a 350-degree oven until golden brown (about 25 minutes). Serves 6.

Moules Marinière

6 TABLESPOONS BUTTER
6 TABLESPOONS CHOPPED SHALLOTS

This is an excellent luncheon or supper dish. Be sure to serve lots of hot crusty French bread with it and follow

3 TABLESPOONS CHOPPED PARSLEY

¼ TEASPOON WHITE PEPPER

3 TABLESPOONS LEMON JUICE

1½ CUPS DRY WHITE WINE

1½ TEASPOONS DRIED THYME

1 BAY LEAF

5 POUNDS MUSSELS, CLEANED (PAGE 20)

3 CUPS WHITE WINE SAUCE

(SEE SAUCES)/

1½ CUPS HEAVY CREAM

3 TABLESPOONS CHOPPED PARSLEY

it by a green salad, served, as in France, as a separate course.

Place ingredients from butter through bay leaf in large saucepan. Place mussels on top and cover. Cook for 8–10 minutes over high heat, until mussels open. Discard top shell. (Discard also any mussels which stay closed.) Lay mussels in serving dish, shells down, and keep warm. To the sauce remaining in pan, add the wine sauce. Reduce by ⅓. Add the cream and heat for a few minutes more. Strain over mussels, sprinkle with parsley, and serve. Serves 6.

Baked Red Snapper

½ CUP OLIVE OIL

6 TOMATOES, PEELED, SEEDED, & CHOPPED/

6 CUPS SLICED ONIONS

8 CLOVES GARLIC, PEELED & LEFT WHOLE/

½ CUP PITTED BLACK OLIVES

1 3-INCH STALK ROSEMARY (OR ¼ TEASPOON DRIED)/

6 STALKS FENNEL

2 BAY LEAVES

1 3-INCH STALK THYME (OR ¼ TEASPOON DRIED)/

SALT & PEPPER TO TASTE

1 RED SNAPPER ABOUT 4 POUNDS, CLEANED/

1 CUP DRY WHITE WINE

½ CUP WHITE WINE SAUCE (SEE SAUCES)/

½ CUP HEAVY CREAM

We've been asked whether one should leave the head on this fish. The French usually leave it on and we happen to think that makes the dish handsomer. However, if you are squeamish, have it removed. You will thus lose some flavor in the sauce, but perhaps it will be worth it to your sensibilities.

Heat oil in a large skillet. Add tomato, onion, garlic, olives, rosemary, fennel, bay leaves, and thyme. Season with salt and pepper and cook until soft but not brown (about 20 minutes). Sprinkle red snapper with salt and pepper. Place half the vegetable mixture on the bottom of a large, shallow baking dish. Place snapper on top and cover with remaining mixture. Pour white wine over and bake in 400-degree oven for 25 minutes. Remove red snapper to serving platter and keep warm. Add white wine sauce to baking dish and mix well. Return to oven for 10 minutes. Mix in cream and heat for another 5 minutes. Strain sauce over fish and serve. Serves 6.

Turban of Sole

6 FILLETS OF DOVER SOLE
(ABOUT 3 POUNDS)/
6 OUNCES CRABMEAT
6 TABLESPOONS CLARIFIED BUTTER
(SEE SAUCES)/
3 TABLESPOONS COGNAC, WARMED
3 CUPS WHITE WINE SAUCE
(SEE SAUCES)/
SALT & PEPPER TO TASTE
FEW DROPS LEMON JUICE
1½ TABLESPOONS MINCED SHALLOTS
½ CUP DRY WHITE WINE
¾ CUP HEAVY CREAM
6 SLICES TRUFFLE

Let fillets stand for 30 minutes in cold water. To prepare stuffing, put the crabmeat into a pan with the clarified butter. Shake the pan gently over medium heat until the crabmeat is hot. Pour in the cognac and flambé it. Add ¼ cup of the white wine sauce and cook for a few minutes. Season with salt and pepper and add lemon juice. Spread a tablespoonful of the stuffing on each fillet and roll fillets up. Place them in a buttered casserole with the shallots and the white wine. Cover the casserole and cook in 350-degree oven for 15 minutes. Meantime, pour the remainder of the white wine sauce into a pot and reduce it by ⅔. Add the heavy cream and cook a few minutes more. The sauce should be light. When the fillets are ready, arrange them in a circle on a serving plate. Reduce their juices and add to the sauce. Strain the sauce over the fillets and decorate with the truffle slices. Serves 6.

Winter Sole Four Seasons

1 TEASPOON OIL
1 TEASPOON BUTTER
2 TEASPOONS CHOPPED GREEN PEPPER
¼ CUP CRABMEAT
1 TABLESPOON COGNAC, WARMED
2 TABLESPOONS WHITE WINE SAUCE
(SEE SAUCES)/
SALT & PEPPER TO TASTE
6 FILLETS BOSTON SOLE
2 TABLESPOONS MINCED SHALLOTS
1 TABLESPOON LEMON JUICE
¼ CUP WHITE WINE
1 CUP WHITE WINE SAUCE
(SEE SAUCES)/
2 TABLESPOONS BUTTER
2 TEASPOONS MINCED FRESH PARSLEY
2 TEASPOONS MINCED FRESH CHERVIL
6 SLICES TRUFFLE

Heat oil and the teaspoon of butter, and in it sauté the green pepper until soft over low heat. Add the crabmeat. When hot, add cognac and flambé. Add the 2 tablespoons of white wine sauce. Season with salt and pepper. Lay the sole fillets out flat and place about a tablespoon of crab mixture on each. Roll up like paupiettes (big corks). Butter a pan and put shallots, lemon juice, salt, pepper, and white wine on the bottom. Place the fillets on top. Cover with buttered parchment paper. Put into a 350-degree oven and poach for 15 minutes. Remove from the oven and place the fillets on a serving platter. Keep warm. Reduce the pan juices by ⅔ and add the white wine sauce. Cook a few minutes more. Add butter and shake the pan until butter is absorbed by the sauce. Add parsley and chervil. Correct seasoning. Pour sauce over paupiettes and decorate each with a slice of truffle. Serves 6.

Roast Duckling, Sauce Bigarade

2 5-POUND DUCKLINGS
SALT & PEPPER TO TASTE
½ CUP OIL

————

Mirepoix: 2 LARGE CARROTS,
PEELED & CHOPPED;
1 MEDIUM ONION, PEELED & CHOPPED;
1 STALK CELERY, CHOPPED;
2 BAY LEAVES; 1 STALK
FRESH THYME (OR ½ TEASPOON DRY)/

————

1 QUART BROWN SAUCE (SEE SAUCES)
1 PINT BEEF STOCK (SEE STOCKS)
5 ORANGES
2 LEMONS

————

Gastrite: ⅔ CUP SUGAR, 3 TABLESPOONS
WATER, 1½ TABLESPOONS RED
WINE VINEGAR/

Salt and pepper the ducklings. Place on a rack in a roasting pan and pour the oil over them. Roast in a 450-degree oven for 10 minutes. Add mirepoix and cook until brown, stirring occasionally. Add brown sauce, brown stock, and 2 of the oranges and 1 of the lemons, cut in quarters. Reduce heat to 350 degrees and cook the ducklings for 1½ hours, basting often. Remove the pan from the oven. Put the ducklings on a large platter and keep warm. Remove the rack and reduce the sauce by ⅓ over low heat.

Cook sugar and water in a saucepan to a blond caramel color. Add vinegar. Cook for 3 or 4 minutes more and add the gastrite to the sauce in the roasting pan. Cook 5 minutes more. Peel and section 2 of the remaining oranges and remove seeds. Arrange the sections around the ducklings. Strain the sauce over them. Meantime, peel the remaining lemon and orange with a vegetable peeler, and cut the peels into very fine julienne. Blanch them 5 minutes in boiling water. Drain. Sprinkle the julienne over the sauce. Serves 6.

NOTE: Bitter Seville oranges are best for this dish. If they are unobtainable, you may use kumquats instead.

Wine-braised Goose

1 8-POUND GOOSE
SALT & PEPPER TO TASTE
½ CUP OIL
1 CARROT, SLICED
½ MEDIUM ONION, SLICED
1 STALK CELERY, SLICED
2 WHOLE CLOVES GARLIC, PEELED
1 CUP DRY WHITE WINE
½ CUP BROWN SAUCE (SEE SAUCES)

You will note that, as is frequently the case, this recipe does not suggest that you stuff the goose. However, if you very much want a stuffing, use whole chestnuts. With your goose, serve sauerkraut, or Red Cabbage au Caramel with diced apples.

Season the goose with salt and pepper. Truss. Heat the oil in a big casserole or covered roaster. Add the goose, carrot, onion, celery, and garlic. Brown the goose well on all sides. Add the wine and brown sauce, cover the pan and bake in a 325-degree oven for 1½ hours. Baste often. (To test for doneness move the legs up and down. They should move easily.) Strain the sauce and serve it separately. Serves 6. *(See illustration, page 94.)*

Stuffed Capon, Sauce Suprême

2 CUPS LONG-GRAIN RICE
2 QUARTS WATER WITH
1 TABLESPOON SALT/
1¼ CUPS JULIENNE-SLICED MUSHROOMS
1¼ CUPS JULIENNE-SLICED
BLACK TRUFFLES/
1 6-POUND PLUMP CAPON
2 QUARTS CHICKEN STOCK
(SEE STOCKS)/
4 CUPS SLICED ONIONS, BLANCHED
½ CUP FLOUR
4 TABLESPOONS BUTTER
1 CUP HEAVY CREAM
SALT & PEPPER TO TASTE

Blanch rice in salted water for 8 minutes. Drain. Mix rice with mushrooms and truffles. Stuff chicken with the mixture and truss. Place in pot with chicken stock and onions. Cook over low heat for 1 hour. Test for doneness by moving leg. Remove capon to a serving platter and keep warm. Off heat, with a whisk, beat together the chicken stock, flour, and butter. Reduce by ⅓ and add cream. Cook over low heat for 10 minutes and strain. Add seasonings. Pour over capon and serve very hot. Serves 4.

Poulet à la Sainte Ménéhould

1 6-POUND CAPON
1½ CUPS DRY WHITE WINE
SALT & PEPPER TO TASTE
SPRIG OF PARSLEY
3 SHALLOTS, CHOPPED
1 CLOVE GARLIC, CHOPPED
¼ TEASPOON THYME
1 BAY LEAF
¼ TEASPOON BASIL
2 CLOVES

As you may imagine when you read the following recipe, the brushing with egg yolk and patting with browned crumbs gives an indescribable texture of crispness to the finished product.

Truss chicken for roasting. Place in a roasting pan with wine, salt, pepper, parsley, shallots, garlic, thyme, bay leaf, basil, and cloves. Cover and leave overnight. Remove chicken, leaving all other ingredients in the pan, and roast in another pan for 20 minutes in a 400-degree oven.

102

½ CUP BUTTER
2 EGG YOLKS
¾ CUP BREAD CRUMBS
2 TABLESPOONS BUTTER

Return the chicken to the pan in which it was marinated, add the butter and roast in 350-degree oven with the other ingredients for about 1¼ hours, basting frequently. When chicken is done (leg moves easily), remove and brush all over with beaten egg yolks. Meanwhile, slightly brown the bread crumbs in the 2 tablespoons of butter. Pat the bread crumbs over the chicken. Return to 400-degree oven for about 10 minutes (until crumbs are dark brown). Put pan gravy through a sieve. Pour some of it over the chicken and serve the rest separately. Serves 6.

Breast of Turkey, Xeres

1 4-POUND TURKEY BREAST
SALT & PEPPER TO TASTE
1 CUP FLOUR
½ CUP CLARIFIED BUTTER
(SEE SAUCES)/
1 CUP DRY SHERRY
¼ CUP BROWN SAUCE (SEE SAUCES)
2 TABLESPOONS SWEET BUTTER

Slice the turkey breast very thin or have your butcher do it. Sprinkle with salt and pepper. Dip each slice in the flour to coat well. Place clarified butter in a large skillet and heat well. Put in turkey slices and cook over medium heat 3 minutes on each side. Remove slices to a serving dish and keep warm. Remove fat from pan. Add the sherry and reduce by ⅔. Add brown sauce and cook a few minutes more. Off heat, add sweet butter and mix well. Strain the sauce over the turkey and serve very hot. Serves 6.

Beef, Veal, Lamb & Pork

English Mixed Grill

6 LITTLE PORK SAUSAGES
6 5-OUNCE RIB LAMB CHOPS

This recipe does not stint in its offering of meats. If you would rather offer less, just choose any three of the meats

105

6 3-OUNCE SLICES CALF LIVER
12 LARGE WHITE MUSHROOM CAPS
BUTTER
6 4-OUNCE SLICES FILLET OF BEEF
6 LAMB KIDNEYS, SPLIT
6 MEDIUM TOMATOES, HALVED
6 SLICES BACON, FRIED CRISP
4 CUPS FRIED JULIENNE POTATOES
6 SLICES MAÎTRE D'HÔTEL BUTTER
(SEE SAUCES)/
WATERCRESS

you like and you will probably satisfy most appetites.

Simmer sausages with 2 tablespoons water, covered, 5 minutes. Remove cover and cook slowly until brown (10–15 minutes). Place chops, calf liver, and mushrooms (brushed with butter) on the broiler pan and broil chops and liver 4–5 minutes on each side. Broil mushrooms 8–10 minutes without turning. After 4 minutes, put in the fillet slices and cook 3 minutes on each side. After 5 minutes put in the lamb kidneys (seasoned with salt and pepper and brushed with butter) and the tomatoes (seasoned with salt and pepper and with a good lump of butter on top of each). Cook all these foods 5 minutes more. Remove from the broiler. Pile the potatoes in the center of a large serving dish. Arrange the meats and the hot bacon around the potatoes, placing a slice of maître d'hôtel butter in the middle of each kidney. Place the tomatoes on the sides of the dish and top each with a mushroom cap. Garnish with watercress sprigs. Serves 6–8.

Boeuf Bourguignon

4 POUNDS TOP ROUND CUT
IN 1½-INCH CUBES/
4 OUNCES PORK BELLY, CUT
IN SMALL CUBES/
⅓ CUP OIL
⅓ CUP CHOPPED ONION
1 TEASPOON MINCED GARLIC
2 TEASPOONS TOMATO PURÉE
⅓ CUP FLOUR
2⅔ CUPS RED WINE
2⅔ CUPS BEEF STOCK (SEE STOCKS)
1 BAY LEAF
1 3-INCH STALK THYME (OR
¼ TEASPOON DRIED)/
1 TABLESPOON SALT
1 TEASPOON FRESHLY GROUND
WHITE PEPPER/
1½ POUNDS CARROTS

Heat oil in large pot and in it brown the beef and pork belly. Add onion and garlic. Stir until brown. Add tomato purée and flour and mix well. Add remaining ingredients except carrots and stir well. Cover and cook over low heat for 3 hours, stirring occasionally. Meanwhile, peel carrots and quarter lengthwise. Halve these pieces and place in boiling water to cover. Cook for 15 minutes and drain. Remove meat to a serving casserole and strain sauce over. Add carrots and heat together for 5 minutes. Serves 6.

Carbonnade of Beef, Flamande

2 TABLESPOONS BUTTER
2 TABLESPOONS OIL OR BACON FAT
3 POUNDS CHUCK OR RUMP OF BEEF,
CUT INTO SLICES ½-INCH THICK/
1½ POUNDS YELLOW ONIONS,
THINLY SLICED/
SALT & FRESHLY GROUND
PEPPER TO TASTE/
2 CLOVES GARLIC, CRUSHED
1 BOTTLE (12 OUNCES) BEER
1 CUP BEEF STOCK (SEE STOCKS)
1 TABLESPOON BROWN SUGAR
BOUQUET GARNI: BAY LEAF,
THYME, PARSLEY/
2 TABLESPOONS CORNSTARCH
2 TABLESPOONS VINEGAR

Here is an example of a very simple, homelike dish which is consistently so good that we often serve it at parties. It can be made the day before and is only the better for being reheated. As the title suggests, it is a Flemish dish and one encounters it everywhere in Belgium. It has become so popular outside that country in recent years that it now belongs to the category of international dishes.

Heat butter and oil together to sizzling. Brown the beef slices well. Remove them as they brown. Reduce heat and brown onions in the same fat. Remove when browned. Season with salt and pepper and stir in the garlic. Layer the browned beef and onions in a casserole. Pour in beer and stock. Stir in the sugar. Poke the bouquet garni down into the casserole. Cover the casserole and cook in a 350-degree oven 2½ hours, or until the meat is fork-tender. Discard bouquet garni. Mix cornstarch with vinegar and stir into the gravy to thicken it. Serves 6 to 8.

Gypsy Beefsteak, Sauce Bordelaise

6 6-OUNCE SHELL STEAKS
SALT & PEPPER TO TASTE
6 MEDIUM ONIONS
FLOUR FOR COATING
FAT FOR DEEP FRYING
6 TABLESPOONS OIL
6 TABLESPOONS BUTTER
1½ CUPS SAUCE BORDELAISE
(SEE SAUCES)/

Trim steaks and season with salt and pepper. Cut the onions into thin rings. Dip them in flour. Fry in 360-degree fat until golden brown. Chop coarsely. Sauté the steaks in butter and oil until done to your taste. Slice them and re-form their shape. Pour the sauce Bordelaise over and top with the chopped fried onion rings. Serves 6.

Pot-au-Feu Ménagère

3 POUNDS BEEF
1 LARGE ONION

This is the frugal pot-on-the-fire which provides soup, meat, and vegetables all in one cooking operation. It

2 CLOVES GARLIC
6 CARROTS, PEELED
2 PARSNIPS, SCRAPED
1–2 MARROW BONES
3 LEEKS
3 STALKS CELERY (WITHOUT LEAVES),
CUT IN 4 PIECES EACH/
1 BAY LEAF
6 STALKS PARSLEY
3 TABLESPOONS SALT
WATER TO COVER
1 3-POUND CHICKEN
3 CUPS OF SOME OR ALL OF THE
FOLLOWING VEGETABLES, DICED: CARROTS,
CELERY, ONIONS, GREEN BEANS,
POTATOES, TURNIPS/
1 SMALL CABBAGE, QUARTERED
(OPTIONAL)/

is served with pickles, coarse salt, and crusty French bread. The browning process in this recipe gives color to the soup and renders off fat. However, this step is a departure from the classic method of making pot-au-feu and may be eliminated.

Place beef, onion, garlic, whole carrots, parsnips, and marrow bones in a large baking pan. Place in a 375-degree oven and brown for 20 to 30 minutes. Remove meat and vegetables and place in a large pot. Discard the top fat from baking pan and place it over direct heat. Pour a small amount of hot water into the pan, and, stirring constantly, scrape up brown residue from bottom of pan. Pour this over meat and vegetables in the pot. Add leeks, celery, bay leaf, parsley, salt, and water to cover and bring to boil. Carefully skim the fat off the top and lower heat. Simmer for about 1½ hours. Add chicken and cook for about ½ hour. The large vegetables will now have imparted their flavor to the soup and will be overcooked. Discard them, if you like, and add the 3 cups of assorted vegetables. Add the cabbage, if desired. Cook for about ½ hour longer. Remove marrow from bones and add to soup. Cut chicken and beef in serving-size portions. Serve pot-au-feu in one large bowl as the main course, or serve the soup separately as one course and the meat and chicken as another. Some guests will appreciate freshly grated Parmesan cheese to sprinkle over their soup. Serves 8–10. *(See illustration, page 91.)*

Steak Tartare

2 POUNDS FINELY GROUND OR
SCRAPED TOP ROUND/
4 TABLESPOONS CHOPPED CHIVES

For this delectable dish you should buy top round of the finest grade with as little fat in it as possible. If you are going to use it ground, get it from your butcher at the last

SALT & FRESHLY GROUND
BLACK PEPPER TO TASTE/
6 EGG YOLKS

———————

Garnishes: ANCHOVY FILLETS,
FINELY CHOPPED PARSLEY, CAPERS,
CHOPPED ONIONS/
Seasonings: DIJON MUSTARD, COGNAC,
WORCESTERSHIRE SAUCE, TABASCO/

possible minute before serving, or grind it yourself at the last minute. The old-fashioned way of preparing Steak Tartare was to scrape the meat, which some people think keeps it juicier. It is not hard to do, just rather time-consuming. If you'd like to try it, here's how: Slice your top round very thin. Hold a slice on a cutting board with your left hand and with a very sharp knife in your right hand scrape firmly at an angle on the edge of the meat slice, until you have reduced all the meat to scrapings. Serve this exactly as you would ground raw meat.

Mix beef and seasonings lightly together. Shape into 6 ovals on wooden board. Place one egg yolk in center of each. Surround with garnishes, each in its dish. (The onions should be placed under cold running water for 30 minutes and squeezed dry before being set out.) Offer seasonings on the side. Each guest is served a portion of Steak Tartare, then chooses garnishes and seasonings to taste. Serves 6.

Tripes à la mode de Caen

6 POUNDS TRIPE
½ CUP OIL
3 CUPS SLICED ONIONS
3 CUPS JULIENNE-CUT CARROTS
5 CLOVES OF GARLIC, FINELY MINCED
3 CALF FEET, BONED
1 QUART DRY WHITE WINE
1 QUART CIDER
BOUQUET GARNI: 2 BAY LEAVES,
1 3-INCH SPRIG OF THYME,
1 STALK OF CELERY/

Tripes à la mode de Caen is one of France's most famous dishes. It requires very long cooking, but is not otherwise complicated and the dish itself is superb. While it is made differently by different chefs—and housewives, too—it is the seasoning that makes the otherwise bland tripe delicious. Cider and Calvados are entirely characteristic of this dish. It can be reheated perfectly, so it can be made ahead of any party.

Cut the tripe in large julienne. Heat the oil in a heavy casserole. Add the onions and carrots, and stir for a few min-

2 TABLESPOONS SALT
2 TABLESPOONS PEPPER
3 TOMATOES, PEELED & CHOPPED
BOUILLON, IF NECESSARY
6 TABLESPOONS CALVADOS
¾ POUND SWISS CHEESE,
GRATED (OPTIONAL)/

utes. Add the garlic and stir for a few minutes more. Place half the tripe in the casserole. Stuff the calf feet with the remaining tripe and place on top of tripe already in the casserole. Pour in the wine and cider. Add the bouquet and salt and pepper. Cover with chopped tomatoes. Cook, covered, in a 250-degree oven for 12 hours. Check occasionally to be sure the liquid covers the ingredients. Add bouillon if necessary. Remove calf feet and cut into small dice. Return to casserole. At the last moment, add the Calvados and mix well. Serve very hot. Serve the grated Swiss cheese separately, if you wish. Serves 6.

Veal Cutlets Grand'mère

6 VEAL CUTLETS, 8 OUNCES EACH
SALT & WHITE PEPPER TO TASTE
FLOUR
9 TABLESPOONS BUTTER
1 CUP OIL
4 CUPS SLICED MUSHROOMS
(WITH STEMS)/
DASH LEMON JUICE
3 CUPS TINY COOKED ONIONS
(PAGE 131)/
¾ POUND PORK BELLY,
CUT INTO STRIPS/
2¼ CUPS POTATO BALLS,
THE SIZE OF THE ONIONS/
1 CUP DRY WHITE WINE
1 CUP BROWN SAUCE
(SEE SAUCES)/
MINCED FRESH PARSLEY

"Grand'mère" is, of course, the style in which grandmother made whatever the dish may be. Any dish Grand' mère involves onions, pork belly or bacon, and potatoes, as does the fine veal dish below.

Sprinkle cutlets with salt and white pepper. Roll in flour. Shake off excess. Heat butter and 6 tablespoons of the oil in a heavy-bottomed pan over medium heat. Add cutlets and cook about 6 minutes on each side to brown well. Poke meat with finger. If it is done, it will be of firm texture, and the juices will run yellow when the meat is pierced with a fork. Meantime, brown mushrooms in 7 tablespoons of the oil, adding lemon juice to keep them white. Add onions and brown them lightly. In another pan brown the pork belly in remaining oil. Add potatoes and continue cooking until they are done (6–8 minutes). When veal is done remove it from the pan and keep warm. Pour off fat in pan and add wine. Reduce by half. Add brown sauce. Correct seasoning with salt and pepper. Place cutlets on a serving dish. Strain the sauce over. Mix mushrooms, onions, potatoes, and pork and place down the center of the cutlets.

Sprinkle with parsley and serve at once. This is a handsome dish for 6.

Sautéed Calf Liver with Avocado

3 SLIGHTLY UNDERRIPE
MEDIUM AVOCADOS/
2 POUNDS CALF LIVER,
THINLY SLICED/
FLOUR
SALT & PEPPER TO TASTE
3 TABLESPOONS OIL
3 TABLESPOONS BUTTER
FEW DROPS LEMON JUICE
CHOPPED PARSLEY

The secret of this dish is its brief cooking, which keeps the liver rare and the avocado slices just right.

Peel, halve, and pit avocados. Cut each avocado into 6 lengthwise slices. Dip avocado and liver in flour to cover lightly. Season. Heat oil and butter in a large skillet. Sauté avocado and liver together over high heat for one minute on each side. Remove to serving platter, alternating slices of liver and avocado. Pour pan gravy over and sprinkle with lemon juice. Garnish with parsley and serve. Serves 6.

Veal Kidneys in Mustard Cream

6 VEAL KIDNEYS
2 TEASPOONS SALT
FRESHLY GROUND PEPPER TO TASTE
6 TABLESPOONS BUTTER
6 TABLESPOONS OIL
1½ CUPS THINLY SLICED MUSHROOMS
¾ CUP BUTTER
6 TABLESPOONS DIJON MUSTARD
1½ CUPS DRY WHITE WINE
1 TABLESPOON CHOPPED FRESH
TARRAGON (OR ½ TEASPOON DRIED)/
3 CUPS BROWN SAUCE (SEE SAUCES)
¾ CUP HEAVY CREAM
1 TABLESPOON CHOPPED SHALLOTS

This is a rich and fabulous dish. The combination of the tarragon flavor with the creamy mustard sauce is superb.

Slice kidneys in half lengthwise and remove fat and tendons. Cut into thin crosswise slices. Sprinkle with salt and pepper. Heat the 6 tablespoons butter and the oil in skillet until very hot. Add kidneys. Shaking pan continuously, cook for 3 minutes. Drain very well on paper towels. Remove all fat from pan. Cook mushrooms in the ¾ cup butter until well browned, about 5 minutes. Add mustard and mix well. Add wine, tarragon, and brown sauce. Mix well and cook until reduced by ⅓. Add cream, shallots, and kidneys to pan. Shaking pan, heat for a few minutes and serve. Serve with rice or Tarhonya Noodles and green beans for color. Serves 6.

Cassoulet de Toulouse

2 CUPS DRIED WHITE BEANS
3 QUARTS COLD WATER
½ POUND PORK RIND
1 TABLESPOON SALT
2 LARGE ONIONS
1 LARGE CARROT
1 POUND PORK BELLY
½ POUND LARGE SAUSAGES
1 POUND SHOULDER OF LAMB
¼ CUP OIL
4 CLOVES GARLIC
1 BAY LEAF
1 3-INCH STALK THYME (OR
¼ TEASPOON DRIED)/
4 LARGE RIPE TOMATOES, DICED
1 QUART DRY WHITE WINE
SALT & PEPPER TO TASTE
1 PRESERVED BREAST OF GOOSE
(PAGE 117)/

If there was ever a dish to make us lyrical it is a cassoulet. It is a superb, if basically simple, creation and the mouth waters just thinking about it. We think that the recipe given below, which is that of Chef Chantreau of The Four Seasons, is the best we've ever tasted, and we've had some fine ones. We had always regretted that the preserved goose, *confit d'oie* (see below), which is delectable, seemed beyond our capability to reproduce. Our delight in learning that it can be made and kept for a long time, with the prospect of using it in many a cassoulet, was great. Chef Chantreau points out that sometimes people sprinkle the cassoulet with bread crumbs and brown them. He does not think this is necessary. The important thing, he says, is to serve the dish very hot.

Soak beans overnight in cold water. Drain. Add the 3 quarts cold water, pork rind, a tablespoon of salt, a whole onion, the carrot, pork belly, and sausage. Simmer until the beans are soft (2 to 3 hours). Meantime, cut the lamb in big dice. Sauté them in the oil in a large casserole. When the lamb is brown, add the second onion, minced, and garlic, herbs, tomatoes, white wine, and a little of the cooking water from the beans. Season with salt and pepper. Simmer for 1½ hours. Ten minutes before the lamb is done, cut the breast of goose into 6 parts and add to the lamb. Mix the beans and meat together, shake the casserole and simmer for 10 minutes longer. Slice the sausage and pork belly and return to the dish. Serve the cassoulet in a large terrine. Serves 6.

Preserved Goose (Confit d'Oie)

1 8-POUND GOOSE
1 TABLESPOON QUATRE ÉPICES
(SEE GLOSSARY)/
1 TEASPOON GROUND THYME
1 TEASPOON GROUND BAY LEAF
3 TABLESPOONS SALT
5 POUNDS LARD
3 POUNDS TINNED GOOSE FAT

Cut goose into quarters. Mix spices and rub into goose. Let stand 24 hours. Melt lard and goose fat together in a large, heavy pot. Add goose. Cook, uncovered, very slowly for 2 hours. Cool. Place pieces of goose on the bottom of a large jar or earthenware terrine. Pour fat, 3 inches deep, over goose. Cover container with parchment or waxed paper and tie with string. Preserved goose will keep for a year.

Moussaka

6 SMALL EGGPLANTS
OIL FOR FRYING
1½ POUNDS LEAN LAMB, DICED
5 TABLESPOONS BUTTER
3 TABLESPOONS CHOPPED ONION
5 TABLESPOONS CHOPPED MUSHROOMS
DASH GARLIC POWDER
3 WHOLE EGGS
¾ CUP BROWN SAUCE (SEE SAUCES)
1 TABLESPOON SALT
1 TEASPOON WHITE PEPPER
1½ TEASPOONS CHOPPED
FRESH PARSLEY/
TOMATO SAUCE (SEE SAUCES),
HEATED TO PIPING/

Moussaka is a typical Middle Eastern dish and is served throughout the area in many guises. The recipe below makes it beautiful to look at in a way that is particularly French—that is, the mold is lined with eggplant skin. The dish, when turned out, is truly stunning.

Split 4 of the eggplants lengthwise and score the cut sides with a fork or the point of a knife, so they will cook quickly. Fry in hot deep oil until eggplant meat is soft. Remove meat with a spoon, keeping both skin and meat. Cook the lamb in 3 tablespoons of butter until it loses color. Cook onion and mushrooms separately, each in one of the remaining tablespoons of butter. Slice the remaining eggplants and fry the slices in deep oil. Grind the lamb and the eggplant meat and mix with the onions, mushrooms, and garlic powder. Add the eggs and mix well. Add brown sauce, salt, pepper, and parsley, and mix well with a wooden spoon. Correct seasoning. Line 6 small molds with the eggplant skin, purple side against the mold. Make layers in the molds of the meat mixture and the fried eggplant slices. Place molds in a pan of hot water and cook 15 minutes in a 350-degree oven. Turn each moussaka out on a plate and pour hot tomato sauce around it. Serves 6.

Boned Roast Suckling Pig

1 12-POUND SUCKLING PIG

3 POUNDS LEAN VEAL

3 POUNDS LEAN PORK

3 POUNDS PORK FAT

2 EGGS

¼ CUP COGNAC

2 TABLESPOONS SALT

1 TEASPOON FRESHLY GROUND PEPPER

1 POUND DRY MORELS, SOAKED IN

WARM WATER 1 HOUR AND DRAINED/

———————

Mirepoix: 2 LARGE CARROTS,
CHOPPED; 1 LARGE ONION, CHOPPED;
3 STALKS CELERY, CHOPPED;
2 4-INCH STALKS THYME (OR ½
TEASPOON DRIED); 2 BAY LEAVES/

———————

½ CUP OIL

½ CUP LARD

SALT & PEPPER FOR SPRINKLING

2 CUPS DRY WHITE WINE

5 CUPS VEAL STOCK (SEE STOCKS)

APPLE & CRANBERRIES TO GARNISH

Have your butcher bone the pig, leaving the head intact. Grind veal, pork, and fat three times. Add eggs, cognac, the 2 tablespoons salt, the teaspoon pepper, and the morels (chopped or whole). Mix together well and stuff into the pig. Re-form the pig into its original shape. Tie with string. Put it into a large roasting pan with the mirepoix, oil, and lard. Sprinkle generously with salt and pepper. Place a raw potato in the mouth and aluminum foil over the ears. Place in a 350-degree oven. When the pig is brown, add wine and veal stock. Cook 3½ hours, basting occasionally. When done, remove foil from ears. Replace potato with an apple and put cranberries in the eyes. Serves 16.

Curried Loin of Pork

3 POUNDS BONED LOIN OF PORK

¼ CUP OIL

———————

Mirepoix: 1 LARGE CARROT,
SLICED; 1 MEDIUM ONION, CHOPPED;
BOUQUET GARNI: 1 BAY LEAF,
1 3-INCH STALK SAGE (OR
¼ TEASPOON DRIED)/

———————

The unusual touch of sprinkling curry powder over the pork as it cooks in this recipe is a great inspiration. Pork curries are certainly not Indian, but we must say that the meat has an affinity for these spices.

Put the meat into a baking pan with the oil and the mirepoix. Sprinkle with salt. Put the pan over medium heat on top of the range and brown the loin and vegetables.

SALT TO TASTE
¼ CUP WHITE WINE
½ CUP BEEF STOCK (SEE STOCKS)
4 TABLESPOONS CURRY POWDER

Add white wine and brown stock. Put into a 350-degree oven and cook for 2¼ hours, sprinkling the meat with 1 tablespoon of curry powder 4 times during the cooking. Strain the sauce over it. Serve with Mango Rice. Serves 6.

Loin of Young Pork with Glazed Apricots

6 POUNDS LOIN OF PORK, TRIMMED
¼ CUP OIL
2 CARROTS, SLICED
1 MEDIUM ONION, CHOPPED
1 STALK CELERY, SLICED
1 3-INCH STALK FRESH SAGE (OR
¼ TEASPOON DRIED)/
1 BAY LEAF
1 TABLESPOON SALT
1 TEASPOON PEPPER
1 CUP DRY WHITE WINE
1 CUP BROWN SAUCE (SEE SAUCES)
1 POUND DRIED APRICOTS
½ CUP HONEY

Cook pork in a roasting pan with the oil in a 450-degree oven for 10 minutes. Add the vegetables and let them take on color. Add herbs and seasonings. Pour in wine and brown sauce. Cover the pan and cook in a 300-degree oven for 2 hours. Remove the loin to a platter. Keep warm. Meantime, poach the apricots in a quart of water for 20 minutes. Strain and put the apricots and honey into a saucepan. Cook over low heat until the apricots are glazed (about 10 minutes). Arrange the apricots gently and decoratively on the loin of pork. Strain the sauce from the roasting pan and pour it around the loin. Serves 6. *(See illustration, page 113.)*

Braised Loin of Pork

3 POUNDS BONED LOIN OF PORK
1 TABLESPOON OIL
2 SMALL CARROTS, SLICED
2 SMALL PARSNIPS, SLICED
2 SMALL GREEN PEPPERS, SLICED
2 SMALL TOMATOES, CHOPPED
1½ TEASPOONS PAPRIKA
2 TABLESPOONS LEMON JUICE
1 BAY LEAF
1 CUP RED WINE
4 DRIED JUNIPER BERRIES
PINCH OF SALT

Heat oil in flame-proof casserole and brown pork quickly and evenly. Add remaining ingredients and cover. Cook over low heat until meat is tender, about 1½ hours. Remove meat to serving platter and slice. Press sauce through a sieve or whirl in blender and pour over meat. Serves 6.

119

Baby Pheasant with Juniper Berries and Gin

6 BABY PHEASANTS,
1½ POUNDS EACH/
SALT & PEPPER
6 SLICES FATBACK
3 TABLESPOONS OIL
½ CUP (1 STICK) BUTTER
3 TABLESPOONS JUNIPER BERRIES
½ CUP GIN, WARMED

Juniper berries are much used in the cooking of game birds. The use of gin to flambé these pheasants simply underlines the juniper flavor already present.

Sprinkle pheasants with salt and pepper. Bard each with fatback (see Glossary). Put in an oven-proof casserole with oil, butter, and juniper berries. Put the casserole into a 375-degree oven for 25 minutes. Baste the pheasants often, or they will become dry. Remove the casserole from the oven and put the birds (but not the juniper berries) in another casserole for serving. Heat gin, pour over pheasants, and flame it at the table before the guests. Serves 6.

Baby Pheasant with Fresh Tarragon

6 BABY PHEASANTS
18 WHOLE FRESH TARRAGON LEAVES
3 CARROTS, CHOPPED
3 ONIONS, CHOPPED
6 STALKS CELERY, CHOPPED
4 CUPS VEAL STOCK (SEE STOCKS)
SALT & PEPPER TO TASTE
1 CUP DRY WHITE WINE
18 TARRAGON LEAVES, CHOPPED
6 TABLESPOONS BUTTER, MELTED
FRESH WATERCRESS SPRIGS

Place 3 whole tarragon leaves inside of each pheasant. Cook carrots, onions, and celery in 3 cups of veal stock 8–10 minutes. Pour this mirepoix around the birds. Season. Roast in a 375-degree oven for 20 minutes. Mix the wine, remaining veal stock, chopped tarragon leaves, and butter. Pour this over the birds and cook for 5 minutes longer. Strain the sauce and serve it in a gravy boat. Serve pheasants on a platter with watercress. Serves 6.

Quail Stuffed with Game Pâté

6 BLACK TRUFFLES
¼ POUND FOIE GRAS
6 QUAIL, CLEANED, WITH GIBLETS
1½ CUPS GAME STOCK (SEE STOCKS)

Chop 3 of the truffles and mix with the foie gras. Stuff into the quail. Wrap each bird in cheesecloth. Heat game stock with quail giblets and Madeira. Poach the birds in this liquid for 15 minutes. Drain, reserving liquid, and remove

½ CUP MEDIUM-DRY MADEIRA
½ CUP (1 STICK) BUTTER
12 MUSHROOM CAPS, THICKLY SLICED
12 COOKED ARTICHOKE
BOTTOMS (PAGE 247)/
½ CUP HEAVY CREAM
SALT & PEPPER TO TASTE

cheesecloth. Pat the quail dry with paper towels. Melt butter in a skillet and brown quail in it. Remove quail to a casserole. In the same skillet sauté the mushrooms and artichoke bottoms for 5 minutes. Add to casserole with remaining truffles, thickly sliced, as a garniture. Boil down the liquid from cooking the quail until it is reduced by ½. Strain. Add cream, correct seasoning with salt and pepper, and pour sauce over quail. Cover the casserole and place in a 350-degree oven for 5 minutes. Serve quail with sauce on the side. Serves 6.

Salmis of Wild Turkey

1 7-POUND WILD TURKEY
1 TABLESPOON SALT
1 TEASPOON PEPPER
½ CUP OIL
½ CUP CLARIFIED BUTTER
(SEE SAUCES)/
¼ CUP COGNAC, WARMED
4 OUNCES TRUFFLE, SLICED
2 POUNDS FRESH WHITE
MUSHROOMS, SLICED/

Salmis Sauce:
BONES FROM TURKEY
2 TABLESPOONS OIL
1 LARGE CARROT, SLICED
1 MEDIUM ONION, SLICED
1 TEASPOON DRIED THYME
1 BAY LEAF
1 BOTTLE RED WINE
½ CUP BROWN SAUCE (SEE SAUCES)
½ CUP (1 STICK) SWEET BUTTER

A salmis is a dish in which meat, usually game, is partially cooked, then finished off at the table—or, in this case, in the oven. Since the wild turkey is inclined to be a bony bird, the only parts really worth eating are the heavy breasts and the leg meat; thus it is perfect for salmis. Wild turkey are available largely from game farms, as they have become rare in the areas where they used to be hunted. They are exceedingly different in flavor from their domestic counterparts, though not a bit gamey, as some wild birds are.

Put the turkey in a large casserole. Sprinkle with salt and pepper. Pour the ½ cup of oil and the clarified butter over. Roast in a 450-degree oven for 20 minutes. It should be rare. Remove the bird and carefully cut out breast and leg meat without bones. Put meat in a casserole and flambé with cognac. Add truffles and mushrooms. Cover. Cook in a 300-degree oven 40 minutes.

Meantime, make the salmis sauce. Chop the bones of the turkey as fine as possible. Put them in a flame-proof cas-

121

16 HEART-SHAPED CROUTONS,
FRIED IN BUTTER/

serole. Brown them in the 2 tablespoons oil. Add carrot, onion, thyme, and bay leaf. Stir with a wooden spoon for a few minutes. Add wine and cook slowly until reduced by ⅔. Add brown sauce. Cook 15 minutes longer. Strain sauce into the other casserole. Add sweet butter and mix well. Remove the turkey. Slice the breast thin, cut the meat of each leg in 4 parts. Arrange pieces of turkey on a large serving dish. Pour the sauce over. Arrange mushrooms and truffles on top. Put croutons around the edge. Serves 6–8.

Saddle of Hare, Chantreau

1 SADDLE OF HARE
FATBACK, CUT IN NARROW LARDOONS/

———

Marinade: 1 ONION, SLICED
1 CARROT, SLICED
½ BAY LEAF
PINCH OF THYME
10 SPRIGS PARSLEY
1 TABLESPOON BLACK PEPPERCORNS
2 TABLESPOONS SALT
4 CUPS DRY WHITE WINE
½ CUP WHITE VINEGAR

———

1 TABLESPOON OIL

If you've forgotten what lardoons and larding are, they are defined under "Larding" in our Glossary of Cooking Terms. The process is important in this recipe, since hare is inclined to be dry. It makes delicious eating when properly cooked, however.

Lard hare on top and bottom, at 1-inch intervals. Let strips of fatback protrude ½ inch. Cook marinade, uncovered, over low heat for 30 minutes. Chill. Pour over hare and marinate, covered, for 48 hours. Remove hare from marinade, dry well with paper towels. Heat 1 tablespoon oil in a roasting pan and turn hare in it for a moment to brown the outside quickly. Roast in a 550-degree oven for 8 minutes.

Sauce:
½ CUP STRAINED MARINADE
1 TABLESPOON PREPARED MUSTARD
1 CUP GAME SAUCE (SEE SAUCES)

Cook together until reduced by ⅓. Place hare on carving board or platter and serve. Serve sauce separately. Serves 6.

Estouffade of Venison

6 POUNDS LEG OF VENISON, CUBED
MARINADE TO COVER (SEE STOCKS)

An estouffade is a dish whose ingredients are slowly stewed. The combination of that sort of cooking with veni-

¼ CUP OLIVE OIL
¼ CUP COGNAC, WARMED
1 TABLESPOON TOMATO PURÉE
1 BAY LEAF
¾ CUP FLOUR
½ BOTTLE CHAMBERTIN WINE
½ BOTTLE RED VIN ORDINAIRE
2 CUPS OF THE MARINADE
SALT & PEPPER TO TASTE
6 TRIANGLE-SHAPED CROUTONS
12 BOILED POTATOES

son which has been well marinated produces tender meat. Chef Chantreau says that some chefs add a garniture of small onions, mushrooms, and diced pork belly to this dish. But he says also that he is not a partisan of this custom, because he thinks that too many additions take away from the flavor of the venison.

Marinate the venison in the marinade for 48 hours, then remove and pat dry with paper towels. Heat the olive oil very hot in a casserole and brown the venison in it. Add the vegetables from the marinade and flambé all with cognac. Add the tomato purée, bay leaf, and flour, and stir well to mix with the meat. Add both wines and the 2 cups of marinade. Simmer 1½ hours. Remove meat to a serving dish and keep it warm. Season with salt and pepper. Strain over the meat. Arrange the croutons and potatoes around the meat. Serves 6.

Saddle of Venison, Sauce Poivrade

9-POUND SADDLE OF VENISON
FAT FOR LARDING
MARINADE TO COVER (SEE STOCKS)
½ CUP OIL
1 CUP MARINADE
4 TABLESPOONS FRESHLY GROUND
BLACK PEPPER/
2 CUPS GAME SAUCE (SEE SAUCES)
¼ CUP SWEET BUTTER
SALT TO TASTE

The piquancy of freshly ground pepper adds great zest to the sauce suggested for this venison dish.

Trim the saddle and lard it. Place it in the marinade for 48 hours. Remove the saddle from the marinade and pat it dry with paper towels. Bring the oil to high heat in a large pan. Add the saddle and roast in a 450-degree oven for 30 minutes. It should be rare. Remove and keep warm. Add the cup of marinade to the pan and reduce to dry. Add the pepper and the game sauce. Cook a few minutes more. Strain. Add the butter and mix well. Correct the seasoning with salt. Serve sauce separately. Serves 6.
NOTE: Serve this dish with Purée of Chestnuts and Bar-le-Duc or currant jelly as accompaniments.

Chartreuse of Vegetables

1 POUND GREEN BEANS OF
UNIFORM SIZE /
2 SUMMER SQUASH
2 LARGE CARROTS
2 ZUCCHINI
¼ CUP FRESH GREEN PEAS
½ CUP BRUSSELS SPROUTS
½ CUP CAULIFLOWER FLORETS
6 CABBAGE LEAVES
SALT & PEPPER
SOFT BUTTER FOR LINING MOLD
1½ CUPS MASHED POTATOES
¼ CUP CLARIFIED BUTTER
(SEE SAUCES) /

If you want to make a production that will dazzle your guests, try this dish which is one of the prettiest vegetable presentations we've ever seen and tastes as good as it looks.

Cut ends off beans. Peel carrots and cut them in pieces the same length as the beans. Slice the zucchini and squash thin. Parboil beans, squash, carrots, zucchini, peas, Brussels sprouts, cauliflower, and cabbage separately in boiling water (the vegetables should still be firm). Drain and season to taste with salt and pepper. Spread the sides and bottom of a 6-inch-diameter mold very thickly with butter. Around the outside edge of the bottom of the mold make a circular border of green peas. The butter will hold the peas in place. Make an outer circle of overlapping slices of squash and an inner circle of overlapping slices of zucchini (the entire bottom of the mold should be covered). Stand alternate slices of green beans and carrot upright on the peas and leaning against the side of the mold. Trim the ends of the beans and the carrots with scissors, so that the ends are even with the top of the mold. With spatula, cover sides and bottom of mold with layer of mashed potatoes. Press potatoes down firmly. Cover the layer of mashed potatoes with cabbage leaves. Place an outer circle of Brussels sprouts on the leaves, and fill the center with cauliflower. Place a new layer of zucchini and squash in overlapping circles. Pour clarified butter over. Cover with cabbage leaves. Now cover with the final layer of mashed potatoes and bake in a 350-degree oven for 20 minutes. Remove from oven and turn out mold onto serving plate. Serves 6. *(See illustration, pages 126-127.)*

1. *Cutting carrots in julienne.*

2. *Slicing zucchini.*

3. *Slicing yellow squash.*

7. *Fill in bottom with zucchini.*

8. *Lining mold with alternate slices of green beans & carrots.*

9. *Trimming beans & carrots flush to rim.*

13. *Space in center of sprouts is for cauliflower.*

14. *Pressing to fill mold firmly.*

15. *Final layer of squash & zucchini.*

16. *Adding final layer of cabbage.*

17. *Again pressing to firm.*

18. *Covering with mashed potatoes.*

Chartreuse of Vegetables

4. Vegetables ready for parboiling.

5. Lining buttered mold with circle of peas.

6. Circling bottom with squash.

10. Inner lining completed.

11. Covering bottom & inner side with mashed potatoes.

12. Placing cabbage leaves, then Brussels sprouts over potatoes.

19. Chartreuse of Vegetables turned out onto serving plate.

A Chartreuse of Vegetables requires patience and a steady hand, but result is infinitely worthwhile. For recipe, see page 124.

Stuffed Cabbage à la Ménagère

4 POUNDS CABBAGE
STUFFING (SEE BELOW)
¼ CUP OIL

Mirepoix: 1 CARROT, CHOPPED;
1 MEDIUM ONION, CHOPPED;
1 POUND PORK SKIN, CUBED;
1 BAY LEAF;
1 4-INCH STALK OF THYME (OR
¼ TEASPOON DRIED)/

1 CUP DRY WHITE WINE
½ CUP BROWN SAUCE (SEE SAUCES)

A ménagère is a thrifty housewife and this is indeed an inexpensive, homely, but still delicious and filling dish to serve to family or guests.

Remove the cabbage leaves carefully, one by one. Blanch them in boiling salted water for 10 minutes. Cool under running water and drain. Arrange the leaves on a cloth on a table. Put 2 tablespoons of stuffing on each leaf. Wrap each leaf into a neat ball shape. If 1 leaf is not enough, use 2 or 3. It is most important that the stuffing doesn't break through the leaves. Press the balls firmly into shape with a cloth. Pour oil into a large, oven-proof casserole. Add mirepoix. Arrange cabbage balls on top. Cover casserole and put it in a 375-degree oven. After 10 minutes add wine and brown sauce. Continue to cook, uncovered, at the same heat, for 1 hour. Remove casserole from oven. Carefully put the cabbage balls on a serving plate. Strain the sauce around them. Serves 6.

Stuffing:
¼ CUP OIL
1 POUND LEAN PORK, CUBED
1 POUND LEAN VEAL, CUBED
1 MEDIUM ONION, SLICED
SALT & PEPPER TO TASTE
2 EGGS

Heat oil in a skillet, add the meat and brown it. Add the onion and brown it. Add salt and pepper. Put meat through the grinder into a bowl. Add eggs and mix well to bind.

1½ POUNDS CARROTS, PEELED & SLICED
1½ TEASPOONS SUGAR
1½ POUNDS SMALL POTATOES, PEELED & SLICED/
3 TABLESPOONS SWEET BUTTER
1 TABLESPOON IMPORTED SOY SAUCE
¾ CUP HEAVY CREAM
MILK TO THIN PURÉE
SALT & PEPPER TO TASTE

Purée of Carrots

Place carrots in boiling water to cover. Add sugar and cook for 8 minutes. Add potatoes and cook for another 10 minutes or until vegetables are soft. Drain. Force through sieve or whirl in blender. Add butter and soy sauce. Mix in the cream. Add milk until purée is light and fluffy. Season and serve. Serves 6.

NOTE: The soy sauce specified here is the imported variety, from Japan or Hong Kong.

Chestnut Purée

3 POUNDS CHESTNUTS
3 CUPS BEEF STOCK (SEE STOCKS)
BOUQUET GARNI: PARSLEY, BAY LEAF,
& SHORT CELERY STALK/
3 TABLESPOONS BUTTER
HEAVY CREAM
SALT & PEPPER TO TASTE

Making chestnut purée from scratch, as suggested below, is something of a chore. You can buy Chestnut Purée Natur (unsweetened), imported from France, in tins. It is very good and we think all that time is worth saving. Add cream and butter to the tinned variety before heating in a double boiler.

Cut slits on the flat side of chestnuts and place in a pan. Put into a 450-degree oven for 5–6 minutes. Remove, peel off shells, and with a sharp knife remove inner skin. This is difficult and must be done when the chestnuts are hot, so you may have to reheat them as you work. Place in a pan with the beef stock and bouquet garni and simmer until chestnuts are cooked through (45–60 minutes). Drain and put through a food mill. Place again in saucepan. Add butter and enough cream to achieve the consistency you like. Season to taste. Serves 6.

Leeks in Cream

12 CLEANED LEEKS (PAGE 66)
1 TEASPOON SALT
2 CUPS SAUCE BÉCHAMEL (SEE SAUCES)
½ CUP GRATED SWISS CHEESE
BUTTER

Place leeks in water to cover. Add salt and bring to a boil. Cook, uncovered, for 15–20 minutes, or until green tops of leeks are tender. Drain thoroughly. Place 1 cup Béchamel on bottom of baking dish. Arrange leeks on top. Pour remaining Béchamel over. Sprinkle with Swiss cheese and dot with butter. Place under broiler for a few minutes until just golden brown. Serves 6.

Onions in Onions

3 LARGE SPANISH ONIONS,
3 INCHES IN DIAMETER OR LARGER/
12 TINY WHITE COOKED ONIONS
(SEE BELOW)/

This is one of The Four Seasons' most popular vegetable dishes, invented by the restaurant and greatly prized by the clientele.

1 TABLESPOON BUTTER
⅓ CUP BREAD CRUMBS
CUPS SAUCE BÉCHAMEL (SEE SAUCES)

Peel large onions, cutting off only minimum amount at root and stem ends. Gently boil in salted water to cover, until barely done (about 25 minutes). Do not overcook or onions will fall apart in handling. Drain and cut each onion in half crosswise. Carefully remove center rings to make a hole 2 inches wide. Peel excess layers from tiny white onions to reduce size to ½-inch diameter or less. Melt butter in a skillet, add bread crumbs, and toss briefly. Place small onions in Béchamel and heat. Arrange the 6 Spanish onion halves on a flame-proof dish. Fill centers first with small onions, then with sauce. Pour remaining sauce over. Sprinkle bread crumbs over onions and brown under broiler. Serves 6.

Boiled Tiny White Onions

2 POUNDS TINY WHITE ONIONS
BOILING WATER TO COVER
2 TEASPOONS SALT

To peel onions, immerse for about 15 seconds in boiling water. Drain. Cut off ends and peel off outer layer and thin layer underneath. Put the onions into a deep saucepan, add water to cover, and the salt. Bring to a boil, cover the pan, and cook until just tender (15–20 minutes). Do not overcook or they will fall apart. Drain well. Add salt, pepper, and clarified butter (see Sauces) to taste, if onions are to be served as a vegetable. As a garniture, they are frequently browned lightly in butter. As a vegetable, serves 6.

Roesti Potatoes

4 MEDIUM POTATOES
⅔ CUP SHREDDED GRUYÈRE CHEESE
¼ CUP MELTED BUTTER
¼ CUP OIL
SALT & PEPPER TO TASTE

This is a national dish of the Swiss, and certainly one of their best inventions. The method of cooking the potatoes is always the same, but sometimes it omits the cheese, and sometimes in country places it calls for bits of ham to be mixed in. Also, in the countryside a great deal of butter or other fat is used, but more sophisticated cooking cuts down on that.

Peel potatoes. Shred in hair-fine julienne and drain on a towel. Mix with cheese. Heat the butter and oil in a large skillet and press the potato mixture into the pan in a thin layer. Sprinkle with salt and pepper. Cook until the bottom is browned, shaking pan constantly. Loosen edges with a spatula and turn as you would a pancake. Brown second side and serve. Serves 6.

Tangerine Sweet Potatoes

6 MEDIUM SWEET POTATOES, BOILED IN THEIR SKINS/ 48 TANGERINE SECTIONS ¾ CUP HONEY

Peel and cut each potato lengthwise in 4 slices. Put 2 sections of tangerine on each slice of potato in a casserole or oven-proof serving dish. Cover with honey. Bake in a 350-degree oven 20 minutes. Serves 6–8.

Mango Rice

¼ CUP CLARIFIED BUTTER 3 TABLESPOONS CHOPPED ONION 1 BAY LEAF 1½ CUPS LONG-GRAIN RICE ½ CUP BOILING CHICKEN STOCK (SEE STOCKS)/ SALT TO TASTE 2 MANGOS, DICED

This makes a delicious accompaniment to a curry.

Put butter and onion into a flame-proof casserole. Stir over fairly high heat until lightly browned. Add bay leaf and rice, and stir well again so that the rice is coated with the butter. Pour in the boiling chicken stock. Season to taste. Cover casserole and bake in a 325-degree oven 18–20 minutes. Remove bay leaf and add mango to the rice. Serves 6.

Saffron Rice

½ CUP CLARIFIED BUTTER (SEE SAUCES)/ ¼ CUP MINCED ONION

Saffron rice is appetite-provoking, if only because of its lovely color. And of course it tastes delicious as well. Though saffron powder is so expensive that few can afford

1 BAY LEAF
1 CUP RICE
¼ TEASPOON SAFFRON LEAVES
2 CUPS CHICKEN CONSOMMÉ
(SEE STOCKS)

to keep it on their spice shelves, the leaves are less expensive and do an equally good job.

Pour butter into skillet and sauté the onion and bay leaf for 1 minute. Add the rice and be sure to coat it well with the butter and onion. Crush the saffron to powder and add to rice. Mix well and add the consommé. Bake in a 400-degree oven for 17 minutes, uncovered. Discard bay leaf before serving. Serves 6.

Shallot Soufflé

9 SHALLOTS, PEELED & CHOPPED
9 TABLESPOONS BUTTER
6 TABLESPOONS FLOUR
1¼ CUPS MILK
1 TEASPOON SALT
DASH TABASCO SAUCE
1¼ CUPS GRATED GRUYÈRE CHEESE
6 EGG YOLKS, LIGHTLY BEATEN
8 EGG WHITES
―――――――――――――――――
PREHEAT OVEN TO 375 DEGREES

Sauté the shallots in 3 tablespoons of the butter over medium heat until soft and slightly colored. Combine remaining butter and flour in a pot and cook for a few minutes, stirring until well blended. Gradually stir in the milk, salt, and Tabasco sauce, and continue to stir until thickened. Add the shallots, cheese, and egg yolks. Cook, stirring, over very low heat until cheese is melted and the mixture well blended. Cool. Beat the egg whites until stiff but not dry. Fold half of the whites thoroughly into the cheese mixture. Add remaining whites and fold in lightly. Pour into a buttered 2-quart soufflé dish and bake in a 375-degree oven 25–30 minutes, or until high and golden brown. Serves 6.

Zucchini with Walnuts

1 CUP WALNUT HALVES
6 MEDIUM ZUCCHINI
2 TABLESPOONS BUTTER
SALT & FRESHLY GROUND PEPPER

Reserve 8 walnut halves for garnish and chop the rest. Cut unpeeled zucchini in slices ⅛-inch thick. Sauté in butter, stirring gently and constantly. When almost tender, add chopped walnuts, salt, and pepper. Continue cooking and stirring until zucchini is tender. Garnish with reserved walnut halves. Serves 6.

133

Pear and Potato Salad

5 MEDIUM BOILING POTATOES
2 LARGE, HARD PEARS
¼ CUP WHITE VINEGAR
½ CUP OIL
¼ TEASPOON PEPPER
½ TEASPOON SALT
½ TEASPOON SUGAR
1 TEASPOON GRATED RAW ONION

This is a hearty yet refreshing and tangy winter salad. It accompanies game dishes well.

Boil potatoes in their jackets until tender (about ½ hour). When potatoes are cool enough to handle, peel and slice (not too thin, or they'll break). Peel pears and slice as thinly as possible, taking out core. Mix vinegar, oil, pepper, salt, sugar, and onion. Mix dressing with potatoes and pear, being careful not to break potatoes. This salad may be served either warm, room temperature, or chilled. *(See illustration, page 128.)*

Beefsteak Tomato Salad

2 MEDIUM GREEN PEPPERS
1 LARGE CUCUMBER
2 TABLESPOONS LEMON JUICE
6 TABLESPOONS OLIVE OIL
SALT & PEPPER TO TASTE
YOGURT DRESSING (SEE SAUCES)
2 LARGE BEEFSTEAK TOMATOES
SPRIG OF DILL

Blanch the green peppers 10 minutes in boiling water. Drain, cool, and chop. Cut cucumber in half, lengthwise. Remove seeds, then cut in quarters and dice. Marinate, with peppers, in lemon juice, oil, salt, and pepper. Drain well and mix with yogurt dressing. Peel the tomatoes, cut into thick slices. Top with the green pepper-cucumber mixture. Decorate with a sprig of dill. Serves 6.

Marinated Turnips, Dill Dressing

2 LARGE TURNIPS
5 TEASPOONS SALT
4 TABLESPOONS SUGAR
1½ CUPS WHITE WINE VINEGAR
3 TABLESPOONS LEMON JUICE
½ CUP DRY WHITE WINE
2 TEASPOONS WHITE PEPPER
1 TABLESPOON FINELY CHOPPED
FRESH DILL (OR ½ TEASPOON DRIED)/

Peel turnips. Cut into rectangles, then trim into ovals about 1 inch long and ½ inch wide. Cover with water. Add 1 teaspoon salt and 1 tablespoon sugar. Cook for 15 minutes and drain. Mix remaining salt, remaining sugar, vinegar, lemon juice, wine, and pepper. Add turnips and marinate for 24 hours. Drain. Sprinkle dill over. Serves 6.

Bûche de Noël

1 RECIPE JELLY ROLL (SEE
DESSERT BASICS)/
2¼ CUPS BUTTER CREAM (SEE
DESSERT BASICS)/
1 OUNCE (1 SQUARE) UNSWEETENED
CHOCOLATE, MELTED & COOLED/
1 TABLESPOON DARK RUM
½ CUP STRAWBERRY OR
CURRANT JELLY/
FEW DROPS VANILLA EXTRACT
¼ CUP COCOA (APPROXIMATE)

One way the French celebrate Christmas is by making or buying a Bûche de Noël, a cake roll artfully cut and decorated to suggest the choice log which, by tradition, is burned in the fireplace at Christmastime.

Make flat cake layer as directed in recipe for Jelly Roll; allow to cool. Meanwhile, mix 2 cups of butter cream with the melted chocolate and rum. Spread the strawberry or currant jelly over the cake. On top of the jelly, spread half the chocolate-flavored butter cream. Roll up. Cut off each end of the roll on a slant and save these cut pieces. Cover outside of roll with more butter cream. Dip a fork in hot water and draw it through the covering butter cream to give the effect of rough bark. Use the cut pieces to simulate knots: place them on top of the roll, one at each end, and cover the rounded sides with chocolate butter cream; repeat bark-like effect with fork. Cover the cut side of each piece and the ends of the roll itself with the remaining ¼ cup of butter cream, flavored with the vanilla. Dip your finger in the cocoa and make a dot in each of the exposed cut sides. Then, take 3 round cookie cutters in graduated sizes, dip in the cocoa, and make circles on the cut sides radiating out from the dots, to resemble the growth rings in the trunk of a tree. Use a fancy cutter to make leaves of green almond paste (see Hacienda Cake, page 138) for decorating one of the "knots" and add little "berries" of red almond paste for a Christmas touch. Serves 10.

Pain Perdu Banane

6 SLICES STALE WHITE BREAD
1 CUP MILK
2 EGGS
¼ TEASPOON SALT

This is an inspired version of the familiar "lost bread" and so easy to prepare. The dash of banana liqueur added at the last lifts the whole dish from the ordinary to the fascinating. The request that you use stale bread, by the

135

Ingredients (left column, top)

¼ CUP BUTTER
2 MEDIUM BANANAS, SLICED CROSSWISE/
1 TABLESPOON BANANA LIQUEUR

Body (right column, top)

way, means that the bread should be several days old, so that it will thirstily drink up the milk mixture—not fresh, but not hard as a rock, either.

Trim crusts from bread and cut each slice in half. Beat milk, eggs, and salt in a platter large enough to hold all the slices of bread. Soak the slices in the mixture, turning once, until they have absorbed it all. Fry in butter until golden brown on both sides. Remove to serving plate. Arrange banana slices in an overlapping row on each piece of bread. Sprinkle with banana liqueur and serve immediately. Serves 6.

Coffee Cup Soufflé

4½ TABLESPOONS BUTTER
4½ TABLESPOONS FLOUR
1½ CUPS MILK
6 EGGS
3 TEASPOONS INSTANT COFFEE
¾ CUP SUGAR
4 TABLESPOONS COFFEE ICE CREAM

PREHEAT OVEN TO 425 DEGREES

This is an original dish from The Four Seasons and a great favorite with its habitués.

Mix flour with butter until all flour is absorbed. Place milk in a saucepan and bring to a boil. Add the butter-flour mixture bit by bit and stir until thick. Cool. Separate the eggs and add the yolks and coffee to the original mixture. Beat the egg whites until they form soft peaks. Continue beating, gradually adding the sugar, until they form stiff peaks. Fold into the yolk mixture. Set aside 4 tablespoons of the resulting soufflé mixture. Butter the insides of 6 oven-proof coffee cups and sprinkle lightly with sugar. Divide the remaining mixture among the prepared coffee cups. Bake in 425-degree oven about 11 minutes. (Eleven minutes will turn out a soufflé of medium consistency. Shorten or lengthen baking time a few minutes if a softer or firmer consistency is desired.) Serve with a sauce made by mixing the reserved soufflé mixture with the coffee ice cream. Serves 6.

Crêpes Aurora

18 COLD DESSERT CRÊPES (SEE
PASTRIES & BATTERS)/
2¼ CUPS CRÈME PÂTISSIÈRE
(SEE DESSERT BASICS)/
JUICE & GRATED PEEL OF 1 ORANGE
JUICE & GRATED PEEL OF 1 LEMON
¼ CUP CHOPPED FRESH PINEAPPLE
POWDERED SUGAR

Spread out the crêpes. Divide the crème pâtissière into 3 parts. Flavor one with orange juice and peel, one with lemon juice and peel, and the third with chopped pineapple. Put one flavor of filling on each of 6 crêpes and roll up. Repeat with the other two flavors. Serve crêpe of each flavor to each guest. Sprinkle with powdered sugar to serve. Serves 6.

Désir de Roi

18 SMALL CREAM PUFFS
(SEE PASTRIES & BATTERS)/
2 CUPS (APPROXIMATE) CRÈME
PÂTISSIÈRE (SEE DESSERT BASICS)
RUM
CHOCOLATE SAUCE (SEE
SWEET SAUCES)/

The combination of flavors—rum in the filling of the cream puffs, and the chocolate sauce—is a great one. Any king would wish for it.

Flavor the crème pâtissière with rum to taste. Using a plain pastry tube, fill cream puffs with crème pâtissière. Place in a crystal bowl. Serve with chocolate sauce. Serves 6.

Diplomat Pudding

1 PINT MILK
5 EGGS
½ CUP SUGAR
½ TEASPOON VANILLA EXTRACT
1 TABLESPOON DARK RUM
¼ CUP SEEDLESS RAISINS
¾ CUP MIXED CANDIED FRUITS
2 SPONGE-CAKE LAYERS, BROKEN UP
(SEE DESSERT BASICS)/
_____
PREHEAT OVEN TO 350 DEGREES

Diplomat Pudding is a classic French dessert. It may be served warm or cold. If you wish to serve it chilled, make it the day before.

Boil milk. Mix eggs with sugar and pour boiling milk over, beating well. Add vanilla and rum. Put custard through a sieve. Mix raisins with candied fruits. In 6-cup cylindrical mold place layers of cake, custard, and fruit mixture, ending with cake. Bake in a pan of hot water in a 350-degree oven 40 minutes. Cool. Chill if desired. Unmold to serve. Serves 6.

Gâteau Progrès

10 EGG WHITES
2 CUPS SUGAR
¼ CUP CORNSTARCH
4 CUPS ALMOND FLOUR
½ CUP PRALINE PASTE
2 CUPS BUTTER CREAM (SEE
DESSERT BASICS)/
DROP OF KIRSCH
¼ CUP MELTED BITTER CHOCOLATE
¼ CUP THINLY SLICED
TOASTED ALMONDS/

PREHEAT OVEN TO 200 DEGREES

This truly marvelous cake was invented by Bruno Comin, The Four Seasons' pastry chef. Though rich, it has a deceptively simple appearance and flavor. If you find you cannot buy almond flour, simply pulverize blanched almonds in your blender (not too many at a time) to achieve an equally good result. Praline paste may be bought in jars.

Beat egg whites with sugar. When thick, add cornstarch. Mix in the almond flour gently with the hands. With a pastry bag or spatula make 3 thin rectangular layers (about 9 x 6 inches) of the above mixture on cooking parchment on a cookie sheet. Bake in a 200-degree oven 30 minutes. When you take this meringue from the oven it will be soft. Turn rectangles over. Cool. Remove paper.

Mix ¼ cup of the praline paste with butter cream and kirsch. Spread ¼ of the mixture on one of the almond meringue layers. Cover with another layer. Spread it with another ¼ of the butter cream mixture. Cover with remaining layer. Spread remaining butter cream mixture over the whole cake. Mix remaining praline paste with melted chocolate. Refrigerate 1 hour. Remove from the refrigerator and work the mixture with a wooden spoon. Roll into a sausage shape. Flatten and use to make a band across the cake from one corner to the other, lengthwise. Sprinkle the almonds on all of the top except the chocolate band.

Hacienda Cake

1 ROUND SPONGE CAKE, 2 INCHES
THICK (SEE DESSERT BASICS)/
½ CUP SIMPLE SYRUP (SEE

Slice the sponge cake into 3 thin layers. Sprinkle layers with simple syrup flavored with kirsch and allow to soak for a little while. Flavor the crème pâtissière and the

138

DESSERT BASICS)/
KIRSCH
2 CUPS CRÈME PÂTISSIÈRE
(SEE DESSERT BASICS)/
½ CUP MIXED CANDIED FRUITS
½ MEDIUM PINEAPPLE
1 QUART WATER
1 POUND SUGAR
BUTTER CREAM (SEE
DESSERT BASICS)/
½ POUND ALMOND PASTE
YELLOW FOOD COLORING
POWDERED SUGAR

candied fruits with kirsch to taste. Core, peel, and slice the pineapple. Poach slices in the water with the sugar for about 10 minutes. Chop coarsely. Over one layer of sponge cake spread ⅓ of the crème pâtissière and the candied fruit. Top with another layer of sponge cake and spread another ⅓ of the crème pâtissière and the pineapple over it. Cover with the third layer of sponge cake and spread with the remaining crème pâtissière. Cover the whole cake with a thin layer of butter cream. Color the almond paste a pale gold with yellow food coloring. Put a bit of powdered sugar on a board, or marble, and knead the almond paste briefly. Roll out very thin in round shape. Put over the cake, patting it gently into the shape of the cake. Cut off any excess. Decorate with thin slices of poached pineapple, representing leaves and a long "stem" of chocolate, if you like—or use your own inventiveness to decorate.

Pineapple Bourdaloue

SWEET DOUGH (SEE PASTRIES &
BATTERS)/
3 TABLESPOONS CRÈME PÂTISSIÈRE
(SEE DESSERT BASICS)/
½ PINEAPPLE
1 POUND SUGAR
1 QUART WATER
FRANGIPANE (SEE DESSERT BASICS)
PINEAPPLE FOR DECORATION
APRICOT GLAZE (SEE DESSERT BASICS)

PREHEAT OVEN TO 300 DEGREES

If you haven't a large flan ring to use on a cookie sheet, for lining with sweet dough, use a pie pan. The charm of the flan is that you remove the ring when you slide the tart from the cookie sheet onto the serving dish, where the tart stands alone and looks very handsome.

Place a 12-inch flan ring on a cookie sheet. Press sweet dough onto the bottom and sides to form a shell ¼-inch thick. (For ease in arranging the dough around the inside of the ring, make a "sausage" of the dough and press it on, fluting the rim.) Chill the prepared shell. Put the crème pâtissière on the bottom of the shell. Core, peel, and slice the pineapple and poach in the water, with the sugar, for 10 minutes. Chop the pineapple (saving a little to slice thinly for decoration) and place on top of the crème pâtissière. Cover with the frangipane, using a pastry tube so that you can make it smooth. Bake in a 300-degree oven about 45 minutes. Cool. When cold, decorate with pineapple slices and brush with apricot glaze.

Paris Brest

2 CUPS PÂTE À CHOUX (SEE
PASTRIES & BATTERS)/
1 CUP CRÈME PÂTISSIÈRE (SEE DESSERT
BASICS), FLAVORED WITH VANILLA,
CHOCOLATE, OR RUM/
2 CUPS WHIPPED CREAM
APRICOT GLAZE (SEE DESSERT BASICS)
¼ CUP SLIVERED, TOASTED ALMONDS
POWDERED SUGAR

PREHEAT OVEN TO 375 DEGREES

This is a well-known French dessert, in fact a classic one.

On a cookie sheet, make a ring of pâte à choux 8 inches in diameter and about 1½ inches thick, using a pastry bag with a large plain tube. Bake in a 375-degree oven 25 minutes. Cool. Split ring in half horizontally. Fill bottom with crème pâtissière, flavored as you wish. Top with whipped cream. Replace top of ring. Spread with apricot glaze. Sprinkle with almonds, then with powdered sugar. Serves 6.

Café Santos Parfait

6 EGG YOLKS
1¼ CUPS CONFECTIONER'S SUGAR
1 TABLESPOON INSTANT COFFEE
2 TABLESPOONS CRÈME DE CACAO
1 PINT HEAVY CREAM, WHIPPED
COFFEE LIQUEUR (LIKE TÍA MARIA)
CANDIED COFFEE BEANS

As you may know, Santos is the great coffee port of Brazil, which obviously inspired the name of this parfait. The candied coffee beans are a very fine finishing touch.

Beat egg yolks with sugar. Add coffee and crème de cacao. Fold in whipped cream. Pour into 6 parfait glasses and chill for 5 hours. (At The Four Seasons the parfaits are unmolded by placing a hot tea towel around them briefly so that they slip out easily. You may unmold them or not, as you wish.) Before serving, pour coffee liqueur over them and place 3 candied coffee beans on top of each. Serves 6.

Zabaglione with Amaretti

8 EGG YOLKS
1 CUP SUGAR
5 TABLESPOONS MARSALA WINE
1 TABLESPOON WHITE WINE
8 AMARETTI (ITALIAN MACAROONS)

Zabaglione is one of Italy's delectable contributions to the dessert department. To be sure, it has to be made at the last minute, but it doesn't take long and is worth the few minutes' wait.

Mix yolks, sugar, and wines together in the top of a double boiler and cook over hot water, beating constantly, until the mixture thickens and becomes warm. Remove from heat and beat until fluffy. Break up the amaretti in the bottom of a serving bowl. Pour zabaglione on top and serve at once. Serves 6.

NOTE: Zabaglione may be flavored to taste with kirsch, or any other liqueur of your choice, in place of the wines suggested here.

Chausson of Strawberries

PUFF PASTRY (SEE PASTRIES & BATCHERS)/
1 EGG, BEATEN
POWDERED SUGAR FOR SPRINKLING
½ CUP CRÈME PÂTISSIÈRE (SEE DESSERT BASICS)/
12 STRAWBERRIES, HALVED

PREHEAT OVEN TO 375 DEGREES

A chausson is a puff pastry turnover, as you will see if you look at the picture of ours on page 145. Some chaussons are baked with their filling in them, but this one is filled after the pastry is baked, which allows the strawberries to be fresh and raw and at their best. In order to provide space and openings for the filling in the baked pastry, one must place an object across the middle of the pastry before folding it over into its half-moon shape. This object must be two inches in diameter in the center, taper toward the ends, and it should protrude beyond the edges of the pastry. It might be a piece of wood, a metal tube of the right size, or one of those very small rolling pins. You might even fashion it by bunching and shaping aluminum foil into the right shape. Whatever you use, wrap it in foil and butter the foil on the outside before placing it on the rolled-out puff pastry.

141

In handling puff pastry, follow these few general rules to insure an even rising of the pastry when you bake it. First, always trim the edges after you have rolled the pastry out. Second, do not handle or leave finger marks in the cut edges of the pastry. Third, do not allow egg white or egg yolk to run over the cut edges when you brush the pastry; it will act as an adhesive in these spots and prevent the pastry from puffing up evenly.

Roll out puff pastry a scant ¼-inch thick in a round 10 inches in diameter. Trim the edges. Put a cylindrical object (described above), wrapped in aluminum foil and buttered, across the center of the pastry; it should be wider than the pastry. Brush pastry with egg to within ⅛ inch of edges, being careful not to let egg run over the cut edges. Slip your hand under one side of the pastry and fold it over to meet the other side so that the edges are even. Press together close to the edges, but be careful not to touch the cut edges themselves. Place on ungreased baking sheet and chill thoroughly in the refrigerator. Bake 30 minutes in a 375-degree oven. Remove from oven and turn up heat to 450 degrees. Sprinkle the chausson with powdered sugar and glaze in the oven for about 5 minutes. Pull out foil-wrapped object. Slit the round side of the chausson with a sharp knife where the edges of the pastry meet. Put in crème pâtissière from the ends with a pastry tube. Poke the strawberry halves in the slit so that they show through.
NOTE: You can vary this dessert by filling it with well-drained stewed rhubarb, cut in 3-inch lengths and cooled— or, for that matter, with any fresh fruit in season that suits your fancy and looks handsome.

After the delights of fall, the winter season brings a different, more dramatic experience. In the western world, Christmas and New Year's and the meaningful days between are a sustained period of celebration offering many opportunities to serve fine wines with typical holiday foods. Now the sun of other seasons can be released at your table. It is time for some of the choice, older wines in your cellar— full-bodied reds and whites, wines of robust character to lend substance and quality to the dishes they accompany. This, of course, includes champagne; no time except the bridal month of June calls so fittingly or so frequently for the serving of this festive wine.

Following are some typical winter dishes with suggestions for appropriate wines, plus a seasonal wine list.

CAVIAR WITH BLINIS: The combination of the soft hot pancakes and the cold caviar and sour cream offers a nice variety of texture and temperature. I recommend a fine chilled vodka here, rather than a wine.

STUFFED MUSSELS: Here I'd settle for one of the good California Pinot Chardonnays, wines with quality and flavor, yet with character enough not to be intimidated by the herbs and seasonings.

LOBSTER QUICHE: This elegant first course will do well with a Corton-Charlemagne, a 1964 or 1966, perhaps—one of the outstanding white wines of the world.

RED SNAPPER OR SOLE: Dishes involving either of these fine fishes would be well balanced by a Chassagne-Montrachet, which has certain dry, fragrant overtones making it an ideal white wine with seafood.

BOEUF BOURGUIGNON: Nothing could express the essence of this dish better than a Chambertin Clos de Bèze. As a matter of fact, to be perfectly in accord, it should be made with the same wine.

POT-AU-FEU MÉNAGÈRE: Somewhat similar to the Bourguignon, the Pot-au-Feu is best with a Juliénas, or a Fixin Clos Napoléon.

CARBONNADE FLAMANDE: Ragoûts and braised dishes come into their own in winter. This is a classic, made with beer, and at its best when accompanied by beer. German, Dutch, Czech, or Danish brews would be in keeping.

CASSOULET DE TOULOUSE: Needs a sense of contrast: A wine from the Beaujolais—a Fleurie, perhaps—or Robert Mondavi's excellent Cabernet Sauvignon from the Napa Valley.

VEAL: An accommodating meat which tastes well with white or light red wine. Among the whites you might choose a Montrachet from the Domaine de la Romanée-Conti; a pleasing red would be the delicious—and somewhat under-estimated—Château La Mission-Haut-Brion, of Graves.

PORK AND SUCKLING PIG: Champagne has the cutting effervescence and fruity flavor necessary to balance the rich and overpowering quality of pork, which somehow destroys other wines. Try the Krug non-vintage, or the rather remarkable Schramsberg Napa Valley champagne.

GAME: The extraordinary game dishes of The Four Seasons all call for red wine. The Estouffade of Venison might well require a wine as significant as

143

Château Cheval-Blanc—a 1955 if you are feeling expansive (and can find it), or a 1961 if your feelings are more moderate. Either year would lend stature to the venison, and to the cheese which might well follow. The Salmis of Wild Turkey would be excellent with a Corton, Cuvée Dr. Peste, 1964, from the noted *proprietaire* in Burgundy. The Quail Stuffed with Pâté deserves a respectable Bordeaux, a St. Estèphe, for example, such as Château Montrose, 1957, a wine which has matured slowly to a peak of excellence.

DESSERTS: Everyone who shares in the Bûche de Noël will want to toast with a superior champagne; we can suggest nothing better than a Dom Pérignon. Or, with something like Crêpes Aurora or the Gâteau Progrès, indulge in a great Château d'Yquem. Its unctuous texture and superb flavor will elevate any sweet.

White:

Montrachet, Domaine de la Romanée-Conti, 1964.
Corton-Charlemagne, 1966—One of the fine white Burgundies, from the commune of Aloxe-Corton; a pressing of the Chardonnay grape.
Chassagne-Montrachet, Ramonet, 1966—A product of the nineteen precious acres comprising Montrachet, whence comes what many consider to be the world's finest dry white wine.
Chablis, Montée de Tonnerre, Grand Cru.
Johannisberger Riesling, California, Joseph Heitz.
Pinot Chardonnay, California, Almadén.

Champagne:

Moët et Chandon, Cuvée Dom Pérignon.
Charles Heidsieck, brut, N.V.
Schramsberg, California, Napa Valley.

Red:

St. Émilion, Château Ausone, 1961, 1964, 1966.
Pomerol, Château Petrus—Among the greatest; wine of a superior year would be an outstanding accompaniment for your *pièce de résistance*.
St. Julien, Château Léoville Poyferré, 1955.
Cabernet Sauvignon, California, Georges De Latour, private reserve.
Vosne-Romanée, Clos de Réas, 1964—A companion of the seven or eight superlative red Burgundies of the Côte de Nuits, velvety soft and with magnificent bouquet.
Corton, Clos du Roi, Baron Thénard, 1962.
Clos Vougeot, Vougeot, 1964—This commune has been producing red wine since the twelfth century.
Pinot Noir, California, Joseph Heitz, 1968.

—JB

144

Spring

Miraculous spring! The sudden bursting of snowdrops through the frozen earth, the first crocus, the first tiny bunch of intoxicatingly perfumed flowers that form on the Daphne bush, and then the appearance of the tender shoots of new vegetables in one's garden—these are the harbingers.

But the pleasure of these joyful sights is given to all too few of us these days. For the city dweller, the first glimpse of spring may well be the arrival of tightly pointed, perfectly matched bunches of green or white asparagus in the markets. How pleasant to have the first shoots, whether purple-tipped white stalks, peeled and cooked to a crisp tenderness, or the richly flavored green stalks, boiled and served forth with the unmistakable flavor of the awakening earth. Somehow one never tires of eating this excellent vegetable. The Egyptians savored it. The Romans honored it as a symbol of fertility, often puréeing other foods and forming them in asparagus shapes in tribute. Accounts survive of the praise lavished on such dishes by noted guests at famous dinners in antiquity.

Make a rite of the first asparagus of the season. Hail it as the herald of further delights—tiny radishes, young onions, the first bits of fabulous green, colors and tastes as stimulating as any in nature, and reminders that once more a cycle has renewed itself, that once more the promise of a season has been fulfilled. —JB

147

Celery with Brandied Roquefort

½ POUND ROQUEFORT CHEESE
2 TEASPOONS COGNAC
3 STALKS CELERY
1 TEASPOON CHOPPED TRUFFLES

This is an appealing hors d'oeuvre to serve with drinks on a warm spring day. The crisp celery is greatly enhanced by the rich Roquefort, the cognac, and truffles.

Crumble Roquefort and mix with cognac thoroughly. Cut celery into 1-inch lengths and stuff with cheese mixture. Sprinkle with truffles and serve. Serves 6.

Lamb in Lettuce Leaves, Sweet and Sour

1 POUND LAMB FROM THE SHOULDER,
CUT INTO 1-INCH CUBES/
1 SMALL ONION
1 BAY LEAF
1 TABLESPOON SALT
1¼ TEASPOONS PEPPER
18 OUTSIDE LEAVES BOSTON LETTUCE
¾ CUP WHITE WINE VINEGAR
4 TEASPOONS LEMON JUICE
¼ CUP DRY WHITE WINE
4 TEASPOONS SUGAR

Little bundles of lamb wrapped in lettuce leaves make a tangy and refreshing first course for a spring meal.

Place lamb in saucepan and cover with water. Add onion, bay leaf, 1 teaspoon salt, and ¼ teaspoon pepper. Cook until lamb is tender. This may take from 20 minutes to an hour, depending on the age of the lamb. Drain meat, reserving a little broth. Discard onion and bay leaf. Put meat through finest blade of grinder. If it seems dry, add a little broth. Place lettuce leaves in boiling water for 3 minutes. Drain. Place about 2 heaping tablespoons of meat in the center of each leaf and roll up securely, tucking ends in. Mix remaining salt (2 teaspoons) and pepper (1 teaspoon) with vinegar, lemon juice, wine, and sugar. Carefully place wrapped lamb in mixture and marinate at least 6 hours. Drain and serve. Serves 6.

Mussels in Pink Sauce

36 MUSSELS
½ CUP MAYONNAISE (SEE SAUCES)
2 TABLESPOONS LOBSTER SAUCE
(SEE SAUCES)/

You will note that this recipe calls for using two tablespoons of lobster sauce, and perhaps you wonder about making the recipe just to provide that small amount. It is vital to the success of this recipe, as you may guess,

148

1 TABLESPOON HEAVY CREAM
4 TEASPOONS CATSUP
LEMON JUICE TO TASTE
SALT & FRESHLY GROUND PEPPER
TO TASTE/
1 TEASPOON PREPARED MUSTARD
RED CAVIAR

and you have only to look for other recipes requiring it to find out how to use up the remainder—or to make an invention of your own for the purpose. You can then plan to serve such a dish next day.

Clean mussels (page 21) and steam in water until shells open. Remove top half of shells. Cool. Mix mayonnaise, lobster sauce, cream, catsup, lemon juice, and seasonings. Top each mussel with ¾ to 1 teaspoon of this pink sauce. (Be sure not to put on too much. Some of the inside shell should show for an attractive appearance.) Top with a bit of caviar. Chill thoroughly. Serve on beds of crushed ice. Serves 6.

Cornets of Smoked Salmon

½ POUND SMOKED SALMON
DASH WHITE PEPPER
1 TABLESPOON COGNAC
½ CUP BUTTER
½ POUND SMOKED SALMON,
SLICED THIN/

A cornet, in food terminology, is any food rolled into the shape of a horn. These are most delicious examples.

Grind the first portion of smoked salmon. Add pepper, cognac, and butter, and mix well. Cut the sliced salmon into 1½-inch squares. Form into cornucopias and, with a pastry tube, fill each with the ground mixture. Arrange the cornets attractively, spaced well apart, on plates or platters, using a few sprigs of parsley or watercress for garnish. Makes about 40 cornets.

The Four Seasons' Mousse of Trout

2 POUNDS TROUT MEAT (AFTER
REMOVING HEAD AND TAIL,
BONING & SKINNING)/
3 EGG WHITES

As suggested below, this steamed mousse of trout, blanketed with white wine sauce, makes a perfect first course. The mousse itself (or any of its variations) is often used for stuffing other fish.

149

1 QUART HEAVY CREAM
2 TEASPOONS SALT
1 TEASPOON GROUND NUTMEG
MELTED BUTTER FOR BRUSHING
1 CUP WHITE WINE SAUCE
(SEE SAUCES)/

Mash the trout meat in a mortar. Put into a bowl set in a larger bowl filled with cracked ice. Add egg whites to trout and beat well with the electric beater. Continue beating, adding heavy cream slowly. Add seasonings. Brush two 6- or 7-inch savarin molds, or 12 individual cups, with melted butter. Fill with the trout mixture. Steam 12 minutes in steamer. Let stand a few minutes before unmolding and serving with white wine sauce poured over. Serves 12.

VARIATIONS:

This mousse may also be made with salmon, pike, lobster, or almost any other fish which strikes your fancy. Substitute an equal amount of whichever one you choose for the trout specified above.

Beignets of Artichoke Bottoms

12 ARTICHOKE BOTTOMS (PAGE 247)
BEIGNET BATTER (SEE PASTRIES
& BATTERS)/
TOMATO SAUCE (SEE SAUCES)

Cut each artichoke bottom into four parts. Dip each piece into the beignet batter and fry in deep fat at 375-degrees until pale golden brown. Serve with Tomato Sauce. Serves 6.

Fish Milt in Shell

1 POUND FISH MILT
3 TABLESPOONS LEMON JUICE
1/4 CUP DRY WHITE WINE
WATER TO COVER
SALT TO TASTE
1 BAY LEAF
6 TART SHELLS (SEE PASTRIES
& BATTERS)/
3/4 CUP WHITE WINE SAUCE
(SEE SAUCES)/

Fish milt has a mild, delicate flavor and is regarded as a great delicacy. It also makes an excellent hors d'oeuvre when breaded and deep fried. Cooked in that manner it is also a good garniture for whole fish.

Let the milt stand in cold water for a couple of hours with 2 tablespoons of the lemon juice. Dry on paper towels and put into a casserole with the white wine and water to cover. Add salt to taste, the remaining lemon juice, and the bay leaf. Poach the milt for 6 minutes. Remove from

½ CUP SLICED COOKED MUSHROOMS
6 TABLESPOONS SAUCE HOLLANDAISE
(SEE SAUCES)/
6 TABLESPOONS UNSWEETENED
WHIPPED CREAM/

the liquid and dry on paper towels. On the bottom of each pastry shell place 2 tablespoons of white wine sauce, then place some milt on top of this. Place a few slices of mushrooms around the shells. Mix Hollandaise with whipped cream and spread 2 tablespoons of the mixture over top of each shell. Put under the broiler for a few minutes to glaze. Serves 6.

Crisped Shrimp with Mustard Fruit

2½ POUNDS SHRIMP (ABOUT
24 LARGE SHRIMP)/
3 CUPS COURT-BOUILLON
(SEE STOCKS)/
1 CUP CREMONESE MUSTARD FRUIT,
WITH LIQUID/
4 CUPS FLOUR
2 TABLESPOONS OIL
1 TEASPOON BAKING POWDER
3 CUPS WATER
2 EGG YOLKS
SALT TO TASTE
FLOUR FOR DIPPING
2 CUPS SAUCE BÉCHAMEL
(SEE SAUCES)/
2 TABLESPOONS DRY MUSTARD
6 TABLESPOONS MUSTARD FRUIT
IN CHUNKS/

This is one of The Four Seasons' best-known dishes. The Cremonese mustard fruit required for it can be bought in cans under the Motta label. The dish is not only a very special first course, it also makes a fine luncheon entrée.

Poach shrimp in court-bouillon until they turn pink (about 4 minutes). Drain. Shell and de-vein. Mince the cup of mustard fruit in their liquid. Slit shrimp halfway through and stuff with the minced fruit. Pat firmly so that stuffing remains in shrimp. Make a thick batter by mixing flour, oil, baking powder, water, egg yolks, and salt. (This may be prepared in advance and refrigerated.) Roll shrimp in flour, dip into batter, and deep fry in 400-degree oil until brown (4–6 minutes). Drain. Mix Béchamel with mustard and the 6 tablespoons of mustard fruit. Heat to piping. Serve in a separate dish as sauce for the shrimp. Fried Parsley makes an attractive garnish for the shrimp. Serves 6 as an appetizer, 4 as a main course.

Shrimp Kiev

18 CLEANED JUMBO SHRIMP
3 TABLESPOONS SHELLFISH BUTTER,
FROZEN (SEE SAUCES)/

Shrimp stuffed with butter—in the manner of the well-known Chicken Kiev—is a Four Seasons' invention, and even better than its namesake.

FLOUR TO COAT SHRIMP
1 TEASPOON SALT
½ TEASPOON PEPPER
4 EGGS, BEATEN
4 CUPS BREAD CRUMBS
FAT FOR DEEP FRYING

Split shrimp from the inside about ¾ of the way through to the back. Place, split side down, between sheets of dampened wax paper. Pound very gently until flattened, taking care not to split shrimp. Place ½ teaspoon frozen shellfish butter inside each shrimp, and fold together. Dip re-shaped shrimp into flour mixed with salt and pepper, then eggs, then bread crumbs. Fry in 450-degree fat until golden brown (about 1 minute). Drain on paper towels and serve. Serves 6.

Soups

Cream of Wild Asparagus

1 TABLESPOON BUTTER
1 SMALL ONION, CHOPPED
½ STALK CELERY, CHOPPED
2 CUPS BEEF STOCK (SEE STOCKS)
1 POUND TINY ASPARAGUS
SALT & PEPPER TO TASTE
¾ CUP HEAVY CREAM

The original Four Seasons recipe for this soup calls for wild asparagus. We have substituted tiny asparagus, such as is sometimes cut at the very beginning of the season; it is thin and delicate in flavor, and more readily available.

Heat butter in saucepan and cook onion and celery until soft but not brown, stirring frequently. Add stock, bring to a boil. Trim asparagus, cutting as little as possible from the bottom. Place in liquid and simmer 5 minutes. Add salt and pepper. Pour stock and asparagus into blender and whirl until liquid. Strain and add cream. Reheat and serve. Serves 6.

Curried Clam Soup

1½ CUPS CHOPPED CLAMS
¾ CUP CLAM JUICE
1½ SHALLOTS, MINCED
3 SPRIGS PARSLEY

The following is a rich yet delicately flavored soup.

Simmer clams, clam juice, shallots, parsley, wine, and curry powder, well mixed, for 5 minutes. Remove parsley.

¾ CUP DRY WHITE WINE
3 TEASPOONS CURRY POWDER
3 CUPS HEAVY CREAM
2 EGG YOLKS
SALT & FRESHLY GROUND PEPPER
TO TASTE/

Add cream and heat well. Beat egg yolks with a bit of the soup, return to soup, and stir until slightly thickened. Season to taste. Serves 6.

Consommé Bellevue

1 DOZEN LITTLENECK CLAMS
1 QUART COLD WATER
SALT & PEPPER
1 QUART STRONG CHICKEN STOCK
(SEE STOCKS)/
WHIPPED CREAM
PAPRIKA

Wash clams well. Place in a saucepan with cold water, bring to a boil. Cover. Reduce heat and simmer until liquid is reduced by half (2 cups). Strain through cheesecloth and season with salt and pepper. Combine clam broth with chicken stock and heat well. Pour into individual broiler-proof soup cups. Top each serving with a thin film of whipped cream and a dash of paprika. Place under broiler for a minute. Serves 6.

Morel Soup

⅔ POUND DRIED MORELS, CHOPPED
¾ POUND FRESH MORELS, CHOPPED
5 CUPS CHICKEN CONSOMMÉ
(SEE STOCKS)/

A description of morels is given together with the recipe for Meadow Veal Cutlet with Morels (page 181). This recipe is presented in case you are lucky enough to find fresh ones.

Add the dried morels to a cup of the consommé and soak for 30 minutes. Add this and the fresh morels to the remaining consommé. Cook 5 minutes. Do not boil. Serve in consommé cups. Serves 4.

Cream of Mushroom Soup

1 CUP DRIED CÈPES
3 CUPS BEEF STOCK (SEE STOCKS)
1 SMALL ONION, SLICED

Cèpes are large mushrooms with bun-shaped caps and pestle-shaped stems. They grow in the United States in shady woods in summer, but not in sufficient quantity to

Ingredients for Celery with Brandied Roquefort and truffles (page 148).
Next three pages: Broccoli Mornay with Smoked Salmon & Shrimp (page 163);
and Spring Squab Chicken in Casserole (page 173).

1 STALK CELERY, CHOPPED
¼ CUP BUTTER
2 TEASPOONS FLOUR
1 CUP HEAVY CREAM, HEATED
SALT & PEPPER TO TASTE
½ CUP VERY FINE JULIENNE
RAW MUSHROOMS/

be marketed commercially. They are imported, dried and in cans, from France and their flavor gives distinction to this soup.

Soak dried cèpes in stock for 3 hours. Cook onion and celery in butter until soft but not brown. Gradually mix in flour, blending well. Strain mushroom stock and mix in. Cook, uncovered, over low heat for 15 minutes. Strain. Add cream, salt, and pepper and heat through. Immediately before serving, float raw mushrooms on soup. Serves 6.

Golden Jellied Onion Soup

2 TABLESPOONS (2 PACKETS) GELATIN
2 QUARTS BEEF CONSOMMÉ (SEE STOCKS)
2 TABLESPOONS BUTTER
1 LARGE BERMUDA ONION
QUARTERED & SLICED/
PINCH OF SAFFRON
SALT & PEPPER TO TASTE

Sprinkle gelatin over 1 cup of cold consommé. Stir for a few moments over low heat until completely dissolved. Off heat, add remaining consommé. Heat butter in a saucepan and sauté onion until golden brown. Add consommé and seasonings. Mix well. Cook, uncovered, over low heat until onions are tender (about 30 minutes), stirring occasionally. Chill. Serves 6.

Vichyssoise

3 LEEKS
1 MEDIUM ONION
3 TABLESPOONS SWEET BUTTER
4 MEDIUM POTATOES
3 PINTS CHICKEN STOCK
(SEE STOCKS)/
DASH NUTMEG
SALT & PEPPER TO TASTE
2½ CUPS MILK
1¾ CUPS HEAVY CREAM
CHIVES

Vichyssoise is a classic cold soup enjoyed by many all during the year. This book contains many variations on the original, which follows.

Slice the white part of the leeks fine. Slice the onion fine. Cook until soft in the butter, but do not brown. Peel potatoes and slice very thin. Add to leeks and onion. Add stock and cook at a low boil for 30 minutes. Rub through a fine sieve or whirl in the blender until smooth. Season. Add milk. Bring to a boil. Cool. Add cream and chill. Serve sprinkled with finely chopped chives. Serves 6.

Bourride

1¼ POUNDS RED SNAPPER
1¼ POUNDS WHITEFISH
1¼ POUNDS STRIPED BASS
1¼ POUNDS TURBOT (OR HALIBUT)
1 LARGE ONION, SLICED IN RINGS
1 LARGE CARROT, SLICED
2 LEEKS, IN JULIENNE
1 BAY LEAF
4 STALKS FENNEL
1 TABLESPOON SALT
1 CUP DRY WHITE WINE
1 CUP WATER
4 EGG YOLKS
1 RECIPE SAUCE AÏOLI (SEE SAUCES)
2 TABLESPOONS CORNSTARCH
12 SMALL BOILED POTATOES
COARSELY CHOPPED PARSLEY
TOASTED CROUTONS

A bourride is a sort of fish stew, the sauce of which is thickened after the fish is cooked. It is typical Provençal cookery. If you like garlic, you will love the way the aïoli flavors the dish.

Cut each kind of fish into 6 pieces. Place in a large, deep pot. Add onion, carrot, leek, bay leaf, fennel, and salt. Mix wine and water, and pour in. Bring to boil and simmer for 12 minutes. Remove from heat. Carefully remove fish to a large serving bowl. Add just enough of the fish stock to keep moist. Keep warm. Mix egg yolks, ½ the aïoli, and the cornstarch. Place in large saucepan and pour in remaining fish stock. Cook until thick and smooth; do not let it boil. Strain into a second serving bowl. Place potatoes around fish and sprinkle with parsley. Serve fish and sauce separately, with toasted croutons and remaining aïoli. Serves 6.

Soft-shell Crabs Amandine

18 SMALL SOFT-SHELL CRABS
½ CUP OIL
½ CUP CLARIFIED BUTTER (SEE SAUCES)/
SALT & PEPPER
FLOUR FOR DIPPING
2 TABLESPOONS SWEET BUTTER
½ CUP COARSELY CHOPPED ALMONDS
¼ CUP RED WINE VINEGAR
½ CUP HEAVY CREAM

Spring is certainly a season of wonderful fresh foods, many of which appear at no other time of year. Soft-shell crabs are one such seasonal delight. Here is a rather unusual amandine dish, richer than the simpler browned almonds-and-butter recipes, and very good.

Have your fish market clean the crabs. Heat oil and clarified butter in a large, heavy skillet until very hot. Sprinkle crabs lightly with salt and pepper, and dip in flour. Place in skillet and cook for about 3 minutes on each side. Remove from pan and arrange in one or two rows down the center of serving platter. Keep warm. Add sweet butter to a skillet and heat until golden brown. Add almonds. Shaking pan, toast them very quickly in the butter—less

than 1 minute. Pour in vinegar and reduce until dry. Pour in cream and cook for 5 minutes, stirring until thick and smooth. Pour sauce over backs of crabs. Serves 6.
VARIATION:
Trout Amandine is made in the identical manner. With small mountain trout, serve a whole trout to each person.

Crabmeat Casanova

3 TABLESPOONS MELTED BUTTER
9 THIN SLICES FRENCH BREAD
12 SLICES LEMON
1 POUND 2 OUNCES LUMP CRABMEAT
3 TABLESPOONS COGNAC, WARMED
6 TABLESPOONS DRY WHITE WINE
1 CUP FISH STOCK (SEE STOCKS)
¾ TEASPOON SALT
SCANT ¾ TEASPOON FRESHLY GROUND BLACK PEPPER/
3 TABLESPOONS LEMON JUICE
1 TABLESPOON FINELY CHOPPED PARSLEY
3 TABLESPOONS THIN CARROT CURLS

Heat the butter in a skillet. Cook the bread until slightly brown. Remove the bread to center of serving platter and put the lemon slices in the pan. Heat for half a minute. Place slices, still in pan, one on top of the other and press down lightly so that a little juice runs out. Remove and arrange at ends of platter. Add the crabmeat to the pan, shaking pan so as not to break lumps. Pour in cognac and ignite. Add remaining ingredients except carrot curls. Heat and reduce for 4–5 minutes, shaking pan over high heat. Spoon crabmeat over bread and pour sauce over. Top with carrot curls and serve. Serves 6.
NOTE: This is served tableside at The Four Seasons. If you do it in a chafing dish, you may find it simplest to prepare a third of the recipe at a time.

Fillet of Sole Sautéed with Shrimp

12 FILLETS OF DOVER SOLE, HALVED LENGTHWISE/
SALT & PEPPER TO TASTE
MILK IN WHICH TO DIP FILLETS
FLOUR IN WHICH TO DIP FILLETS
8 TABLESPOONS BUTTER
12 COOKED JUMBO SHRIMP,

This simple and easy recipe makes an excellent main course to follow a rich soup, or to be followed by a rich dessert. Serve it with sautéed potatoes and a green vegetable—perhaps mange-touts.

Season fillets. Dip in milk and then flour. Sauté in butter until golden brown. Remove to serving platter. Slice

PEELED & CLEANED/
1 TABLESPOON LEMON JUICE

shrimp slantwise in four pieces. Place in butter remaining in pan and cook for just 1 minute. Add lemon juice, swirl in pan. Place shrimps on sole and pour sauce over. Serves 6.

Baked Baby Flounder Stuffed with Crabmeat

6 BABY FLOUNDERS, ABOUT
12 OUNCES EACH/
SALT & PEPPER TO TASTE
10 OUNCES CRABMEAT
6 HEAPING TABLESPOONS MOUSSE
OF PIKE (PAGE 149)/
¼ CUP CLARIFIED BUTTER
(SEE SAUCES)/
2 TABLESPOONS MINCED SHALLOTS
1 CUP SLICED MUSHROOMS
½ CUP DRY WHITE WINE
1 CUP WHITE WINE SAUCE
(SEE SAUCES)/
½ CUP HEAVY CREAM
1 TABLESPOON LEMON JUICE

Have your fish market bone and skin the flounders. Sprinkle them inside and out with salt and pepper. Mix crabmeat with mousse of pike. Stuff into the flounders. Put the clarified butter, shallots, and mushrooms in a large baking pan. Lay the flounders on top and pour white wine over. Put the pan in a 375-degree oven for 20 minutes. Remove the pan from the oven, put the fish on a platter and keep warm. Pour the white wine sauce into the pan and reduce it by ⅓. Add cream, cook for 10 minutes, and reduce by ⅓ again. Correct the seasoning. Add lemon juice. Strain the sauce over the flounders. Serve very hot. Serves 6.

Frogs' Legs in Vermouth with Truffles

48 FROGS' LEGS
5 TABLESPOONS FLOUR
8–10 TABLESPOONS OIL
SALT & PEPPER TO TASTE
6 TABLESPOONS DRY VERMOUTH
¾ CUP WHITE WINE SAUCE
(SEE SAUCES)/
3 TABLESPOONS JULIENNE-SLICED
TRUFFLES/
3 TABLESPOONS CHOPPED PARSLEY

Dip frogs' legs in flour. Heat the oil to very hot in a skillet. Sauté the frogs' legs very quickly, shaking pan. Add salt and pepper. Add the vermouth and let sauce reduce by ⅓. Add the white wine sauce and cook for a few minutes more. Place frogs' legs and sauce on a serving dish or platter. Sprinkle the truffles and parsley on top and serve very hot. Serves 6.

Lobster Thermidor

3 LOBSTERS, ABOUT 2 POUNDS EACH
¾ CUP CLARIFIED BUTTER
(SEE SAUCES)/
3 TABLESPOONS COGNAC, WARMED
3 TABLESPOONS DRY MUSTARD
4½ CUPS THICK SAUCE BÉCHAMEL
(SEE SAUCES)/
SALT & PEPPER TO TASTE
3 CUPS GRATED GRUYÈRE CHEESE
LIGHT CREAM
PARSLEY SPRIGS
LEMON SLICES

There are few French creations in the fish category more justly famous than this. You will notice that one is instructed to place the lobsters on a platter with a napkin on it. Classic French cookbooks generally specify this. If you don't like the idea, simply ignore it. The Thermidor will be just as good.

Poach lobsters as described on page 35. Split lobsters in two. Take out intestinal vein, liver, and stomach. Save coral, if any. Remove tail meat, saving shells. Remove legs. Put shells in 350-degree oven 5 minutes to dry. Crack claws and remove meat. Slice body meat. Leave claw meat whole. Heat the butter. Sauté lobster meat in it about 5 minutes. Flame with cognac. Shake pan until flames die. Take out lobster meat. Add mustard and lobster coral to pan and stir well. Add Béchamel. Season. Add 6 tablespoons of the cheese. If sauce becomes too thick, thin it with light cream. Spoon some of the sauce into lobster shells and follow with the lobster meat. Cover with remaining sauce. Cover thickly with remaining cheese. Run under broiler to glaze. Remove lobster to a platter with a napkin on it. Decorate with parsley sprigs and lemon slices, also with lobster legs, if desired. Serves 6.

Quenelles of Pike

1 CUP FLOUR
¼ CUP BUTTER
1 TEASPOON SALT
DASH PEPPER
DASH FRESHLY GROUND NUTMEG
1 CUP BOILING WATER
8 EGGS
1 POUND FILLET OF PIKE,
GROUND TWICE/

Quenelles are a sort of dumpling, made with fish or meat forcemeat bound with eggs. They can be large or small. When, as in the following recipe, they are to be served as a luncheon entrée, they are fairly large. When they are floated in soup or used as a garnish for other dishes, they are small. It is most important, as instructed below, to poach a test quenelle before you cook them all, to make sure that your mixture is of the right consistency and that the quenelles will hold together.

2 EGG WHITES
2 POUNDS SWEET BUTTER
FLOUR TO COAT QUENELLES
2 CUPS LIGHT SAUCE NANTUA
(SEE SAUCES)/

Add the cup of flour, the ¼ cup butter, salt, pepper, and nutmeg to the boiling water. Mix well over heat for a few minutes. Remove from heat and add 4 eggs, one at a time. Beat each in well. Place again over heat and stir constantly for 5 minutes. Place mixture in a large bowl. Add the pike and mix well. Add the remaining eggs and whites one by one, beating very hard after each addition. Add the butter, bit by bit, still beating very hard. Poach a test quenelle— a ball of paste the shape of a large walnut—in simmering water. If the mixture is too soft to hold together, add 1 or 2 more egg whites (but never more than 2, or the mixture will become rubbery). Cover mixture and refrigerate for several hours, or overnight. Form quenelles by hand or with 2 tablespoons dipped in cold water. Roll as lightly as possible in flour. Poach in very gently simmering salted water to cover for 15 minutes. Remove from water with a slotted spoon and place in an oven-proof serving dish. Cover with sauce Nantua. Place in 400-degree oven for 15 minutes. The quenelles will double in size. Serves 6–8.

Broccoli Mornay with Smoked Salmon and Shrimp

3 POUNDS FRESH BROCCOLI
3 TABLESPOONS BUTTER
12 SLICES SMOKED SALMON
12 COOKED SHRIMP
SLICED IN TWO LENGTHWISE/
¾ CUP SAUCE MORNAY
(SEE SAUCES)/

Here is a rich and filling dish for a spring luncheon. The combination of flavors is superb.

Cut off tough ends of broccoli stems and peel stems about an inch up. Trim off wilted leaves. Soak in cold, salted water for 15 minutes. Drain. Put into a kettle with boiling, salted water to cover and cook at a low boil for 10 to 15 minutes, until stems are easily pierced with a fork. Drain. Sauté drained broccoli briefly in a skillet with the butter. Butter a broiler-proof dish. Put 6 slices of the salmon on the bottom, then 12 shrimp halves. Place broccoli on top.

163

Put remaining salmon and shrimp halves on top of broccoli. Pour sauce Mornay over and run under broiler to brown lightly. Serves 6. *(See illustration, pages 156–157.)*

Salmon Chaud-froid

3 cups court-bouillon
(see stocks)/
6 fresh salmon steaks,
about 8 ounces each/
1 cup mayonnaise for
chaud-froid (see sauces)/
6 slices truffle
few sprigs parsley

A chaud-froid is cooked like a hot (*chaud*) dish, but served cold (*froid*). Using mayonnaise for chaud-froid, as this recipe does, produces a perfect entrée for a warm day.

Bring court-bouillon to a simmer. Poach the salmon steaks in it over low heat for 12 minutes. Let fish cool in the court-bouillon. Take fish out carefully. Remove skin and fat, so that only pink meat remains. Put salmon on a platter and coat lightly with mayonnaise for chaud-froid. Refrigerate for 5 minutes. Repeat the process 3 or 4 times. When ready, the salmon should be shiny with the chaud-froid. Arrange steaks on a serving platter and place a slice of truffle on each. Decorate with parsley sprigs. Serve with dilled cucumbers. Serves 6.

Shad Roe in Lemon Butter

6 large pairs shad roe
salt & pepper to taste
flour for dipping
¼ cup oil
½ cup butter
6 large pieces toast
½ cup sweet butter
¼ cup lemon juice
2 tablespoons minced parsley

One of the greatest treats of spring is the roe of shad. The point is not to overcook them. They should be nicely browned on the outside and moist on the inside.

Sprinkle roes with salt and pepper. Dip them in flour. Heat the oil and the ½ cup butter in a large skillet. Put in the roes. Sauté gently for 5 minutes on each side. Put the toast on a serving dish and place a pair of roes on each piece of toast. Remove the fat from the skillet and replace it with the sweet butter. Brown it. Pour the lemon juice over the roes and then the browned sweet butter. Sprinkle the roes with parsley. Serves 6.

Scallops with Mushrooms and Shrimp

¾ CUP CLARIFIED BUTTER
(SEE SAUCES)/
¾ CUP OIL
3 POUNDS SCALLOPS
1½ TEASPOONS SALT
¾ TEASPOON FRESHLY GROUND
WHITE PEPPER/
2¼ CUPS COARSELY CUT MUSHROOMS
1½ CUPS COARSELY CUT
COOKED SHRIMP/
½ CUP COGNAC, WARMED
2 CUPS DRY WHITE WINE
½ CUP SAUCE BÉCHAMEL
(SEE SAUCES)/
½ CUP SAUCE HOLLANDAISE
(SEE SAUCES)/

Heat butter and oil in skillet. Add scallops, salt, and pepper. Cook for 2 minutes. Remove scallops and set aside in flame-proof dish. Sauté mushrooms in same skillet for 2 minutes. Remove mushrooms and pour over scallops. Sauté shrimp in same skillet for 2 minutes. Remove shrimp and pour over scallops. Pour the cognac over the scallops, ignite, stir. Pour white wine over scallops. Heat through. Mix Béchamel and Hollandaise sauces, pour over the scallops. Brown under broiler until golden. Serves 6.

Boned Trout à la Point

6 TROUT, 8–12 INCHES LONG
SALT & PEPPER TO TASTE
½ CUP MOUSSE OF PIKE (PAGE 149)
¼ CUP CLARIFIED BUTTER
(SEE SAUCES)/
1 TABLESPOON CHOPPED SHALLOTS
½ CUP PORT WINE
1 QUART HEAVY CREAM
½ CUP WHITE WINE SAUCE
(SEE SAUCES)/
2 BLACK TRUFFLES, SLICED

Have your fish market bone the trout. Sprinkle trout with salt and pepper. Stuff them with the mousse of pike. Put the butter and shallots in a large baking pan. Add the trout. Pour in the port wine. Put the pan in a 350-degree oven. Bake for about 20 minutes. Remove from oven. Take out the trout and put them carefully on a platter. Keep them warm. Reduce the cooking liquid by ⅔. Add the cream. Cook for a few minutes and add the white wine sauce. Cook the sauce for 5 minutes more to reduce it by ⅓. Strain the sauce over the trout. Sprinkle with truffles and serve very hot. Serves 6.

Whole Trout in Soufflé

6 TROUT, 8–12 INCHES LONG
3 TABLESPOONS BUTTER
2 HEAPING TABLESPOONS FLOUR
2 CUPS MILK
3 EGG YOLKS
¾ CUP GRATED SWISS CHEESE
DASH GRATED NUTMEG
SALT & FRESHLY GROUND PEPPER
MILK & FLOUR FOR DIPPING
BUTTER FOR BROWNING TROUT
6 EGG WHITES
_____
PREHEAT OVEN TO 375 DEGREES

This dish turns out to have an intriguing appearance because the heads and tails of the trout are likely to turn up in the baking and protrude through the soufflé—a gay and inviting presentation.

Have your fish market clean and bone the trout, leaving heads and tails on. In a small, heavy saucepan, melt 3 tablespoons of butter and stir in the 2 tablespoons of flour. Stir over moderate heat for 2 or 3 minutes. Do not brown. Add milk and stir constantly until the sauce boils. Remove from heat and stir in the egg yolks, 1 at a time. Stir in the cheese and season lightly with nutmeg, salt, and pepper. Set aside. Wash the trout, dip them in milk, then coat lightly with flour. In a large skillet melt enough butter to completely cover the bottom of the pan. When the butter is sizzling, brown the trout in it, 1 or 2 at a time, turning them once. Add more butter if necessary to cook all the trout. When they are brown, arrange them in a lightly buttered shallow baking dish. Beat the egg whites stiff and fold the cheese sauce into them gently. Cover the trout with this mixture and bake in a 375-degree oven for 20–30 minutes, until soufflé is golden brown. Serves 6.

Snails à la Mistral

¾ CUP BUTTER
36 CANNED SNAILS
2 CLOVES GARLIC, MINCED
¾ CUP TOMATOES CONCASSÉES,
(SEE SAUCES)/
PERNOD TO TASTE

The northwest wind that blows through southern France is called the mistral. Even without that cue, you could spot the southern French influence in this dish with its garlic and its tomato sauce. The Pernod gives an exactly right finishing touch.

Melt butter in a skillet and sauté snails 5 minutes. Add garlic and tomatoes concassées, and heat for a few minutes more. Remove from heat. Flavor with a few drops Pernod. Serve with toasted French bread. Serves 6.

Baked Young Chicken with Two Cheeses

BREASTS OF 3 YOUNG CHICKENS
HALVED, BONED, & SKINNED/
6 SLICES GRUYÈRE CHEESE
SALT & PEPPER TO TASTE
¼ CUP CHOPPED SHALLOTS
¼ CUP BUTTER
¼ CUP OIL
¼ CUP DRY WHITE WINE
¾ CUP GRATED PARMESAN CHEESE
½ CUP TOMATO SAUCE (SEE SAUCES)

The two cheeses here turn this into a marvelously flavorsome spring chicken dish.

Split open the breasts lengthwise and stuff them with the slices of Gruyère. Sprinkle with salt and pepper. Put the breasts in a flame-proof casserole with shallots, butter, and oil. Cook over low heat until lightly browned (about 25 minutes). After 20 minutes add the white wine. Remove the breasts and put them on a broiler-proof serving dish. Sprinkle with the Parmesan and run under the broiler to brown lightly. Add tomato sauce to the pan in which chicken was cooked and heat to piping. Pour around chicken. Serves 6.

Breast of Chicken Monte Carlo

3 MEDIUM-SIZED CHICKEN BREASTS,
HALVED, BONED, & SKINNED/
¼ CUP CLARIFIED BUTTER
(SEE SAUCES)/
1 TEASPOON MINCED SHALLOTS
¼ CUP RED PORT WINE
6 SLICES TOAST
½ CUP MOUSSE OF CHICKEN LIVERS
(PAGE 23)/
½ CUP BROWN SAUCE (SEE SAUCES)
1 TABLESPOON LEMON JUICE
2 TABLESPOONS SWEET BUTTER
SALT & PEPPER TO TASTE
3 TABLESPOONS CHOPPED
BLACK TRUFFLES/

You may be tempted to provide yourself with tinned chicken liver pâté in place of the homemade one suggested here. It will probably be very good, but will not be as interesting as the one you make yourself. You can find many uses for it in your cooking and we think it's worth the effort required to make it.

Roll the chicken breasts into the shape of snail shells. Secure them with cocktail picks. Put them in a flame-proof casserole with the clarified butter, shallots, and wine. Cook 5 minutes over medium heat. Cover casserole and place in a 350-degree oven for 12 minutes. Remove the casserole and keep the contents warm. Spread chicken liver mousse on each piece of toast. Arrange on a platter. Place a half chicken breast on each. Keep warm. Reduce the liquid in the casserole by ⅓. Add the brown sauce and lemon juice. Cook 5 minutes. Add the 2 tablespoons of sweet butter and stir well. Correct seasoning. Strain the sauce over the breasts and sprinkle them with chopped truffles. Serves 6.

Young Chicken Baked in Applejack and Cream

2 3-POUND CHICKENS
SALT & PEPPER
¾ CUP BUTTER
1 SMALL ONION, SLICED
1 CARROT, CHOPPED
1 STALK CELERY, CHOPPED
½ CUP APPLEJACK
½ CUP WATER
½ CUP HEAVY CREAM
2 LARGE APPLES

The flavor added to this dish by the use of applejack is interesting and richly rewarding. The French would probably use Calvados, the Normandy apple brandy, but since we have a native equivalent, using it seems a good idea.

Halve chickens and sprinkle lightly with salt and pepper. Brown chicken on all sides in ½ cup of the butter. Add vegetables. Mix applejack and water and pour in. Cover and cook until chicken is tender, about 15 to 20 minutes. Remove chicken and keep warm. Reduce sauce by half. Add cream, mix well, and reheat. Strain sauce over chicken. Meanwhile, peel and core apples. Cut each apple into 4 slices and sauté in remaining butter. Serve with chicken. Serves 6.

NOTE: If you wish more sauce you may add more applejack and/or more cream to taste.

Truffled Chicken in Champagne

3 WHOLE CHICKEN BREASTS
¼ CUP MELTED BUTTER
SALT & PEPPER TO TASTE

When a chicken breast is skinned, halved and boned, it is a *suprême*. When the upper part of the wing is left on, as in the recipe below, it becomes a *cotelette*. The sauce for this dish is as great as its ingredients would indicate.

Have the chicken breasts skinned, halved, and boned, leaving the upper part of the wing on and removing the wing tip. Place breasts in a shallow baking dish and brush them all over with melted butter. Season lightly. Cover dish. Bake in a 375-degree oven 8 to 12 minutes, or until chicken springs back when pressed with finger. Remove to serving platter, cover each wing tip with a paper frill, if desired, and keep warm in a low oven.

Sauce:
½ cup chopped shallots
¼ cup butter
1½ cups champagne
½ teaspoon salt
½ teaspoon sugar (optional)
1 tablespoon flour
2 white truffles, sliced
½ cup heavy cream

Cook shallots slowly in butter until soft, but not brown (about 8–10 minutes). Add champagne, salt, and sugar. Bring to a boil, reduce heat, and cook at a low boil for 10 minutes. Blend flour with a few drops of water. Quickly stir into sauce, stirring constantly until sauce is thickened. Scrape pan drippings from the chicken into the sauce and add the truffles. Lower heat and stir in the cream. Heat gently. Do not boil. Serve over chicken breasts. Serves 6. NOTE: At The Four Seasons the chicken is placed on a serving dish with frills facing outward, the sauce poured over, and a garnish of parsley sprigs is added.

Poulet Sauté Beaulieu

3 large potatoes cut into large even chunks/
¾ cup oil
2 tablespoons butter
1 3½-pound chicken, cut into frying pieces/
¼ cup minced onion
2 cloves garlic, minced
4 medium tomatoes, peeled, seeded & cut in chunks/
1½ cups dry white wine
⅓ cup sliced ripe olives, or small whole olives/
salt & pepper to taste
4 cooked artichoke bottoms (page 247), quartered/

Sauté potatoes 2–3 minutes in 3 tablespoons of the oil plus the butter in a flame- and oven-proof pan. Sprinkle lightly with salt and place in a 350-degree oven until brown and cooked through (about 15 minutes). Discard back and breast bones of chicken, and trim away loose skin. Sprinkle with salt and pepper, and sauté in remaining oil on high heat until brown (about 5 minutes). Add onion and cook for 2 minutes. Add garlic, tomatoes, and wine, and cook for another 2 minutes. Add olives, salt, and pepper, and continue to cook on lowered heat until chicken is tender. Add cooked potatoes and artichoke bottoms, cook for 3 minutes and serve with pieces of chicken piled on top of vegetables. Serves 6.

Potted Pigeon, Nutted Wild Rice

6 young pigeons
6 slices pork fat

Clean the pigeons and bard (see Glossary) with the slices of pork fat. Sprinkle them with salt and pepper. Heat oil

SALT & PEPPER TO TASTE
¼ CUP OIL
¼ CUP CLARIFIED BUTTER
(SEE SAUCES)/

———————

Mirepoix:
1 LARGE CARROT, CHOPPED
1 MEDIUM ONION, CHOPPED
1 STALK CELERY, CHOPPED
1 BAY LEAF
¼-INCH STALK THYME (OR
¼ TEASPOON DRIED)/

———————

½ CUP DRY WHITE WINE
½ CUP BROWN SAUCE (SEE SAUCES)

and butter in a large, oven-proof casserole. Add pigeons and place in a 375-degree oven to brown (about 10 minutes). Add the mirepoix and brown it. Pour in wine and brown sauce. Cover the casserole and cook for 45 minutes. Remove casserole from the oven and arrange pigeons on a platter. Strain sauce over them. Serve Nutted Wild Rice separately. Serves 6.

Pigeon with Candied Figs

6 YOUNG PIGEONS
SALT & PEPPER TO TASTE
6 SLICES PORK FAT
¼ CUP OIL
½ CUP CLARIFIED BUTTER
(SEE SAUCES)/
½ CUP SUGAR
¼ CUP WATER
2 POUNDS SMALL DRIED WHITE FIGS

Clean pigeons and sprinkle them with salt and pepper. Bard them each (see Glossary) with a slice of pork fat, tied in two places with white string. Pour oil and butter into a large, flame-proof casserole. Add the pigeons and cook, uncovered, in a 375-degree oven for 35 minutes. Baste often to keep the birds juicy and tender. Make a syrup with sugar and water. Cook it until thick (about 6 minutes). Cook the figs in it for 5 minutes. Remove the casserole from the oven. Remove pork fat from pigeons and arrange them on a round platter. Put the candied figs in the center. Serve the gravy (see below) separately. Serves 6.

Gravy:
¼ CUP DRY WHITE WINE
¼ CUP WATER

Heat the casserole on top of the range for a few minutes, until contents in the bottom brown. Pour off the fat. Add wine and water. Cook for 5 minutes, strain into bowl.

172

Spring Squab Chicken in Casserole

1 POUND TURNIPS
1 POUND ASPARAGUS
1 POUND GREEN BEANS
1 POUND CARROTS
2 POUNDS POTATOES
½ CUP OIL
½ CUP CLARIFIED BUTTER
(SEE SAUCES)/
6 SQUAB CHICKENS, 1 POUND EACH
SALT & PEPPER TO TASTE
2 TABLESPOONS BUTTER (OR
MORE, AS NEEDED)/
1 TEASPOON SUGAR
¼ CUP DRY WHITE WINE
¼ CUP WATER OR BEEF STOCK
(SEE STOCKS)/

You will find in the recipe below a technique which appears frequently in this book and which is often done at The Four Seasons—that of sautéing cooked vegetables briefly in butter before serving them. It is done to warm them up and to add flavor.

Clean all the vegetables. Cut the carrots and turnips in attractive shapes. Peel the asparagus (page 192). Cook each vegetable, except potatoes, separately in boiling, salted water. Drain each when it is done to your taste. Peel potatoes and cut with a small ball cutter. Soak in ice water for an hour. Dry on paper towels. Sauté in a skillet with ¼ cup of the oil, ¼ cup of the clarified butter, and salt to taste. Put the chickens in a large casserole. Sprinkle them with salt and pepper. Pour over them the remaining oil and clarified butter. Put into a 400-degree oven for 20–30 minutes. Put the 2 tablespoons butter into a skillet and briefly sauté, first the asparagus, then the turnips, then the green beans, adding more butter if necessary. Last, sauté the carrots, sprinkling them with the sugar. Arrange each vegetable in a bouquet around a large silver platter. Put the 6 chickens in the middle. De-glaze the casserole in which the chickens were cooked with white wine and water or beef stock. Cook for 5 minutes. Strain over the chickens. Serves 6. *(See illustration, page 158.)*

VARIATION:
Veal Cutlet with Primeurs: In place of the chickens use 12 very thin slices of veal from the leg (about 4 ounces each). Dip them in flour and sauté them in ½ cup butter for 5 minutes on each side. De-glaze the pan as in the original recipe. Use the same vegetables and the same presentation.

Twin Tournedos with Woodland Mushrooms

12 TOURNEDOS, 4 OUNCES EACH
SALT & PEPPER TO TASTE
6 TABLESPOONS BUTTER
3 TABLESPOONS CHOPPED SHALLOTS
6 TABLESPOONS COGNAC, WARMED
1½ CUPS TINY CHANTERELLES
(WOODLAND MUSHROOMS),
CANNED OR FRESH/
1 CUP MEDIUM-DRY MADEIRA
3 CUPS BROWN SAUCE (SEE SAUCES)
MINCED PARSLEY

Tournedos are rounds cut from the heart of fillet of beef. Chanterelles are yellow mushrooms shaped like cups with frilled edges. They have thick, vein-like gills. Their stems are short and fleshy. In the United States they can be found in clusters in bogs or on dry hillocks from June to September. Like morels, they do not grow in sufficient quantity to be marketed commercially. However, they can be obtained, dried or in cans, imported from France; either form may be substituted for fresh chanterelles.

Season tournedos with salt and pepper. Melt 3 tablespoons of the butter and heat to sizzling. Brown tournedos rapidly on both sides (3 minutes per side for rare). Add shallots. Turn tournedos over in the butter a few times. Flame with the cognac. Remove tournedos to a serving dish and keep warm. Add mushrooms to pan and sauté briefly (about 4 minutes), but do not brown. Add Madeira and cook for 2 minutes. Add brown sauce. Reduce by ⅓. Correct seasoning. Add remaining butter to finish the sauce, stirring until well incorporated. Pour over tournedos. Sprinkle with minced parsley and serve. Serves 6. *(See illustration, page 167.)*

Sirloin Steak Bercy

6 8-OUNCE SHELL STEAKS
SALT & PEPPER TO TASTE
¾ CUP (1½ STICKS) BUTTER
2 TABLESPOONS CHOPPED SHALLOTS
½ CUP DRY WHITE WINE
2 TABLESPOONS CHOPPED PARSLEY
FEW DROPS LEMON JUICE

The Sauce Bercy with which this steak is dressed lends a piquant flavor to the meat.

Heat 6 tablespoons butter in a skillet and sauté steaks (5 minutes on each side for rare, 7 minutes for medium, 10 minutes for well done). Season, and place on serving platter. Add shallots to the skillet and cook until soft but not brown. Add wine and reduce by half. Off heat, add remaining butter bit by bit and mix well. At the last moment, add parsley and lemon juice. Pour sauce over steaks and serve immediately. Serves 6.

Sirloin Steak Niçoise

6 TABLESPOONS OIL
6 8-OUNCE SHELL STEAKS
SALT & PEPPER TO TASTE
6 TABLESPOONS CHOPPED ONION
5 TOMATOES, PEELED & CHOPPED
18 PITTED BLACK OLIVES
12 FILLETS OF ANCHOVY
2 TABLESPOONS DRIED MARJORAM

The sauce for this steak is a proper Niçoise, with onion, tomatoes, olives, and anchovies. If you are a steak sauce fancier we think you will find it an interesting departure from familiar prepared sauces.

Heat oil in skillet. Sauté steaks (5 minutes on each side for rare, 7 minutes for medium, or 10 minutes for well done). Season, remove to serving platter and keep warm. Add onion to same skillet and cook until browned, stirring often. Add tomato and cook for an additional 5 minutes. Pour sauce over steak. Arrange olives and anchovies on steaks. Sprinkle with marjoram and serve. Serves 6.

Rack of Veal with Creamed Wild Mushrooms

4 POUNDS LOIN OF VEAL WITH BONE
¼ CUP OIL
1 LARGE CARROT, SLICED
1 MEDIUM ONION, SLICED
BOUQUET GARNI (SEE GLOSSARY)
2 RIPE TOMATOES, PEELED & CUBED
1 CUP DRY WHITE WINE
½ CUP BROWN SAUCE (SEE SAUCES)
2 POUNDS FRESH CHANTERELLES (OR
8 OUNCES DRIED, SOAKED 1 HOUR)/
¼ CUP CLARIFIED BUTTER
(SEE SAUCES)/
1 QUART HEAVY CREAM

The chanterelles in cream served with this loin of veal give an elegant touch to an already beautiful meat dish.

Brown the loin in the oil on all sides. Add carrot, onion, and bouquet garni, and brown them. Add tomatoes and wine. Put into a 325-degree oven and cook for 2 hours, turning meat over several times. Remove the veal from the pan. Reduce the cooking liquid by half. Add the brown sauce and cook a few minutes more. Strain the sauce. Keep veal and sauce warm. Put the mushrooms in a pan with the clarified butter and cook until brown and dry. Add cream, nutmeg, salt, and pepper. Reduce cream by ⅓. Add lemon juice and taste for seasoning. Put the veal

175

1 TEASPOON NUTMEG
SALT & PEPPER TO TASTE
FEW DROPS LEMON JUICE

on a serving platter, whole or sliced. Pour the sauce over it. Serve the chanterelles in cream separately. Serves 6.

Veal Pojarski

4 POUNDS VEAL FROM RACK
4 SLICES WHITE BREAD
MILK FOR SOAKING
¼ POUND SWEET BUTTER
1 TABLESPOON SALT
1 TEASPOON PEPPER
FLOUR FOR ROLLING VEAL
3 TABLESPOONS OIL
3 TABLESPOONS BUTTER

Pojarski was a famous Russian innkeeper in the town of Torjok many years ago. He is said to have invented the idea of making a "cutlet" out of ground meat, his original being made of game meat. Nowadays, Pojarski Kotleti are usually made of veal, chicken, or beef. Due to the butter which is incorporated into them, they are quite rich. The use of the veal bones to simulate chop bones is, one presumes, a French addition to the recipe.

Bone the veal and keep the bones. Remove the fat and tendons. Soak the bread in milk and squeeze dry. Grind together through the finest blade the veal, bread, and sweet butter. Add salt and pepper. Divide mixture into 6 parts and form each into shape of veal chop. Coat each "chop" in flour. Heat oil and butter in skillet. Handling gently, cook "chops" over low heat for 6 minutes on each side. Remove to serving platter. Meanwhile, heat bones in 250-degree oven until warm. Place next to "chops" to complete illusion and decorate with white paper frills. Serves 6. NOTE: Veal Pojarski may be served with or without sauce. If sauce is served, the garniture should be served separately. Some possibilities are: Sautéed Potatoes, beignets of asparagus (for batter, see Pastries & Batters), french fried potatoes, Sautéed Artichoke Bottoms, Petits Pois à la Française, noodles.

A sauce may be served separately (for recipes, see Sauces): light Tomato Sauce, Madeira Sauce, natural veal gravy, Sauce Suprême.

1. Bending lamb bones back.

2. Cutting ribs off.

3. Removing excess fat.

7. Sautéing stuffing while lamb browns.

8. Rolling brioche dough.

9. Centering prosciutto. Cover with stuffing.

12. Trimming dough.

13. Brushing lamb and edges of pâte with egg yolk.

14. Folding dough . . .

18. Brushing overall with egg.

19. Braiding strip cut from pâte.

20. Placing braid on brioche;

Boned Rack of Lamb in Crust

4. Chopping mushrooms.

5. Sautéing shallots, bay leaf, carrots, celery.

6. Adding mushrooms, lemon juice & seasoning.

10. Covering lamb with stuffing . . .

11. and with more prosciutto.

15. to encase lamb.

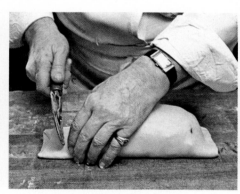
16. Trimming ends, leaving flaps . . .

17. to fold underneath.

21. egg will help it to adhere.

22. As it appears at table.

For recipe, see page 186.

Veal Chops Stuffed with Foie Gras

6 LARGE VEAL CHOPS
SALT & PEPPER
6 SLICES BLOCK FOIE GRAS,
EACH ABOUT ½-INCH THICK AND
1-INCH SQUARE/
½ CUP FLOUR
3 TABLESPOONS OIL
¼ CUP CLARIFIED BUTTER
(SEE SAUCES)/
½ CUP RED PORT WINE
¼ CUP BROWN SAUCE (SEE SAUCES)

Almost any stuffed chop is bound to be rich, indeed. These are probably the richest you'll ever eat. Serve with a buttered green vegetable for color and perhaps plain dry rice to help absorb the gravy.

Split and open chops almost all the way through to the bone. Sprinkle lightly with salt and pepper. Place in the split of each chop a slice of foie gras and press the two sides together. Dip chops in flour. Heat oil and butter in large skillet and sauté chops over very low heat for 10 minutes on each side. Remove chops to serving platter and keep warm. Pour off grease from skillet and discard. Add port and cook until reduced by ⅓, scraping up the brown bits sticking to pan. Add brown sauce and cook for 5 minutes more, still scraping and stirring. Strain sauce over chops and serve immediately. Serves 6.

Meadow Veal Cutlets with Morels

6 LARGE, VERY THIN SLICES VEAL
FROM THE LEG (6 OUNCES EACH)/
SALT & PEPPER TO TASTE
FLOUR FOR DIPPING
¼ CUP BUTTER
¼ CUP OIL
4 OUNCES DRIED BLACK MORELS,
SOAKED 1 HOUR IN WARM WATER,
OR 1 POUND FRESH MORELS/
¼ CUP DRY WHITE WINE
1½ PINTS HEAVY CREAM
2 TEASPOONS LEMON JUICE

Morels are among the world's most prized mushrooms. Usually the caps are oval in shape, though sometimes rounded. They are beige, grayish, or almost black according to the species. The caps are honeycombed and the stalks frequently shorter than the caps. In the United States they can be found in sandy places in May and June, but do not grow in sufficient quantity to be marketable. Imported fresh morels from France can occasionally be found in the markets of our larger cities. They are very expensive. Fortunately, however, French morels can be bought dried or in cans and, though not up to the fresh in flavor, are still delicious and unusual.

Sprinkle the cutlets with salt and pepper. Dip into flour. Heat butter and oil in a large skillet. Put in cutlets and

181

cook 3 minutes on each side. Put them on a platter. Keep warm. Put the morels into the skillet and sauté for a few minutes. Add the wine. Reduce a little. Add the cream. Reduce by ⅓. Add lemon juice. Pour the morels in cream over the cutlets. Serves 6.

Bouchée à la Toulousaine
(*Ris de Veau*)

2 POUNDS CALF SWEETBREADS
6 COCKS' COMBS
1 LARGE CARROT, CHOPPED
1 MEDIUM ONION, CHOPPED
BOUQUET GARNI: 1 BAY LEAF,
1 STALK THYME, 1 STALK PARSLEY,
1 STALK CELERY/
½ CUP CLARIFIED BUTTER (SEE SAUCES)
½ CUP MEDIUM-DRY MADEIRA WINE
½ CUP DRY WHITE WINE
SALT & PEPPER TO TASTE
1 POUND CHICKEN KIDNEYS
½ CUP BROWN SAUCE (SEE SAUCES)
½ CUP FINELY CHOPPED MUSHROOMS
PARSLEY FOR DECORATION
6 OVAL BOUCHÉES (SEE PASTRIES
& BATTERS), 3 INCHES ACROSS,
2½ INCHES HIGH/

A bouchée is a pastry case which can be filled in a great variety of ways, in this case, with sweetbreads. You will note the recipe calls for chicken kidneys. Unfortunately, they are not usually obtainable in retail butcher shops in this country. If you can't find them, simply leave them out.

To prepare sweetbreads see Talmouse with Sweetbreads and Brains, page 25. Cook the cocks' combs in boiling salted water for 1 hour. Drain. Brown the mirepoix of carrot, onion, and bouquet garni in the clarified butter in a casserole. Add sweetbreads, wines, salt, and pepper. Cover the casserole and cook in a 325-degree oven 35 minutes. Poach the kidneys in boiling water for 15 minutes. Remove the sweetbreads from the casserole, divide into 6 pieces, and keep warm. Strain the juice in the casserole into a saucepan. Add the brown sauce. Put over low heat and add kidneys, cocks' combs, and mushrooms. Simmer very gently for 15 minutes. Put 3 tablespoons of the sauce, mixed with mushrooms and kidneys, in the bottom of each bouchée. Reserve the cocks' combs for decoration. Put a piece of sweetbread on top of each bouchée. Add the rest of the sauce. Arrange the cocks' combs around the sweetbreads. Decorate the serving dish with parsley. Serves 6.

Veal Parisienne

6 LARGE VEAL CUTLETS, POUNDED VERY THIN/
FLOUR FOR DIPPING
SALT & PEPPER TO TASTE
¼ CUP BUTTER
¼ CUP OIL
6 COCKS' COMBS, COOKED FOR ONE HOUR, THEN DICED/
12 CHICKEN KIDNEYS, BLANCHED
½ CUP PORT WINE
1 PINT HEAVY CREAM
⅓ CUP BROWN SAUCE (SEE SAUCES)
6 SLICES BLACK TRUFFLE

This is a very rich, very French entrée and delicious even if you can't get the cocks' combs and chicken kidneys listed in the ingredients.

Dip the cutlets in flour. Sprinkle them with salt and pepper. Heat oil and butter in a large skillet or skillets. Add the cutlets and cook for 5 minutes on each side. Put the cutlets on a serving platter. Keep warm. Put cocks' combs and the chicken kidneys in the same skillet. Sauté them for a few minutes. Add the port wine, reduce to dry. Add heavy cream and brown sauce. Cook the sauce for a few minutes more, and pour it on the cutlets. Put 1 slice of black truffle on each. Serves 6.

Scallops of Veal with Lemon Butter

18 SMALL, VERY THIN VEAL SCALLOPS
SALT & PEPPER TO TASTE
¾ CUP FLOUR
3 EGGS, BEATEN
1½ CUPS BREAD CRUMBS
¾ CUP OIL
⅔ CUP CLARIFIED BUTTER (SEE SAUCES)/
3½ TABLESPOONS LEMON JUICE

Season scallops. Dip in flour, eggs, then bread crumbs. Heat the oil and half of the butter in a skillet. Sauté scallops for 3 minutes on each side. Remove to serving plate. Add remaining butter and lemon juice to pan. Swirl together for a few minutes and pour over scallops. Serve with Saffron Rice. Serves 6. *(See illustration, page 168.)*

Deviled Calf Brains

3 CALF BRAINS, ABOUT 10 OUNCES EACH/
3 TABLESPOONS DIJON MUSTARD
6 TABLESPOONS FLOUR
2 EGGS, MIXED WITH

Breaded, fried calf brains are a delicious combination of soft and crisp texture, and the Dijon mustard with which these are coated adds a piquant note.

For preparing brains see Talmouse with Sweetbreads and

2 TABLESPOONS WATER/
6 TABLESPOONS BREAD CRUMBS
1 PINT OIL
FRIED PARSLEY (PAGE 196)
SAUCE DIABLE (SEE SAUCES)

Brains, page 25. Slice each cooked brain into 8 pieces. Spread each side of the slices with mustard. Dip each slice in flour, the egg-and-water mixture, then in bread crumbs. Fry in the hot oil until golden. Put the brain slices on a serving dish on a napkin with a bouquet of fried parsley in the center. Serve with Sauce Diable. Serve very hot. Serves 6.

Eggs with Sweetbreads, Sauce Béarnaise

2 PAIRS VEAL SWEETBREADS
BOILING SALTED WATER
2 TABLESPOONS LEMON JUICE
BOUQUET GARNI: BAY LEAF,
PEPPERCORNS, CELERY, PARSLEY/
BREAD CRUMBS
½ CUP PLUS 1 TABLESPOON BUTTER
6 TABLESPOONS CHOPPED MUSHROOMS
6 TART SHELLS (SEE PASTRIES
& BATTERS)/
6 POACHED EGGS, NEATLY TRIMMED
2 TRUFFLES, GRATED
6 TABLESPOONS SAUCE BÉARNAISE
(SEE SAUCES)/

This is a delicious main course for a spring luncheon. All it needs as accompaniment is the simplest possible green salad, preferably of Bibb lettuce.

Cover sweetbreads with boiling, salted water and add lemon juice and bouquet garni. Bring to a boil, reduce heat, and simmer 20 minutes. Drain, remove membrane and tubes, and cut into 1-inch cubes. Roll sweetbreads in crumbs and sauté lightly in the ½ cup butter. Sauté mushrooms lightly in remaining butter. Place sweetbreads in bottom of tart shells. Place the eggs on top. Spread mushrooms over the eggs and strew truffle gratings on the mushrooms. Cover with sauce Béarnaise and run under the broiler for 2–3 minutes to glaze. Serves 6.

Medallions of Sweetbreads
Sautéed with Mustard Crumbs

6 SWEETBREADS, ½ POUND EACH
PINCH OF SALT

Place sweetbreads in water to cover and bring to boil. Drain. Place again in water to cover and add salt, bay leaf,

1 BAY LEAF
2 CLOVES
1 SMALL ONION
1½ TEASPOONS DRY MUSTARD
MILK FOR DIPPING SWEETBREADS
1 CUP BREAD CRUMBS
8 TABLESPOONS BUTTER

cloves, and onion. Bring to a boil, cover and boil for 5 minutes. Drain. Cut in half lengthwise. Sprinkle both sides lightly with dry mustard. Dip lightly in milk, then bread crumbs. Sauté in butter until golden brown and serve. Serves 6.

Roussette of Lamb

3 POUNDS BONED LEG OF
LAMB, CUBED/
3 TABLESPOONS OIL

—————

Mirepoix: 1 CARROT, SLICED;
½ MEDIUM ONION, CHOPPED;
1 STALK CELERY, SLICED

—————

2 TABLESPOONS FLOUR
1 CUP DRY WHITE WINE
2 CUPS CHICKEN STOCK (SEE STOCKS)
1 BAY LEAF
1 TEASPOON THYME
1 TABLESPOON SALT
1 TEASPOON PEPPER
½ CUP HEAVY CREAM
3 EGG YOLKS
FEW DROPS LEMON JUICE
1 LARGE CARROT, SLICED JULIENNE
& COOKED/
½ CUP FRESH GREEN PEAS, COOKED

This lamb casserole transforms a rather simple basic dish into a rich and elegant entrée to be served with pride.

Blanch the meat in boiling water for 4 minutes. Drain and dry with paper towels. Heat oil in a casserole. Put in meat and the mirepoix. Cook until meat is brown. Add the flour and mix well with a wooden spoon. Add the wine, stock, and seasonings. Cook very slowly for 1 hour and 15 minutes. Remove meat to another casserole. Mix cream and egg yolks and add to the sauce in the original casserole. Cook 3 minutes, stirring constantly, and strain over meat. Add lemon juice and stir well. Sprinkle top with julienne carrots and peas, and serve. Serves 6.

Stuffed Legs of Baby Lamb en Brioche

2 4-POUND LEGS OF BABY LAMB
SALT & PEPPER TO TASTE

Consider this when you want a handsome, rich, and superb dish to serve at a springtime dinner.

¼ CUP OIL
6 OUNCES FOIE GRAS
1 RECIPE PÂTE BRIOCHE
(SEE PASTRIES & BATTERS),
WITH DASH OF SUGAR/
2 EGGS BEATEN WITH
2 TABLESPOONS WATER/

Have your meat market bone the legs of lamb. Wipe with a damp cloth. Sprinkle with salt and pepper inside and out. Place in roasting pan. Pour oil over. Roast 15 minutes in a 400-degree oven. Cool. Stuff the legs with the foie gras. Wrap each leg in pâte brioche. Make a round knob of the pâte on top of each. Brush with the beaten eggs. Allow to stand for 25 minutes. Bake in a 375-degree oven until crust is brown and shiny (about 30 minutes). Serve Sauce Périgourdine (see Sauces) on the side. Serves 6–8.

Boned Rack of Lamb in Crust

1 BONED RACK OF LAMB,
ABOUT 1¼ POUNDS/
¼ CUP OIL
SALT & PEPPER

There is no question about it, this dish is elegant and spectacular to look at. While it is a long recipe, there is nothing really complicated about it. Do not be surprised, by the way, at the small quantity of meat required. The whole dish is so rich that it should be carved into quite thin slices for serving and this amount will be entirely adequate for four people. If you wish to double the number of guests, this is the kind of recipe which can be doubled simply by making it twice. (The preparation is illustrated in detail on pages 178–179.)

Rack of lamb is described in American meat books as a wholesale cut. It is actually the loin, and the boned rack of lamb required in this recipe is the tenderloin. A *matignon* is what the French call a fondue of vegetables. Often they cook it until it is practically a pulp, though the way it is made in the following recipe is more to our taste.

Have your butcher bone rack of lamb, or do it yourself. Sprinkle the lamb with salt and pepper on all sides. Heat the oil in a skillet and cook lamb on high heat for 15 minutes, turning often to avoid burning. Remove meat from skillet. Cool.

Stuffing à la Matignon:
¼ CUP CLARIFIED BUTTER
(SEE SAUCES)/
2 TABLESPOONS MINCED SHALLOTS
½ BAY LEAF
½ CUP FINELY CHOPPED CARROTS
½ CUP FINELY CHOPPED CELERY
1½ CUPS FINELY CHOPPED MUSHROOMS
¾ TEASPOON SALT
¼ TEASPOON WHITE PEPPER
2 TABLESPOONS LEMON JUICE
½ CUP DRY WHITE WINE

Pour butter into a skillet and add shallots, bay leaf, carrots, and celery. Cook over medium heat for 10 minutes. Add mushrooms, salt, pepper, and lemon juice. Cook 15 minutes longer over high heat, stirring occasionally. Add wine and continue cooking and stirring until carrots are soft. Discard bay leaf. Set aside.

The Assembly:
PÂTE BRIOCHE (ABOUT ½ RECIPE,
SEE PASTRIES & BATTERS)/
8 THIN SLICES PROSCIUTTO
1 EGG YOLK

PREHEAT OVEN TO 375 DEGREES

In this step, the lamb with its stuffing is completely wrapped in rolled brioche dough. Sprinkle pâte lightly with flour. Roll out about 10 inches long, or long enough to completely encase the cooked lamb. Lay 5 slices of the prosciutto in center of pâte, covering an area about equal in size to that of lamb. Spread half of the stuffing over the prosciutto. Place the cooked lamb on top. Spread remaining stuffing over the top and sides of the meat. Pat remaining slices of prosciutto over this. Trim edges of dough. Dilute egg yolk with 2 tablespoons water. Brush the egg yolk mixture on the outer edges of the pâte and the lamb. Enclose the meat with the pâte by folding both edges to meet and overlap in the center. The egg yolk you have brushed on the outside edges will help the pâte to adhere. After you have done this, turn the whole thing over, exposing the neat underside on which you will put the decoration. Cut off extra pâte from both ends, leaving enough to fold under (about 1 inch). Fold ends under. Brush entire surface with egg. Roll the cuttings from the edges of the pâte about 3 inches wide and 6 inches long. Make two parallel slits about ¾ of the way down the strip. You will have 3 strips, uncut at one end. Braid the 3 strips and place

187

on top of the brioche. Brush with egg yolk. Set aside in a warm place for 30 minutes while dough rises. Bake in a 375-degree oven 12–15 minutes, or until beautifully brown. Serves 4.

Roast Rack of Lamb Persillée

1 DOUBLE RACK (LOIN) OF LAMB, 6–8 POUNDS/ COOKING OIL
BONES (TRIMMED FROM RACK AND RESERVED)/
1 CARROT, DICED
1 ONION, DICED
1 CLOVE GARLIC, CRUSHED
DASH THYME, CRUSHED
1 BAY LEAF, CRUSHED
1 CUP DRY WHITE WINE
6 TABLESPOONS BUTTER
1 CUP BREAD CRUMBS
3 SHALLOTS, CHOPPED
½ CUP CHOPPED PARSLEY
SALT & PEPPER TO TASTE

We think you will agree, if you've never tried it before, that this is one of the most delicious ways to present a lamb rack.

Have your meat market trim the rack of lamb and tie the ribs securely with string, so that they will not spread in the cooking. Wrap the ends of the ribs in aluminum foil to prevent burning. Sear the rack on all sides in oil. Place in a pan with a few bones reserved from the trimming, the carrot, onion, garlic, thyme, bay leaf, and wine. Cook in a 350-degree oven 45 minutes (for medium-rare). Every 10 minutes baste the rack with the pan juices. Meantime, brown the butter and in it sauté the crumbs and shallots for about 5 minutes. Stir in the parsley. When the lamb is done place it on an oven-proof platter. Pat the crumb mixture firmly on top and return to oven for 5 minutes. Remove from oven and keep warm. Add a cup of water to the pan juices, season with salt and pepper, and reduce for 10 minutes. Strain. Serve as gravy with the lamb. Serves 6. *(See illustration, page 180.)*

Noisette of Young Lamb

15 POUNDS RACK (LOIN) OF LAMB
18 SLICES BACON
SALT & PEPPER TO TASTE

A noisette is a small individual portion of meat. It must be round in shape, as are these cut from the rack of lamb. Three of these to a person is the usual serving. Placing

188

1 TABLESPOON MARJORAM
6 TABLESPOONS OIL
18 ROUND PIECES MARROW BONE
1-INCH THICK/
2 CUPS BOUILLON, OR SALTED WATER
MINTED FLAGEOLETS (PAGE 195)

them on little rounds of marrow bone with the marrow in it makes an amusing presentation. Have your butcher cut the marrow rounds for you.

Bone the rack (or have your meat market do it), taking out all fat and sinews. What remains is the loin. Slice into 18 noisettes (fillets). Put a slice of bacon around each noisette and fasten with a toothpick. Sprinkle with salt, pepper, and marjoram. Heat oil in a pan, add noisettes and cook over medium heat 4 minutes on each side. Poach marrow bones in simmering bouillon or salted water for 4–5 minutes. Place the cooked marrow pieces on a serving dish. Put a noisette of lamb on each. Pour the flageolets around the noisettes. Serves 6.

Lamb Chops Braised in Lettuce

12 BONED LOIN LAMB CHOPS
SALT & PEPPER
12 SLICES BACON
¼ CUP OIL
24 LEAVES BOSTON LETTUCE
½ CUP BROWN SAUCE (SEE SAUCES)

Sprinkle chops lightly with salt and pepper. Wrap a slice of bacon around the outside of each chop and secure with a toothpick. Heat oil in an oven-proof skillet and sauté chops for 4 minutes on each side. Remove chops from skillet and carefully remove toothpick, leaving bacon intact. Wrap each chop in 2 leaves of lettuce. Replace chops in skillet, pour brown sauce over and cover. Cook in a 400-degree oven for 20 minutes. Remove chops to serving platter. Strain sauce over. Serves 6.

Roast Epaulets of Baby Lamb with Rosemary

3 BONED EPAULETS (SHOULDERS)
OF BABY LAMB,
ABOUT 2 POUNDS EACH/
SALT & PEPPER TO TASTE

Rosemary makes this dish, simple as it is, something truly memorable.

Sprinkle insides of the epaulets with salt, and pepper, and

191

1½ TEASPOONS DRIED ROSEMARY
¼ CUP OIL
¼ CUP CLARIFIED BUTTER
(SEE SAUCES)/
6 4-INCH STALKS OF
FRESH ROSEMARY/

dried rosemary. Re-form epaulets and tie them each with 3 rings of white kitchen string. Heat oil and butter with the stalks of rosemary in a large casserole. Add the epaulets. Cook for a few minutes on top of the range to brown lightly. Put the casserole into a 350-degree oven. Cook 35 minutes, adding ¼ cup water from time to time to make a good juice. Remove the casserole and put the epaulets on a serving dish. Remove string. Put stalks of rosemary on each epaulet. Pour the pan juices around them. Serves 6. NOTE: To accompany this dish, try Purée of Flageolets. Or you may prefer to cook quartered potatoes in the casserole.

Vegetables

Artichoke Bottoms Stuffed with Spinach

1 POUND FRESH SPINACH
4 TABLESPOONS BUTTER
SALT TO TASTE
DASH NUTMEG
DASH FRESHLY GROUND PEPPER
12 COOKED ARTICHOKE BOTTOMS
(PAGE 247)/
1½ CUPS THICK SAUCE BÉCHAMEL
(SEE SAUCES)/
6 TABLESPOONS GRATED PARMESAN

There are many ways to stuff artichoke bottoms, but this is one of the simplest and most satisfactory.

Blanch the spinach for 3 minutes in boiling water, drain well, and mince fine. Sauté in the butter and add seasonings. Heap the mixture on the artichoke bottoms. Top each with 2 tablespoons Béchamel. Sprinkle with grated cheese. Run under broiler to brown. Serves 6.

Asparagus

4 POUNDS ASPARAGUS
BOILING, SALTED WATER TO COVER

Though the season for asparagus has been extended a good deal, thanks to improved transportation methods,

192

it still seems a spring vegetable to many of us. And certainly the special flavor of the fresh-cut spears is one of the glories of this time of year. While we think all of the special suggestions supplementing this recipe are very good, we cannot resist saying that the Asparagus Polonaise, is, for our taste, the best of all.

Cut the woody ends off the asparagus and, with a vegetable peeler, peel off the skin from the bottom of the stalks up to the tender heads. Wash. Tie into bundles with white kitchen string. Cook bundles in a large pot full of boiling, salted water for 10–15 minutes, or until done to your taste. The spears should be tender, but still crisp. Run cold water over the asparagus. (This is called "refreshing" and is done to stop the cooking and set the color.) Drain well. Serves 6. Serve with the sauce you prefer: clarified butter, lemon butter, Sauce Hollandaise, Sauce Maltaise, or Sauce Mousseline (see Sauces). Asparagus may also be served in any of the special ways set forth below.

Asparagus Mornay

4 POUNDS ASPARAGUS, COOKED AS ABOVE/
1 CUP SAUCE MORNAY (SEE SAUCES)
6 TABLESPOONS GRATED SWISS CHEESE

Arrange the asparagus on a buttered flame-proof dish. Pour the sauce Mornay over the tips. Sprinkle with the grated cheese and run under the broiler to brown lightly.

Asparagus Parmesan

4 POUNDS ASPARAGUS, COOKED AS ABOVE/
¼ CUP GRATED PARMESAN CHEESE
½ CUP CLARIFIED BUTTER (SEE SAUCES)

Arrange asparagus on a buttered, flame-proof dish. Sprinkle the cheese over the tips. Pour butter over. Run under the broiler to brown.

193

Asparagus Polonaise

4 POUNDS ASPARAGUS,
COOKED AS ABOVE/
½ CUP CLARIFIED BUTTER
(SEE SAUCES)/
3 TABLESPOONS FRESHLY GRATED
BREAD CRUMBS/
3 TABLESPOONS GRATED
HARD-COOKED EGG YOLK/
3 TABLESPOONS GRATED
HARD-COOKED EGG WHITE/
3 TABLESPOONS MINCED PARSLEY

Arrange asparagus on a buttered flame-proof dish. Heat butter in a skillet. Mix remaining ingredients and add to butter. Sauté for a few minutes. Sprinkle over the tips of the asparagus. Run under the broiler for a few minutes, being careful not to burn.

Wild Asparagus Chinoise

3 POUNDS TINY ASPARAGUS
¼ CUP CLARIFIED BUTTER
(SEE SAUCES)/
¼ CUP IMPORTED SOY SAUCE
SALT TO TASTE

If true wild asparagus is not obtainable, you may substitute very thin asparagus. Though scorned by admirers of heavy spears, thin "tiny" asparagus is cherished by many —and eaten raw by some.

Clean and wash the asparagus. Cut on the bias into 2-inch-long pieces. Get butter very hot in a skillet, put in the asparagus and sauté very fast, stirring, for 3 minutes. Add soy sauce and mix lightly. Correct seasoning with salt if necessary. Serves 6.

Fiddlehead Ferns

3 QUARTS BOILING WATER
2 TABLESPOONS SALT
2 POUNDS FIDDLEHEAD FERNS
⅓ CUP CLARIFIED BUTTER
(SEE SAUCES)/

Fiddlehead ferns grow along the eastern seaboard of the United States, particularly in Maine, but not in sufficient quantity to be widely available in the markets. Their season is early spring and they are a vegetable of unique flavor and delightful appearance—tightly curled, green sprouts, known by the French designation of *croisiers*. They come in cans, too, but, as is usually the case, the canned variety bears little relation to the fresh.

Add salt and fiddleheads to boiling water and blanch for 5 minutes. Drain and dry on paper towels. Heat clarified butter in large skillet until golden brown. Add fiddleheads and shake pan over heat for 3 minutes. The ferns won't change color. Heat and serve. Serves 6.

Fiddlehead Ferns Gratinées

3 QUARTS BOILING WATER
2 TABLESPOONS SALT
2 POUNDS FIDDLEHEAD FERNS
1 CUP LIGHT SAUCE BÉCHAMEL
(SEE SAUCES)/
½ CUP FRESHLY GRATED
SWISS CHEESE/
2 TABLESPOONS BUTTER

Follow directions for cooking fiddlehead ferns above. Then mix with Sauce Béchamel. Remove from heat and sprinkle cheese over. Dot with butter. Brown for a few minutes under broiler. Serves 6.

Risotto con Pignole

1½ CUPS RICE
10½ TABLESPOONS BUTTER
3 CUPS CHICKEN STOCK (SEE STOCKS)
½ TEASPOON SAFFRON POWDER
½ TEASPOON SALT
6 TABLESPOONS GRATED
PARMESAN CHEESE/
½ CUP PINE NUTS

Melt 4½ tablespoons of the butter in a deep saucepan. Add the rice and stir to coat it with butter. Add the stock, saffron, and salt. Bring to a boil and cook until stock is absorbed and rice is done (about 14 minutes). It should be rather damp, not dry. Toss with cheese, remaining butter (6 tablespoons), and the pine nuts.

Minted Flageolets

3 CUPS FLAGEOLETS
1½ TEASPOONS SALT
1 ONION, STUCK WITH A CLOVE
BOUQUET GARNI (SEE GLOSSARY)
SALT & PEPPER TO TASTE
3 TABLESPOONS SWEET BUTTER
2 TABLESPOONS CHOPPED FRESH MINT

Flageolets are tiny pale green kidney beans, fresh or dried, not commonly grown in this country, but available, dried and imported from France, in fine grocery and department stores. They also may be available in jars ready-cooked. The ready-cooked flageolets can be used in this recipe by flavoring with salt, pepper, butter, and mint as directed. Flageolets have an affinity for lamb.

Soak the beans in cold water for 2 hours. Drain. Cover with fresh cold water. Add salt, onion, and bouquet garni, and bring to a boil. Reduce heat and simmer gently, covered, until done (2 to 3 hours). Drain. Remove onion and bouquet garni. Correct seasoning with salt and pepper. Add butter and mint, and mix well. Serves 6.

Fried Parsley

SPRIGS OF PARSLEY
DEEP FAT
SALT

Wash sprigs of parsley well. Dry thoroughly with paper towels. Heat fat to 375 degrees. Toss in parsley sprigs, a few at a time, and remove with a slotted spoon the minute they rise to the surface, at which point they will be delicately crisp (1 to 2 minutes). Season lightly with salt.

Glazed Sweet Potatoes

3 LARGE SWEET POTATOES
DASH SALT
FAT FOR DEEP FRYING
APRICOT GLAZE (SEE DESSERT BASICS)

Place sweet potatoes in their skins in water to cover with a dash of salt. Boil until tender, about 15 minutes. Drain and peel. Cut into ⅓-inch slices. Deep fry until brown. Drain and cover with apricot glaze. Serves 6.

Purée of Pimientos

2 POUNDS FRESH SWEET
RED PEPPERS/
¼ CUP OIL
1 CUP RICE
4 CUPS WATER
SALT TO TASTE
6 TABLESPOONS SWEET BUTTER

When sweet red peppers are in season, they make a delicious vegetable to serve with chicken or meat.

Remove seeds and stems from peppers and cut them coarsely. Put oil into an oven-proof casserole, add peppers, and cook in 400-degree oven 15 minutes. Baste peppers with oil frequently. Add rice, water, and salt. Cook in 350-degree oven 30 minutes. Put through a fine sieve or whirl in the blender. Add the butter and mix well. The purée should be light. Serves 6.

196

Mange-touts

1 POUND MANGE-TOUTS
2 TABLESPOONS OIL
SALT TO TASTE

Mange-touts, also known as Chinese snow peas, are exactly what the French name implies—something to be eaten whole. The whole thing is an edible pea pod with tiny undeveloped peas inside. They are a botanical variety of the common pea which never develops beyond the state just described. Mange-touts are delicate and delicious in flavor, bright green in color. They are cooked only enough to warm them through, and remain crisp and brilliantly colored as a result. Their peak season is from May to September. Mange-touts should be soaked briefly in ice water, then the ends trimmed off, together with any fine string which may run along the stem. They should be used as soon as possible after they are purchased, but if wrapped tightly in plastic bags will keep several days in the refrigerator. Mange-touts now can be purchased frozen, but are not nearly so flavorful as the fresh ones and almost impossible to cook so that they retain their admirable crispness.

Prepare mange-touts as described above. Dry thoroughly on paper toweling. Heat the oil in a large skillet. Add mange-touts and cook, stirring constantly—what the Chinese call stir-frying—for about 1 minute. Taste for doneness, remembering that the mange-touts should be crisp and hot. Season to taste with salt. Serve at once. Serves 6.

Julienne of Potatoes

2 POUNDS POTATOES
FAT FOR DEEP FRYING
SALT TO TASTE

Peel potatoes and cut into very fine slices. Then cut the slices lengthwise, like matches. Wash them and dry on paper towels. Put into 350-degree deep fat to brown lightly and become crisp. Drain on paper towels and sprinkle with salt. Serves 6.

197

Nutted Wild Rice

1½ CUPS WILD RICE
6 CUPS BOILING SALTED WATER
7 TABLESPOONS CLARIFIED BUTTER
(SEE SAUCES)/
¾ CUP COARSELY CHOPPED WALNUTS

Cook wild rice in boiling water for 22 minutes. Drain and mix with 4 tablespoons of clarified butter. Sauté walnuts in remaining butter for 3 minutes until golden brown. Mix with rice. Serves 6.

Salads

Dandelion and Egg Salad

1½ POUNDS DANDELION LEAVES
3 TABLESPOONS FRENCH DRESSING
(SEE SAUCES)/
2 HARD-COOKED EGGS

Dandelion leaves make one of the best green salads. They have a pleasingly bitter flavor, admired by connoisseurs. You can perhaps pick them along roadsides, and they are frequently found in fine markets. When picking dandelion leaves, select very young plants before the plant has flowered. After it flowers the leaves become tough and bitter.

Wash leaves and tear into 1½-inch pieces. Toss with French dressing. Sieve whites and yolks of eggs separately and sprinkle both on top of salad. Serve with croutons rubbed with garlic. Serves 6.

Onion and Ripe Olive Salad

1 LARGE BERMUDA ONION
12 JUMBO PITTED BLACK OLIVES
¼ CUP OIL
¼ CUP VINEGAR
1 TABLESPOON TOMATO JUICE
1½ TEASPOONS FINELY DICED
RED PEPPER/
1½ TEASPOONS FINELY DICED
GREEN PEPPER/
DASH SUGAR
SALT & FRESHLY GROUND
BLACK PEPPER TO TASTE/

Slice onion into very thin rings. Arrange in overlapping row on each salad plate. Slice olives and place down center of row of onions. For dressing, mix remaining ingredients and pour over.

198

Cucumber Salad Ilona

3 MEDIUM CUCUMBERS
¾ CUP SOUR CREAM
1 TABLESPOON PAPRIKA
2 TEASPOONS FRESH CHIVES
FEW DROPS LEMON JUICE
SALT & FRESHLY GROUND
WHITE PEPPER TO TASTE/

Peel and halve cucumbers lengthwise. Scrape out seeds and cut cucumber into thin slices. Mix remaining ingredients and spoon over cucumber. Serves 6.

Pickled Veal and Mange-tout Salad

1½ POUNDS ROAST VEAL
3 TABLESPOONS WHITE
WINE VINEGAR/
1 TEASPOON LEMON JUICE
2 TABLESPOONS WHITE WINE
½ TEASPOON SALT
¼ TEASPOON FRESHLY GROUND
WHITE PEPPER/
2 TEASPOONS SUGAR
1 POUND MANGE-TOUTS

Of course one cooks mange-touts very briefly in any case, but if you haven't tasted them raw, as they are in this salad, you have a pleasant surprise in store. The finished dish makes an excellent luncheon entrée—especially for dieters.

Slice veal into fine julienne. Mix vinegar, lemon juice, wine, salt, pepper, and sugar. Add veal and marinate for a minimum of 3 hours. Slice mange-touts into fine julienne. Drain veal and mix immediately before serving. Serves 6.

Zucchini and Hearts of Palm

12 HEARTS OF PALM
1 ZUCCHINI
6 BIBB LETTUCE LEAVES
FRENCH DRESSING (SEE SAUCES)

Heart of palm is a delicate vegetable which comes to us in cans from Brazil and also from Florida, where the State tree, Sabal palmetto, is the source. The hearts are canned in water, either raw or lightly blanched. They are excellent in salads and appear, too, in many cooked dishes in the cuisine of Brazil.

Split hearts of palm lengthwise. Arrange 4 in a row on individual salad plates, with a lettuce leaf at one end. Cut zucchini into thin slices crosswise and arrange between heart-of-palm halves. Serve with French Dressing. Serves 6.

Harlequin Crêpes

1½ CUPS CRÈME PÂTISSIÈRE (SEE DESSERT BASICS)/
1 SQUARE UNSWEETENED CHOCOLATE, MELTED & COOLED/
1 TEASPOON VANILLA
12 5-INCH DESSERT CRÊPES (SEE PASTRIES & BATTERS)/

This dessert is named for the particolored costume of the Harlequin of pantomime. It seems to us that two crêpes per person is enough, but if you think your guests could eat three, flavor an extra ¾ cup of crème pâtissière with 2 tablespoons of very strong coffee and stuff six extra crêpes.

Mix half of the crème pâtissière with the chocolate and half with the vanilla. Put chocolate crème on half of the crêpes and vanilla on the remainder. Roll up. Serve one chocolate and one vanilla crêpe to each person with powdered sugar sprinkled over the top. Serves 6.

Strawberry Vacherin

3 ROUND MERINGUE LAYERS, 8 INCHES IN DIAMETER, ¼-INCH THICK (SEE PASTRIES & BATTERS)/
1 PINT STRAWBERRY SHERBET
4 CUPS WHIPPED CREAM, LACED WITH FRAMBOISE TO TASTE, AND 1 TABLESPOON RASPBERRY PRESERVES/
CANDIED VIOLETS OR GLAZED STRAWBERRIES/
FRESH STRAWBERRIES IN CASSIS (SEE BELOW)/

The classic vacherin consists of a base of meringue (as in the following recipe), with several rings of meringue piled on top of it to form a sort of bowl, which is then filled with whatever you may wish. This one differs in that it is made of meringue layers, which allows more variety of filling than in the bowl type of base.

Spread sherbet on the first meringue layer. Put second layer on top. Cover with 2 cups of the whipped cream. Put third meringue layer on top. Cover the whole vacherin with remaining whipped cream. Decorate with candied violets or glazed strawberries. Serve with Fresh Strawberries in Cassis. Serves 6.

Fresh Strawberries in Cassis

Poach 2 cups halved strawberries in ¾ cup Melba Sauce (see Sweet Sauces) for about 5 minutes. Cool, flavor to taste with crème de cassis. Chill.

Semolina Pudding

1 PINT MILK
½ CUP SEMOLINA (CREAM OF WHEAT)
DASH VANILLA EXTRACT
DASH SALT
1 ENVELOPE PLAIN GELATIN,
DISSOLVED IN ¼ CUP BOILING WATER/
DROP OF KIRSCH
1½ CUPS WHIPPED CREAM

We believe this pudding to be of Italian ancestry. It is a marvelous dessert, especially when accompanied by Strawberries in Cassis.

Boil milk. Add semolina slowly, stirring. Cook 10 minutes, stirring occasionally. Add vanilla and salt. Cool. Add gelatin, kirsch, and whipped cream. Fold together and put into a ring mold. Chill. Unmold carefully and serve with Fresh Strawberries in Cassis in the center of the ring. Serves 6.

Toasted Strawberry Crêpes

12 5-INCH DESSERT CRÊPES (SEE
PASTRIES & BATTERS)/
2 CUPS SLICED STRAWBERRIES
¼ CUP MELBA SAUCE (SEE
SWEET SAUCES)/
PREHEAT OVEN TO 400 DEGREES

No doubt you've heard of or enjoyed Oeufs sur le Plat. Eggs cooked in this manner are baked in the oven in shallow round dishes, called "plats." It is that sort of dish to which we refer here for baking your toasted crêpes.

Fill crêpes with a mixture of the strawberries and Melba sauce. Roll them up and put into a baking dish or 2 each into 6 individual oven-proof plats. Place in a 400-degree oven until lightly browned (about 6 minutes). Sprinkle with powdered sugar and serve hot. Serves 6.

Mousse of Rhubarb

1¼ POUNDS RHUBARB
1 CUP SUGAR
FEW TABLESPOONS WATER
1 ENVELOPE PLAIN GELATIN
2 CUPS SWEETENED WHIPPED CREAM

Cut the rhubarb into 1-inch lengths. Put it into a saucepan with the sugar and water. Bring to a boil. Lower heat, cover pan, and simmer until just tender (20–25 minutes). Remove from the heat and take out enough of the rhubarb to make ½ cup. Reserve. Drain the remaining rhubarb and put it through a food mill to purée it. Dissolve gelatin in ¼ cup boiling water and add it to 2 cups of the purée. Cool slightly. Fold in the cut rhubarb and the whipped cream. Put into a mold and chill thoroughly. Unmold to serve and decorate top with pieces of rhubarb or straw-berry.

If you would like to serve a sauce with this, cook enough rhubarb to make an extra cup of the purée (about another ½ pound). Mix 1 cup of the purée and a little of the juice with Simple Syrup (see Dessert Basics) to taste—not too much, the sauce should be nicely tart. Put through a sieve or whirl in blender. Pour around the mousse. Serves 6.

Hungarian Cheese Cake

½ RECIPE SWEET DOUGH
(SEE PASTRIES & BATTERS)/
1 POUND COTTAGE CHEESE
4 EGGS, SEPARATED
1¼ CUPS SUGAR
DASH SALT
GRATED RIND OF 1 LEMON
1 TABLESPOON LEMON JUICE
3 TABLESPOONS SEMOLINA
½ CUP SOUR CREAM
¼ CUP VANILLA SUGAR (SEE
DESSERT BASICS)/

PREHEAT OVEN TO 350 DEGREES

The addition of semolina to the mixture for this cheese cake surprised us, but we found that the consistency and the flavor are excellent.

Roll out dough about ¼-inch thick and line bottom of 7-inch spring-form pan. Prick well with a fork. Bake in a 350-degree oven until pale golden brown (20–25 minutes). Remove from oven and cool. Lower oven temperature to 300 degrees. Press cottage cheese through a sieve. Mix with beaten egg yolks, 1 cup of the sugar, the salt, lemon rind, lemon juice, semolina, and sour cream. Pour into the spring-form pan on top of the crust. Bake in a 300-degree oven 40 minutes, or until set. Beat egg whites with remaining ¼ cup of sugar and, with a pastry tube, form a lattice on top of the cake. Place in a 350-degree oven until me-ringue sets (about 10 minutes). Dust with vanilla sugar.

Black Forest Cake

5 WHOLE EGGS
5 EGG YOLKS

Beat whole eggs, egg yolks, and sugar together. Add flour, baking powder, and cocoa, and blend in. Add melted but-

½ CUP SUGAR
½ CUP FLOUR
½ TEASPOON BAKING POWDER
1 CUP UNSWEETENED COCOA
¼ POUND (1 STICK) BUTTER,
MELTED/
½ CUP SIMPLE SYRUP (SEE
DESSERT BASICS),
FLAVORED WITH A DROP OF KIRSCH/
1 PINT WHIPPED CREAM, FLAVORED
WITH 2 TABLESPOONS OF KIRSCH/
1 1-POUND CAN PITTED BLACK
BING CHERRIES/
2 OUNCES SWEET CHOCOLATE

PREHEAT OVEN TO 350 DEGREES

ter and mix well. Butter a cake pan (8 inches in diameter, 2 inches high) thoroughly. Pour in cake mixture. Bake in a 350-degree oven 25–30 minutes, or until a cake tester inserted in the middle comes out clean. Turn cake out of pan onto a rack and cool it. When completely cool, slice into 3 layers. Spoon the simple syrup over each layer and allow to soak in. Place 2 heaping tablespoons of the whipped cream on each layer and smooth over with a flat knife or spatula. Drain cherries well and place half of them on the bottom layer of the cake. Place second cake layer on top and add remaining cherries. Place third layer, cream side down, on top. Smooth the balance of the whipped cream over the top and sides of the cake. Shave the sweet chocolate with a vegetable peeler and sprinkle over top and sides of cake so that it adheres to the whipped cream.

Croquembouche Bruno

The beautiful dessert pictured on page 207 represents a classic French dessert. As done at The Four Seasons it is more colorful than the usual and, we think, more beautiful.

PÂTE À CHOUX (SEE PASTRIES
& BATTERS)/
1½ CUPS (APPROXIMATE) CRÈME
PÂTISSIÈRE (SEE DESSERT BASICS)/
DASH CREAM OF TARTAR
⅔ CUPS WATER
2 CUPS SUGAR
40 LARGE STRAWBERRIES
(NOT HULLED)/
30 CANDIED VIOLETS
3 STICKS ANGELICA, CUT INTO
DIAMOND SHAPES/

Using pâte à choux, bake an 8-inch ring ½-inch high and 40 cream puff shells, the size of the strawberries. Cool them and fill the cream puffs with crème pâtissière. Dip point of knife in cream of tartar and then in the water. Cook sugar and water together, stirring constantly, to "crack" stage, 270 degrees on the candy thermometer. Keep pot holding syrup warm in a pan of hot water. Dip the strawberries into this syrup and place them on an oiled pan so that they will not stick as the syrup hardens. Put the ring of pâte à choux on a flat tray (a cookie sheet is good for this). In the center of the ring put an oiled bowl, bottom up; it should be 8 inches high and fit loosely into the middle of the ring. Now start to build your croquembouche. Dip the cream puffs into the syrup, one at a time. Place first a cream puff, then a glazed strawberry, with the stem toward the outside, then a cream puff, all around the ring. Continue building a sort of cupola, following the shape of the bowl, alternating cream puffs and strawberries, until you have covered the top. When all the caramel syrup in your croquembouche is cold, carefully lift the croquembouche off the bowl and place it on a silver tray. There will inevitably be some small spaces between rings of the croquembouche. Dip violets and angelica into the warm caramel syrup, just enough to make them stick, and place them in the spaces which occur between the cream puffs and strawberries. Place one glazed strawberry on top.

White Chocolate Ice Cream

24 EGG YOLKS
2½ CUPS SUGAR
2 QUARTS MILK
2 POUNDS WHITE CHOCOLATE, MELTED/
¾ CUP MARASCHINO LIQUEUR

This is a delicious ice cream. The white chocolate adds a slightly different flavor from the ordinary which is most appealing. What to do with twenty-four egg whites? Freeze them. They keep practically indefinitely and are so handy to have for that extra white you need for a good soufflé, for meringues, and the like. The handiest way to freeze them is in ice cube trays, as one white usually just about fills one cube section and thus you know exactly how much you have when you take them out to defrost.

Beat egg yolks and sugar together. Bring milk to a boil and add egg-sugar mixture. Heat together, stirring, until mixture is thick enough to coat a spoon. Mix in chocolate. Remove from heat and add liqueur. Freeze in electric freezer for 25 minutes. Makes about 3 quarts.

Asparagus, shad, fiddlehead ferns, strawberries, artichokes, baby lamb, squab, brook trout, fresh greens—the vernal season provides new delights from the earth, the rivers, and the seas. New wines appear. The whites predominate. The heavier red wines of winter are stored for another season, until the game and red meats of autumn return.

Following are some of the pleasurable foods of spring, with suitable wines in attendance and a suggested seasonal list.

CRISPED SHRIMP WITH MUSTARD FRUIT: A very old specialty, this is delicious with young Muscadet or Gros Plant—light, dry, typical Loire Valley wines. One might turn, too, to Pinot Chardonnay, which has more suavity, more quality.

MOUSSE OF TROUT: A superb Rhine wine, such as the Schloss Vollrads Graf Matuschka-Greiffenclau, would not be too elaborate for this great dish. A fine Meursault would also serve.

SNAILS À LA MISTRAL: Most people serve a dry white wine with snails, but they can take a light red. A lightly chilled Beaujolais Villages, or Brouilly at cellar temperature, go harmoniously with snails.

BOURRIDE: This creamy, garlicky fish stew demands a brisk, chilled wine —for instance, a Chablis or Muscadet—to cut through its rich taste and yet give a contrast of texture and flavor.

FROGS' LEGS IN VERMOUTH AND TRUFFLES: A well-chilled Chablis Vaudésir.

QUENELLES OF PIKE: This dish requires a wine of some stature and of charming mien—possibly a Chassagne-Montrachet of 1966, or an earlier year if it has been treated well. Quenelles may also be complemented with an Alsatian Riesling or a California Pinot Noir.

SHAD ROE IN LEMON BUTTER: My choice would be a Marcobrunner Riesling or a fine Chablis.

YOUNG CHICKEN BAKED IN APPLEJACK AND CREAM: A typically American dish, it should have a pleasing American white wine with it. Try the Joseph Heitz Pinot Blanc from California.

SPRING SQUAB CHICKEN IN CASSEROLE: A red wine, a Morgon, perhaps, from the Beaujolais district, would do very well—not overpowering, but a nice balance of flavors.

LAMB: A versatile meat which can be prepared in a number of interesting ways, lamb is at its peak in spring. Baby lamb and baby racks—crumbed, parsleyed, and baked—will be delightful with a light red Bordeaux, such as a Château Bouscaut, from Graves. Roasted epaulets call for a brisk young wine, such as the current year's Beaujolais—Château de Chaize is a good one—the moment it is imported into the country. The boned leg of lamb encased in brioche—a monumental dish—can take a very big wine; my personal choice would be a great red from the Rhône Valley, the Hermitage, 1961.

VEAL: The rack of veal with wild mushrooms calls for a good red, not too powerful but with good balance. Some Spanish wines answer this description. An interesting variation on conventional choices would be the Rioja Gran Reserva. Another delightful accompaniment for many veal dishes is the Château Pichon-

Longueville-Lalande, of even so recent a year as 1964. On the other hand, the very elegant veal chop stuffed with *foie gras* requires something a bit more important, perhaps the Corton-Bressandes, 1966, from the cellars of the Prince de Mérode.

White:

Muscadet—*De l'année*, "of the current year"—whatever bottling of this light Loire wine that is freshest and most recent.
Gros Plant—Another product of the Loire district, but a bit more tart than Muscadet.
Chablis Vaudésir—From one of the seven grand cru vineyards of Chablis.
Quincy
Gewürztraminer—A soft pinkish wine from Alsace.
Alsatian Riesling
Schloss Vollrads, Graf Matuschka-Greiffenclau—One of the treasures of the Rhineland, pressed from the Riesling grape.
Marcobrunner Riesling, Cabinet, 1969—Lively, hearty, spicy.
Forster Jesuitengarten Riesling Spätlese, Dr. Burklin Wolf—A famous and full-bodied wine from the little town of Forst, in the German Palatinate.
Spätlese refers to a wine whose grapes were picked late in the growing season and were, therefore, riper and a bit sweeter than the normal crop.
Pinot Blanc, California, Joseph Heitz, Napa Valley.

Champagne:

California, Korbel brut.
Louis Roederer brut.

Red:

Banda Azul Tino, Rioja (Spain), 1964.
Gran Reserva, Rioja, 1949.
Valpolicella, Cantina Sociale (Italy), 1966.
Chianti Risèrva, Ducale—A superb Italian wine.
Dão—A smooth, limpid wine from a wild and mountainous area of Portugal, south of the Douro River.
Cahors Rouge, 1966—A delightful, offbeat wine, made north of Toulouse, it is the deepest, darkest red of all French wines.
Hermitage, Rhône Valley, 1961.
Châteauneuf-du-Pape, Rhône Valley, 1962.
Beaujolais, Château de Chaize—Of the most recent year.
Nuits St. Georges, Les Saint-Georges, 1962—One of the "big Burgundies" from the Côte de Nuits.
Morgon, H. Cotillon, 1969—An exceptional Beaujolais.

Rosé:

Anjou—As young as you can find it.
Bandol, Chateau Braquet, 1968—Made east of Marseilles.
Alouette, Rosé de Cabernet.
Tavel, Union Viticole, 1967—Probably the greatest of the rosés.
Grenache Rosé, California, Almadén—Finest of the Californias.

—JB

Summer

As the gastronome's spring begins with asparagus, so his summer arrives with the first tiny new potatoes and tender green peas. Shelling fresh peas, putting them in a pot with butter, lettuce leaves, and a bit of water, and cooking them to a peak of sweetness is a savory realization of the richness and abundance of summer.

Summer also is the time of cherries: brilliant red Montmorencys, Kentish, May Dukes for tarts and clafouti or a fine duckling, gargantuan Bings, and juicy, black and purple Lamberts. One's thoughts turn as well to raspberries with their gracious softness and striking flavor. One doesn't really chew them; they are crushed with the tongue and slowly swallowed, while each breath is imbued with their bouquet.

Summer means food which has been cooked and allowed to cool to room temperature, or cold food. Meat and fish which taste well when first cooked are certain to taste better if given time to absorb the flavorings one has used for enhancement. Chicken or tiny pigeons, crisp brown and succulently tender under the skin, yield their best flavors at room temperature. Thin slices of braised veal smothered with tuna-and-anchovy-scented sauce are excellent served cold with a complementary rice salad. Such summery dishes are picnic food, to be sure, but they are the food of romance—food one eats sitting by a small stream or on a dune overlooking the sea, listening to music, reading poetry, and being very deeply alive. —JB

Eggs Tartare

3 MEDIUM TOMATOES
SALT & FRESHLY GROUND PEPPER
TO TASTE/
6 COLD POACHED EGGS
½ CUP CURRY MAYONNAISE
(SEE SAUCES)/
2 CUPS RAW CARROTS, CELERY, AND
GREEN BEANS, CUT HAIR-THIN/
LETTUCE

This dish may be served as an appetizer, or you might serve two tomato halves per person as a very fine summer luncheon dish. The raw vegetables and cold poached eggs are light and refreshing, and the curry mayonnaise adds just the right touch of sparkle to the whole.

Cut the tomatoes in half and scoop out the centers. Drain shells well. Dice the centers, drain thoroughly, and reserve. Sprinkle tomato halves with salt and pepper. Trim edges of the egg whites to shape the eggs uniformly. Place in scooped-out tomato halves. Add tomato dice. Mask with mayonnaise. Place raw carrots, celery, and beans on top. Serve on lettuce leaves.

NOTE: To prepare poached eggs which you wish to use cold, cook them as you usually do, so that the whites are set and the yolks soft. Trim the edges of the whites neatly, and place eggs in cold water in the refrigerator until ready to use.

Escabèche of Scallops

2 POUNDS BAY SCALLOPS
FLOUR FOR DREDGING
¼ CUP BUTTER
½ CUP JULIENNE CARROTS
¼ CUP JULIENNE CELERY
½ CUP OLIVE OIL
1 CUP WHITE VINEGAR
SALT TO TASTE
1 TABLESPOON WHOLE PEPPERCORNS
1 LEMON, PEELED, SEEDED, & DICED
2 STALKS FENNEL

Escabèche is a marvelous summer dish. It originated in Spain and Provence, where it is usually made with small fish, or fillets of larger fish cut into narrow slices. You can, however, use any fish or seafood you like, and scallops are excellent when cooked and served this way. Serve the escabèche with some of the marinade sprinkled over it and accompany it with crusty French bread and sweet butter for the perfect marriage of taste and flavor. While you should refrigerate escabèche for twenty-four hours, as instructed in the recipe, you are advised not to keep it longer than forty-eight hours. Fish, cooked or raw, doesn't keep well and you cannot preserve this dish successfully in your freezer.

Dredge scallops lightly with flour. Sauté in butter until just barely golden brown. Mix remaining ingredients and pour over scallops. Refrigerate for at least 24 hours. Serves 6.

Mousse of Ham in Whole Peaches

1 POUND COOKED HAM
⅓ CUP MAYONNAISE (SEE SAUCES)
CAYENNE PEPPER & SALT TO TASTE
⅓ CUP BUTTER, SOFTENED
2 TEASPOONS MEDIUM-DRY PORT
6 LARGE, RIPE PEACHES

This is a most unusual and handsome dish for the start of a summer meal. Because ham and fruit combine so well, the flavor is superb.

Cut ham into very small pieces and put through the finest blade of meat grinder. Place in mixing bowl. Beat mayonnaise, pepper, salt, butter, and port very slowly into ham to make a fine mousse. Cool 1 hour. Peel peaches (or not, as you prefer). Remove pit by placing knife in the stem of the peach and encircling pit. This will leave a center core of approximately ¾ inch for stuffing. Stuff peaches with mousse. Serve in coupe glasses lined with Bibb lettuce leaves. Serves 6. *(See illustration, page 217.)*

Smoked Salmon with Caviar

½ POUND SMOKED SALMON,
SLICED VERY THIN/
3 TABLESPOONS BLACK CAVIAR

The Four Seasons uses imported smoked Scotch salmon, but you can use the fine Nova Scotia variety which is more readily available here and, while not cheap, is somewhat less expensive than the Scotch. While there are indeed gradations in the quality of smoked salmon—the best is least salty—if you buy a good one it will do nicely for this dish.

Divide caviar on the slices of salmon. Fold into small envelopes, taking care not to crush caviar. Serves 6.

Seviche à la Four Seasons

1½ POUNDS BAY SCALLOPS
⅘ LEMON JUICE AND ⅕ LIME
JUICE TO COVER SCALLOPS/
6 TABLESPOONS FINELY CHOPPED
GREEN PEPPER/
6 TABLESPOONS CHOPPED RED ONION
6 TABLESPOONS ORANGE JUICE
4 TABLESPOONS LEMON JUICE
4 TABLESPOONS TOMATO CATSUP
SALT, PEPPER, & TABASCO TO TASTE

Seviche is a South American dish, especially Peruvian, in which fish (sometimes fillets of very tender fish are used instead of scallops) is "cooked" by letting it marinate in citrus juice for twenty-four hours. In Peru, only lime juice is used.

Marinate scallops in lemon and lime juice for about 24 hours. Drain thoroughly, discarding juice. Four to 5 hours before serving, mix drained scallops with remaining ingredients. Serves 6.

Avocado Crêpes Filled with Crabmeat

Crêpes:
1 CUP MASHED AVOCADO PULP
(ABOUT 1 LARGE AVOCADO)/
8 EGGS
1 CUP FLOUR
½ TEASPOON SALT
¾ CUP MILK
¾ CUP WATER
2 TABLESPOONS BUTTER

This is a really inventive and very pretty dish. It freezes well, so why not make at least double the recipe and freeze the rest for another occasion? (Line the baking dish with freezer-weight foil. Put in crêpes as instructed in the recipe. Fold foil over to cover the crêpes completely. Freeze. When frozen, lift out crêpes in their foil and store in the freezer. When ready to cook, thaw package in refrigerator for 2 to 3 hours, then place in a baking dish and heat in a 400-degree oven 15 minutes, still wrapped in foil. Fold back foil and bake for an additional 15 minutes.)

To the avocado add eggs, flour, and salt. Beat with a whisk until smooth. Slowly stir in milk and water. Melt a little butter in a 7-inch crêpe pan. Pour in a scant ¼ cup of batter, tilting the pan to spread the batter evenly. Cook the crêpe until lightly browned (about 1 minute). Turn and cook the other side. Continue until all batter is used. Makes about 24 crêpes.

Filling:
¼ CUP BUTTER

Melt butter in a saucepan and add the flour, stirring constantly until smooth. Gradually add the hot milk and

6 TABLESPOONS FLOUR
2½ CUPS HOT MILK
½ CUP HOT LIGHT CREAM
1 CUP DICED SWISS CHEESE
1 TEASPOON WORCESTERSHIRE SAUCE
SALT & PEPPER TO TASTE
2 POUNDS LUMP CRABMEAT

Topping:
1½ CUPS COARSELY GRATED
SWISS CHEESE/
½ CUP BUTTER

PREHEAT OVEN TO 400 DEGREES

cream, stirring constantly until mixture begins to thicken. Add the cheese and cook until very thick. Remove from heat and add Worcestershire and seasonings. Fold in the crabmeat. Spread this filling on ½ of each crêpe and roll them up. Place, seam side down, in well-buttered baking dish or dishes.

Sprinkle the crêpes with the cheese and dot with the butter. Bake in a 400-degree oven for 10–15 minutes, or until crêpes are hot and cheese is melted. Serves 12.

Deviled Clams Fried in Shell

½ CUP SOFTENED BUTTER
¼ CUP FINELY MINCED PARSLEY
2 CLOVES GARLIC, FINELY MINCED
2 TABLESPOONS WHITE WINE
18 CHERRYSTONE CLAMS
ON HALF SHELL/
1 QUART BEIGNET BATTER
(SEE PASTRIES & BATTERS)/
FAT FOR DEEP FRYING

When we first heard about this appetizer, we couldn't believe it would work, and you may read the recipe with the same feeling. But we assure you that it does work, and that it is delicious to eat. It might be well to have oyster forks handy, even if you serve these as appetizers, to ease the clams out of the shells. But we've eaten them straight from the hand neatly, so it is possible also to serve them quite informally.

Mix butter, parsley, garlic, and wine. Spread on clams, completely covering them. Dip clams (in half shells) in batter and deep fry in 375-degree oil until lightly golden brown, about 2 minutes. Serves 6.

Morel Soufflé in Crust

1 RECIPE RICH PASTRY
(SEE PASTRIES & BATTERS)/
1 RECIPE ENTRÉE SOUFFLÉ
(SEE BASIC SOUFFLÉS)/

This is a very fancy, light, and delicate first course for a grand dinner party—or a lovely main course at luncheon, accompanied only by a simple salad with French dressing.

½ POUND FRESH MORELS
(OR 2 OUNCES DRY)/

PREHEAT OVEN TO 400 DEGREES

Roll out the pastry about ⅛-inch thick. Line ramekins 3 inches deep and 2½ inches in diameter with the pastry, then with buttered lightweight foil. Fill with any kind of dried beans (to prevent the sides from collapsing and the bottom from puffing up.) Bake in a 400-degree oven 8 to 9 minutes, or until pastry is set. Remove beans and foil. Prick bottoms of crusts and return to oven for 2 to 3 minutes. Cool and remove crusts from ramekins.

PREHEAT OVEN TO 350 DEGREES

If you are using dry morels, soak them first in warm water for 1 hour. Drain. Before adding the egg whites to your basic soufflé mixture stir the morels, coarsely chopped, into the yolk mixture. Then proceed as directed with the egg-white addition. Fill the crusts with the soufflé mixture and bake in a 350-degree oven 25 minutes, or until soufflé is puffed and browned. Serves 6.

Poached Eggs Armenonville

6 TABLESPOONS PARBOILED
TINY CARROTS/
6 TABLESPOONS PARBOILED
TINY GREEN PEAS/
¾ CUP SAUCE VELOUTÉ
(SEE SAUCES)/
6 POACHED EGGS
6 TART SHELLS
(SEE PASTRIES & BATTERS)/
18 COOKED ASPARAGUS TIPS

Warm the carrots and peas in the velouté. Place the eggs in the tart shells. Cover with the sauced vegetables and garnish with the asparagus tips. Serves 6.
NOTE: It is important that the vegetables be fresh. If necessary, the asparagus may be replaced by broccoli flowerets.

Omelette Grand'mère

1 TABLESPOON BUTTER
2 TABLESPOONS CRISPLY FRIED

Heat omelette pan until a drop of water tossed upon it bounces and disappears. Add butter and bacon to pan, and

214

AND CRUMBLED BACON/
3 EGGS
DASH SALT
DASH TABASCO
1 TEASPOON CHOPPED CHIVES
1 TEASPOON CHOPPED PARSLEY
2 TABLESPOONS FRESHLY GRATED
GRUYÈRE CHEESE/

when the butter sizzles add eggs, beaten very lightly with salt, Tabasco, chives, and parsley. Shake the pan with your left hand, while stirring the mixture with the fork held in your right, using the back of the fork and being careful not to scrape the pan. When mixture is set, sprinkle the cheese in the center of it. Hold the handle of omelette pan with the palm of the left hand *up* (just the reverse of the way you ordinarily hold it). Tilt the pan and roll the omelette onto a warm plate, working gently and lightly. The outside of the omelette should be golden yellow, not brown, and the inside soft. Serves 1. Do not try to make larger omelettes. If you want to serve more people, simply make more omelettes. It takes about a minute for each one, and they are well worth waiting for.

Soups

Jellied Beet and Onion Consommé

1 QUART BEEF STOCK (SEE STOCKS)
3 LEEKS, CHOPPED
1 STALK CELERY, CHOPPED
2 MEDIUM ONIONS, QUARTERED
6 PEPPERCORNS
6 LARGE BEETS
3 EGG WHITES & SHELLS
1 ENVELOPE PLUS 1 TEASPOON
PLAIN GELATIN,
DISSOLVED IN ¼ CUP COLD WATER/
SALT & PEPPER TO TASTE
6 TABLESPOONS SOUR CREAM

A jellied soup served solidly jelled is not attractive. This one is just barely jelled, which is the way madrilene and similar soups should be served.

Place beef stock in a saucepan and add leeks, celery, onion, peppercorns, beets, egg whites, and shells. Simmer 1 hour, or until beets are cooked. Strain through cheesecloth, into stainless-steel bowl. Reserve beets. Remove fat from the surface. Add dissolved gelatin. Taste for seasoning. Peel beets and cut into julienne strips. Add to consommé. Place the bowl in larger vessel filled with cracked ice and chill, stirring constantly, until consommé jells lightly; or chill in refrigerator, stirring now and then. Serve in individual bowls. Garnish each serving with a tablespoon of sour cream. Serves 6.

Spiced Carrot Vichyssoise

5 POTATOES, PEELED & SLICED
7 LARGE CARROTS, SLICED
2 LARGE LEEKS, SLICED
1½ QUARTS CHICKEN STOCK
(SEE STOCKS)/
1 HAM SHANK
1 TEASPOON SUGAR
SALT TO TASTE
DASH FRESHLY GROUND PEPPER
1 QUART HEAVY CREAM
1 RAW CARROT CUT IN FINE JULIENNE

Originally leek and potato soup, now called vichyssoise, or sometimes "à la bonne femme" or "crème Gauloise," this version served at The Four Seasons provides a milder but surprising variation.

Simmer vegetables and ham shank in stock until potatoes and carrots are done (40–50 minutes). Remove ham shank and whirl soup in blender. Season. Cool. Add cream. Serve thoroughly chilled with julienne of raw carrots on top. Serves 6 to 8.

Watercress Vichyssoise

4 LEEKS
1 MEDIUM ONION
2 TABLESPOONS BUTTER
1½ BUNCHES WATERCRESS,
FINELY CHOPPED/
5 MEDIUM POTATOES, PEELED
& SLICED/
1 QUART CHICKEN STOCK
(SEE STOCKS)/
1 TABLESPOON SALT
2 CUPS MILK
2 CUPS LIGHT CREAM
SALT & PEPPER TO TASTE
1 CUP HEAVY CREAM

Slice the white parts of the leeks very fine. Slice the onion. Cook with leeks in butter until they just begin to turn golden. Add the watercress, potatoes, chicken stock, and the tablespoon of salt. Cook at a low boil 35–40 minutes. Rub the mixture through a fine sieve, or whirl in blender. Return to the heat and add the milk and light cream. Correct seasoning with salt and pepper. Bring to a boil. Cool. Chill. When cold, blend in the heavy cream. Serves 8.

Cream of Sorrel Soup

¾ POUND SORREL
1½ QUARTS CHICKEN STOCK
(SEE STOCKS)/
3 EGG YOLKS
3 TABLESPOONS CREAM
SALT & PEPPER TO TASTE
1½ CUPS SOUR CREAM

Sorrel, sometimes known as sour grass, is good for salads, for purées, or cooked until just barely wilted in salted water and dressed with melted butter. But it is at its best in cold sorrel soup. Sorrel is usually gathered in the United States from wild plants, but in Europe it is frequently cultivated. If you learn to recognize the leaves, you may be able to find it growing wild. The sourness in the flavor of the leaves is greater in some varieties of sorrel than others, but in any case the plant is always well worth picking.

Clean sorrel thoroughly and chop fine. Simmer 10 minutes in the chicken stock. Mix egg yolks with cream and add slowly to soup, beating constantly with a wire whisk. Season. Cool and chill. Just before serving, beat in the sour cream. Serves 6.

NOTE: This soup may also be served hot. Warm it to piping after beating in the sour cream.

Cream of Avocado Soup

1 LARGE AVOCADO
1 PINT CHICKEN STOCK (SEE STOCKS)
1 TEASPOON CHILI POWDER
¼ TEASPOON GROUND CORIANDER
1 CUP HEAVY CREAM
RED CAVIAR

This soup has an excellent flavor, and the contrast of its soft green color with the red caviar is most appealing.

Peel and cut up avocado. Whirl in the blender with chicken stock, chili powder, and coriander. Heat in top of double boiler for 10 minutes. Cool, add cream, and chill thoroughly. Float a teaspoon of caviar on each portion. (If you prefer to serve this soup without caviar, you may find it needs salt.) Serves 6.

221

Cream of Squash

2 POUNDS SUMMER SQUASH
2 QUARTS SAUCE VELOUTÉ
(SEE SAUCES)/
HEAVY CREAM TO TASTE
SALT & PEPPER TO TASTE
YELLOW FOOD COLORING

Slice squash but do not peel. Simmer with the velouté for 20 minutes. Strain. Reheat the soup. It will thicken as you do so. Thin to desired consistency with the cream. Season. Add a few drops of yellow vegetable coloring, if desired. Cool. Chill. Serves 6.

NOTE: The only reason for using vegetable coloring is to intensify a principal ingredient which, in its natural state, is too pale. It may be flavorful, but its appearance is unappetizing. This can be true of squash, certain varieties of avocado, and other foods. Since eye appeal is highly important in good cooking, the use of artificial color to attain it seems quite justifiable. However, we urge you to use coloring with discretion, since food that is too highly and unnaturally colored will be as unattractive as that which is pallid.

Mulligatawny

1 MEDIUM ONION, SLICED
4 TABLESPOONS BUTTER
1 TEASPOON CURRY POWDER
10 DRIED APRICOTS, CHOPPED FINE
2 QUARTS CHICKEN STOCK
(SEE STOCKS)/
1 TABLESPOON CORNSTARCH
SALT & PEPPER TO TASTE
6 TABLESPOONS DICED COOKED
CHICKEN BREAST/
1 CUP HEAVY CREAM, CHILLED

The word "Mulligatawny" is spelled according to the English pronunciation of two East Indian words: *molagu* (pepper) and *tunni* (water). Originally, "pepper water" was a dish of the very poor, but as time went by the English and Indians added ingredients and strength to the soup until it became the varied and delicious thing it is today. Serving it cold, as we do, certainly has nothing to do with Indian cookery, but it is a good idea just the same. This recipe was improvised by our test chef from a title we found on one of the restaurant's early menus and for which we could find no instructions. The result is splendid and we recommend it highly. The base of dried apricots may surprise you, but it makes a perfect foil for the rest of the ingredients. And you may be surprised to learn also that the amount of curry powder used, which seems little to a curry lover, turns out to be the perfect seasoning for this particular soup.

Cook onion in butter until soft but not brown. Mix in curry and apricots. Pour in stock. Simmer for 15 minutes. Add cornstarch, salt, and pepper. Strain. Add chicken. Cool and chill. Mix in cream just before serving. Serves 6.

Senegalese Soup

5 TABLESPOONS BUTTER
1 SMALL ONION, COARSELY CHOPPED
1 CARROT, COARSELY CHOPPED
1 STALK CELERY, COARSELY CHOPPED
1 HEAPING TEASPOON CURRY POWDER
3 SMALL CINNAMON STICKS
2 BAY LEAVES
1 TEASPOON WHOLE CLOVES
5 CUPS STRONG CHICKEN BROTH
1 TABLESPOON TOMATO PURÉE
2 HEAPING TABLESPOONS ALMOND PASTE
1 TABLESPOON RED CURRANT JELLY
3 TABLESPOONS FLOUR
SALT & FRESHLY GROUND WHITE PEPPER
2 CUPS HEAVY CREAM
TOASTED COCONUT

Cold Senegalese soup should have a delicate curry flavor, and this does. But the almond paste and red currant jelly are surprising. However, they blend into a delicious whole.

Melt 2 tablespoons of the butter in a heavy saucepan. Add the onion, carrot, and celery. Cook over moderate heat, stirring occasionally, until the vegetables have taken on a little color. Stir in the curry powder until well blended. Add cinnamon sticks, bay leaves, cloves, broth, tomato purée, almond paste, and jelly. Mix well, bring to a boil, and simmer for 1 hour. Skim off any foam that rises to the surface. Knead the remaining butter together with the flour. Add this (called beurre manié), bit by bit, to the soup, stirring until well blended. Cook for 5 to 6 minutes, or until soup has thickened slightly. Strain, taste for seasoning, cool, and refrigerate. Just before serving combine with the cream. Serve in well-chilled soup cups with a sprinkling of toasted coconut on top. Serves 6 to 8.

Fish & Seafood

Cold Striped Bass

1 4-POUND STRIPED BASS
1 RECIPE COURT-BOUILLON (SEE STOCKS)/

Lay bass on a length of cheesecloth in a shallow poaching pan. Let long ends of cheesecloth hang over the edges of

Garnitures:

HARD-COOKED EGGS, TOMATOES, PEAS,
CARROTS, OR OTHER VEGETABLE
OF CHOICE/

————

1 RECIPE PORT ASPIC (SEE STOCKS),
COOLED TO THE CONSISTENCY
OF HEAVY OIL/
CHERRY TOMATOES
LEMON, CUT PAPER-THIN
IN HALF-SLICES/
1 RECIPE GREEN MAYONNAISE
(SEE SAUCES)/

the pan so you can lift fish out easily when it is done. Pour in enough cool court-bouillon to cover bass. Bring to a simmer and poach fish gently 20 minutes. Remove pan from heat and let fish cool in the court-bouillon. Remove fish to a rack to drain. Cut eggs and/or vegetables into any shapes you like and arrange on the bass. Spoon the aspic over fish. Place fish (still on rack) in refrigerator for 15 minutes. Remove and place fish on an oval platter. Alternate cherry tomatoes and slices of lemon (cut side in) in a border around the edge of the platter. Serve green mayonnaise separately. Serves 6.

Barquette of Flounder

3 EGGS
SALT & PEPPER TO TASTE
6 ½-POUND FILLETS OF FLOUNDER
FLOUR FOR DIPPING
BREAD CRUMBS FOR ROLLING
½ CUP OIL
½ CUP BUTTER
3 CUPS DICED APPLE
3 CUPS DICED CANTALOUPE
6 BARQUETTE TARTS (SEE PASTRIES &
BATTERS) CUT TO SIZE OF FILLETS/
6 TABLESPOONS LEMON JUICE
6 TABLESPOONS BUTTER, BROWNED
2 TABLESPOONS FINELY CHOPPED PARSLEY
18 THIN SLICES OF LEMON, CUT IN HALF

Beat eggs and season with salt and pepper. Dip fillets in flour and then eggs. Roll in bread crumbs. Heat the oil and 4 tablespoons of the butter in a skillet. Add fillets and sauté for 8–10 minutes, or until lightly browned on both sides. Sauté apple and cantaloupe in the remaining butter until tender. Fill the barquettes with the sautéed fruit and sprinkle lemon juice over. Top each barquette with a fillet. Mix remaining lemon juice with the browned butter, pour over fish. To garnish, make "spine" of chopped parsley down middle of fillets. (An easy way to do this is to cut a narrow slit in a piece of cardboard the length of the fillets and sprinkle parsley onto the fish through the cardboard.) For "scales," arrange overlapping slices of lemon with cut edges at an angle to the line of parsley. Serves 6.

Lobster Américain in Croustade

3 1-POUND LIVE LOBSTERS
SALT & PEPPER
¾ CUP OIL
1 MEDIUM ONION, CHOPPED
3 CLOVES GARLIC, MINCED
1 4-INCH STALK TARRAGON, CHOPPED
(OR ¼ TEASPOON DRIED)/
3 RIPE TOMATOES, PEELED & DICED
3 MEDIUM CARROTS, PEELED & SLICED
6 TABLESPOONS COGNAC, WARMED
1½ CUPS DRY WHITE WINE
1½ CUPS WHITE WINE SAUCE,
OR BROWN SAUCE (SEE SAUCES)/
3 TABLESPOONS TOMATO PURÉE
¾ CUP HEAVY CREAM
½ CUP SWEET BUTTER
FEW DROPS TABASCO
1½ TEASPOONS LEMON JUICE
2 TABLESPOONS LONG-GRAIN RICE
1 TEASPOON SWEET BUTTER
6 CROUSTADES, HEATED
(SEE PASTRIES & BATTERS)/

The name of this dish has been a matter of controversy for a long time. Originally it was Lobster Provençal, because ingredients characteristic of Provence—tomatoes, onions, and garlic—are present. Others argue that the dish came from Brittany and that the proper title is Lobster Armoricain. This has been transposed into Américain, which currently is the most widely accepted title. Yet how *that* title came about is also argued at length; so if you would like to decide that it was named in honor of some restaurant's favorite American patron, that will be all right. You'll have plenty of company. Note that everything except the last three ingredients are constituents of the Sauce Américaine (see Sauces).

Split the lobsters lengthwise. Reserve the coral. Sprinkle the lobster meat with salt and pepper. Bring the oil to high heat in a large, flame-proof casserole. Put in the lobsters and cook, turning, until the shells turn red and the meat is seared. Remove lobsters. Add onion, garlic, tarragon, tomatoes, and carrots, and cook until brown. Place the lobsters on vegetables, pour in the cognac and flambé. Pour in the white wine and reduce by ⅓. Add the white wine sauce, or brown sauce. (If you use the white wine sauce, add the tomato purée. With the brown sauce it is not necessary.) Add salt and pepper to taste. Cook in a 300-degree oven for 20 minutes. Remove lobster from casserole. Take out the meat and cut it in medium dice. Keep warm. Put the heavy cream into the sauce and let it reduce by ⅓. Strain. Add the ½ cup sweet butter and mix well. Add Tabasco, lemon juice, and lobster coral, and mix well again. This sauce Américaine should be light and delicate.

While the lobster is cooking, cook the rice in ¾ cup boiling water until tender. Drain and mix with the teaspoon sweet butter. Arrange the heated croustades on a serving plate. Put a tablespoon of rice in the bottom of each. Cover with lobster meat and fill with the sauce. Put some sprigs of parsley between the croustades to decorate. Serves 6.

Broiled Lobster with Tarragon Butter

6 2-POUND LOBSTERS
SALT
OIL FOR BASTING
LIVER OF LOBSTERS
6 TABLESPOONS CHOPPED TARRAGON
(OR 2 TEASPOONS DRY)/
2 TABLESPOONS CHOPPED SHALLOTS
3 CUPS CLARIFIED BUTTER (SEE SAUCES)

There are more exciting ways to prepare lobster than by broiling it, but broiled lobster is such a universal favorite it should be in every cook's repertoire. Enhance it, however, with the sauce suggested here.

Have your fish market split and clean the lobster (saving the liver), or, if you prefer, do it yourself. Remove the legs and crack the claws. Salt the meat and paint the lobster all over with oil. Place on the broiler rack, flesh side up, and broil 7 inches from heat until cooked, but not overdone, basting frequently with more oil. The cooking time should be about 12 to 15 minutes. Be careful not to overcook, or it will be dry. Meantime, put the liver, tarragon, shallots, and clarified butter into a saucepan and simmer 5 minutes. Pour over the lobster meat. Run under the broiler for 2–3 minutes. Serves 6.

Salmon Steaks en Papillote

6 LARGE SALMON STEAKS, ABOUT
8 OUNCES EACH/
SALT & PEPPER
1 CUP VEGETABLE OIL
6 SLICES BACON, COARSELY CHOPPED
½ POUND MUSHROOM CAPS, CHOPPED
3 TABLESPOONS MINCED SHALLOTS

Fresh salmon is a treat in any guise. In the United States, the custom of cooking this and other fish in paper is most characteristic of New Orleans. The puffed, browned parchment in which the fish is brought to the table is very alluring: one is eager to know what treat will be found inside.

Sprinkle salmon steaks with salt and pepper, and sauté

¼ CUP BUTTER
1 EGG
2 TABLESPOONS FLOUR
SAUCE DIABLE (SEE SAUCES)

them in the oil for 5 minutes on each side (or longer, depending on thickness). Drain. Sauté bacon, mushrooms, and shallots in butter, with a dash of pepper, for 5–8 minutes. Cut 6 pieces of parchment paper in heart or diamond shapes twice the size of the steaks. Place a portion of the bacon-mushroom mixture at one side of each sheet. Place a salmon steak on top of mixture, then cover each steak with remaining bacon and mushrooms. Beat egg with flour and moisten edge of paper with this mixture. Fold paper over and press edges together. Bake for 5 minutes in a 425-degree oven, during which parchment will puff and brown. Serve on individual plates with sauce diable on the side to be placed on the fish after each diner has opened his parchment. Serves 6.

Summer Sole Four Seasons

6 FILLETS SOLE
6 TABLESPOONS MOUSSE OF
SALMON (SEE MOUSSE
OF TROUT, PAGE 149)/
2 TABLESPOONS MINCED SHALLOTS
1 TABLESPOON LEMON JUICE
SALT & PEPPER TO TASTE
¼ CUP WHITE WINE
1 CUP WHITE WINE SAUCE
(SEE SAUCES)/
2 TABLESPOONS BUTTER
6 SLICES TRUFFLE

There is no true sole fished in American waters, though "sole" is the most popular fish here. When we use the term, we are referring to the numerous members of the flat-bodied flounder family which we can, and do, buy in quite large quantities. These are winter flounder, lemon sole, dabs, yellowtails, and gray sole. While their flavor and texture cannot compare with that of Channel or Dover sole (which is imported to the United States frozen and is astronomically expensive), any recipe that calls for sole will turn out well if made with one of our native species of flounder.

Lay the fillets out flat and put a tablespoon of salmon mousse on each. Roll them up. Butter a pan and put shallots, lemon juice, salt, pepper, and white wine on the bottom. Place the rolled fillets (paupiettes) on top. Cover with buttered parchment paper. Put into a 350-degree

227

oven and poach for 15 minutes. Remove from the oven and place the paupiettes on a serving platter. Keep warm. Reduce the pan juices by ⅔ and add the white wine sauce. Cook a few minutes more. Add butter and shake the pan until it is absorbed. Correct seasoning. Pour sauce over paupiettes and decorate each with a slice of truffle. Serves 6.

Fillet of Sole Caprice

6 8-OUNCE FILLETS OF SOLE
½ CUP CLARIFIED BUTTER (SEE SAUCES)
2 CUPS BREAD CRUMBS
½ CUP BUTTER
3 BANANAS
2 TABLESPOONS BUTTER

Dip each fillet in the clarified butter, then in the bread crumbs. Melt the ½ cup of butter in a pan and sauté the fillets until browned. Remove to a serving platter. Meanwhile, slice the bananas lengthwise and sauté in the 2 tablespoons butter for a few minutes, just until softened. Place a slice of banana on each fillet. Pour the butter from the pan over and serve. Serves 6.

Fillet of Sole Béarnaise

6 8-OUNCE FILLETS OF SOLE
½ CUP CLARIFIED BUTTER
(SEE SAUCES)/
2 CUPS BREAD CRUMBS
2 TABLESPOONS SAUCE BÉARNAISE
(SEE SAUCES)/
POTATOES PARISIENNE (PAGE 249)

Dip fillets into clarified butter, and then bread crumbs. Grill under broiler until browned (6–7 minutes), turning over once. Place on serving platter. On each fillet place a teaspoon of sauce Béarnaise. Serve surrounded with Potatoes Parisienne. Serves 6.

Fillet of Sole Orly

3 DOVER SOLE
(ABOUT 12 OUNCES EACH)/

Have your fish market fillet the sole. Flatten them lightly with the flat of a cleaver. Sprinkle with salt and pepper.

SALT & PEPPER TO TASTE
½ CUP FLOUR
ENGLISH MIXTURE (PAGE 247)
½ CUP BREAD CRUMBS
FAT FOR DEEP FRYING
3 LEMONS CUT INTO WEDGES
PARSLEY SPRIGS
1 CUP TOMATO SAUCE (SEE SAUCES)

Dip fillets into flour, then into English mixture, then the bread crumbs. Fry the fillets in 375-degree deep fat until golden brown (about 3 minutes). Put fillets on serving plate with lemon wedges and parsley. Serve tomato sauce separately. Serves 6.

NOTE: You may also fold the fillets onto skewers and fry in the same way. The presentation is handsome, because the folded sole holds its serpentine curves as it comes off the skewer.

Baked Whitefish with Crabmeat, Gratinée

3 POUNDS SKINNED FILLET
OF WHITEFISH/
SALT & PEPPER TO TASTE
BUTTER
1½ CUPS DRY WHITE WINE
½ POUND FRESH CRABMEAT
1 CUP HEAVY CREAM
1 CUP SAUCE MOUSSELINE (SEE SAUCES)

Whitefish is one of the popular and important freshwater fishes of the United States. In the following recipe, enhanced by crabmeat, cream, and mousseline, it becomes a regal and extremely rich dish. Serve before it a jellied soup, and with it crisp potatoes and buttered green peas or beans. For dessert, a sherbet would be perfect.

Season fish. Butter a flame-proof baking dish in which fillets will fit as closely as possible. Place fillets in dish. Pour wine over. Bake in a 400-degree oven for 10 minutes. Arrange crabmeat over fillets. Pour on cream. Bring to boil on top of range. Spread sauce mousseline on top. Glaze under broiler for a few minutes until golden brown. Serves 6.

Bouillabaisse

1 MEDIUM ONION, COARSELY CHOPPED
2 TOMATOES, COARSELY CHOPPED
2 LEEKS, COARSELY CHOPPED

While there is no question that this is a soup, it is also a meal in itself and should be served as such. Along the Mediterranean coast, a variety of bouillabaisses is to be

⅓ cup olive oil
6 stalks fennel
1 tablespoon tomato purée
2 tablespoons salt
1 teaspoon pepper
¼ teaspoon saffron powder
10 cloves garlic
¾ pound red snapper
¾ pound whitefish
¾ pound striped bass
¾ pound turbot (or halibut)
2 pound mussels,
cleaned (page 20)/
3 1½-pound live lobsters
3 quarts fish stock (see stocks)

found. But the most famous is that of Marseilles, which is considered by connoisseurs to be the best and only authentic one. It is said by natives of Marseilles to have been invented by fishermen who used whatever their catch had provided to make a hearty and satisfying dish for meals aboard ship. It includes always a variety of fish and seafood, plus tomatoes and saffron. The fact that all sorts of fish are used in the soup should be a comfort to you, because most of those caught in the Mediterranean are unavailable elsewhere. Fish used in the Marseilles bouillabaisse are: racasse, chapon, saint-pierre, conger-eel, lophius, red mullet, ronquier, and sea-perch. The recipe which follows includes turbot, which is extremely difficult to obtain in the United States; the best substitute for it is halibut. Any fish used should preferably be lean.

Place onion, tomato, leek, olive oil, fennel, tomato purée, salt, pepper, and saffron powder in a large, deep pot. Mash garlic with the flat of a cleaver. Remove skin. Add garlic to pot. Cut each kind of fish into 6 pieces and add to pot. Add mussels. Cut lobsters through lengthwise and remove stomach and intestinal vein. (You may cut them in quarters, if desired.) Add lobsters to pot and pour in stock. Bring quickly to a boil, and boil hard for 8 minutes. Reduce heat and cook at a simmer for 12 minutes more. Remove from heat. Very carefully remove fish to a shallow serving bowl. Strain stock. Pour ½ cup of stock over fish and the remainder into a soup tureen. Serve fish and stock separately, with toasted garlic croutons and rouille sauce. Serves 6–8.

Rouille:
1 recipe sauce aïoli (see sauces)
½ teaspoon saffron powder
tabasco

Mix aïoli and saffron powder. Add Tabasco to taste. Rouille should be strong.

Mountain Trout Filled with Salmon Mousse

6 FRESH TROUT, BONED
2 CUPS MOUSSE OF SALMON
(SEE MOUSSE OF TROUT, PAGE 149)/
1 TABLESPOON CHOPPED SHALLOTS
1 CUP SLICED FRESH MUSHROOMS
1 TEASPOON LEMON JUICE
¼ CUP BUTTER
½ CUP DRY SHERRY
½ CUP FISH STOCK (SEE STOCKS)
2 TABLESPOONS SALT
1 TEASPOON PEPPER
1 CUP HEAVY CREAM
6 SLICES TRUFFLE

Though it may seem to people of simple tastes that stuffing a trout is overdoing it, anyone who has tried the dish below will admit that it is a glorious concoction and well worth the mild effort of preparation. It's perfect for lunch, dinner, or supper. Serve with it sautéed potatoes and whatever available green vegetables you like—except members of the cabbage family, whose flavor will overwhelm the delicacy of the fish.

Bone the trout, or have your fish market do it. Sauté shallots with butter and lemon juice in a flame-proof casserole for 4 or 5 minutes. Peel the mushrooms and slice. Add to the shallots. Divide the mousse into 6 parts and stuff the trout. Place trout gently in casserole. Put strips of parchment paper over the trout to keep mousse in place. Add sherry, stock, salt, and pepper to casserole. Cook, uncovered, in a 350-degree oven for 15 minutes. Remove paper gently and place trout on serving platter. Keep trout warm. Reduce liquid by ⅔. Add cream to stock sauce and cook for 5 minutes. Pour sauce over trout and decorate with truffle slices. Serves 6. *(See illustration, pages 240–241.)*

Chicken & Duck

Breast of Chicken Polignac

3 CHICKEN BREASTS, BONED,
SKINNED & HALVED/
6 TABLESPOONS SWEET BUTTER
1½ CUPS DRY WHITE WINE
6 OUNCES MUSHROOMS

Put the chicken breasts in a flame-proof casserole with 1 tablespoon of the butter and the white wine. Poach them over low heat for 12 minutes. Meantime, cook the mushrooms in water to cover for 5 minutes. Drain and cut into julienne. When chicken is done remove to a serving dish

½ cup flour
1½ pints chicken stock
(see stocks)/
1½ pints heavy cream
salt & pepper to taste
3 ounces black truffles,
cut julienne/

and keep warm. Save the gravy. Melt remaining butter and stir in flour smoothly. Add chicken stock and the gravy from the chicken. Mix well and reduce by ⅓. Add heavy cream and again reduce the resulting sauce by ⅓. Season with salt and pepper to taste. Strain over the chicken breasts and garnish with the mushrooms and truffles. Serves 6.

Chicken Scallops

12 half breasts of chicken,
boned & skinned/
salt & pepper
flour for dipping
3 eggs, beaten
1 cup butter
lemon wedges or halves

Calling these pieces of chicken "scallops" is taking a liberty, yet after they are pounded they very much resemble veal scallops and they are cooked in much the same way. They make a light and lovely summer entrée.

Place chicken on large sheets of waxed paper. Sprinkle with a few drops of water and cover with waxed paper. Pound chicken with the flat of a cleaver until each piece has about tripled in size. Be careful to pound evenly; uneven blows may tear meat. Remove paper. Sprinkle chicken very lightly with salt and pepper. Dip in flour, then eggs. Sauté in butter until golden brown on both sides. It will be necessary to keep adding butter to pan as scallops are finished. Serve with lemon. Serves 6.

Poule-au-Pot

1 4–5 pound chicken
3 leeks (white part only)
3 carrots
2 turnips
3 parsnips
3 stalks celery

The reason for blanching the chicken in this recipe is to get rid of the scum which would otherwise form in the cooking. Cutting the vegetables into ovals adds interest and charm to their appearance but, needless to say, wastes all the trimmings. You might put them into the next soup you make. Just store in the refrigerator in a tightly sealed plastic bag until you're ready to use them.

1 MEDIUM ONION
1 BAY LEAF
2 TABLESPOONS SALT
3 QUARTS WATER
6 OUNCES VERMICELLI

Blanch the chicken in boiling water for 5 minutes. Drain. Place in a casserole. Add leeks. Cut carrots, turnips, and parsnips in 4 lengthwise pieces each, then into smaller rectangles. Pare these pieces into ovals and add to casserole. Cut the celery stalks in half and add the bottom halves only to the casserole. Add the onion, bay leaf, and salt, and cover with water. Boil slowly for 1 hour. Add the vermicelli for the final 10 minutes. Carve the chicken and cut celery into quarters before serving in soup bowls. Serve with mustard, pickles, and sea salt. Serves 6.

Squab Chicken Crapaudine

6 1-POUND SQUAB CHICKENS, BONED
DASH PEPPER
DASH SALT
DÜSSELDORF OR DIJON MUSTARD
6 EGGS, BEATEN
3 CUPS SOFT BREAD CRUMBS
4 TABLESPOONS BUTTER
6 SLICES HARD-COOKED EGG WHITE
2 SLICES TRUFFLE
MINCED PARSLEY
SAUCE DIABLE (SEE SAUCES)

A crapaudine is the common frog. These chickens are prepared so as to resemble frogs, and are decorated to carry out that amusing illusion. This is a perfect instance of the French use of a sense of humor in food garniture.

Cut open the boned chickens down the breast leaving the chicken in one piece. Season with salt and pepper. Rub with mustard. Dip in beaten eggs, then lightly in bread crumbs. Melt butter in skillet and sauté chickens over low heat until golden brown, about 15–20 minutes. Remove to platter. Make 12 rounds of egg white about ¼ inch in diameter. To form "eyes," place 1 round of egg white at the tip of each wing and add a small dot of truffle in the center. Sprinkle chickens with parsley and serve with sauce diable. Serves 6.

Breast of Chicken with Herbed Mushrooms

½ CUP BUTTER
1½ TABLESPOONS CHOPPED SHALLOTS

It is important to remember that a suprême of chicken is a very delicate piece of meat. It can be absolutely ruined

3 CHICKEN BREASTS, BONED,
SKINNED & HALVED/
¾ CUP MEDIUM-DRY MADEIRA WINE
¾ CUP BROWN SAUCE (SEE SAUCES)
DASH LEMON JUICE
SALT & PEPPER TO TASTE
1 POUND MUSHROOMS, SLICED
4 TABLESPOONS SWEET BUTTER

by overcooking, so be very careful about your timing.

Melt the ½ cup butter in a flame-proof casserole. Add shallots and cook gently for 5 minutes. Place chicken breasts on top. Add the Madeira, cover the casserole, and cook in a 400-degree oven 8 to 10 minutes. Remove the breasts and place them on a serving dish. Keep warm. Reduce the sauce in the casserole by ⅔. Add brown sauce and cook 5 minutes. Correct the seasoning with lemon juice, salt, and pepper. Strain. Meantime, sauté the mushrooms in 2 tablespoons of the sweet butter, stirring occasionally, for 5 minutes. Add to the strained sauce. Add remaining sweet butter and heat well, but do not boil. Pour over breasts of chicken to serve. Serves 6.

Breast of Chicken with Cheese and Tongue

3 CHICKEN BREASTS,
BONED, SKINNED & HALVED/
FLOUR FOR COATING
2 TABLESPOONS OIL
2 TABLESPOONS BUTTER
SALT & PEPPER TO TASTE
1 CUP GRATED SWISS CHEESE
1 CUP MINCED COOKED TONGUE
½ CUP TOMATO SAUCE (SEE SAUCES)
½ CUP CHICKEN STOCK (SEE STOCKS)

Flatten and thin the suprêmes with the flat of a cleaver. Coat with flour and brown in the oil and butter briefly (5 minutes) in a flame- and oven-proof pan. Remove from pan. Season with salt and pepper. Mix cheese and tongue, and coat each suprême with the mixture. Add tomato sauce and stock to the pan juices. Place suprêmes in this sauce. Put pan in a 300-degree oven until cheese melts and sauce thickens (about 10 minutes). Serve with sauce poured over the chicken. Decorate the platter with cooked green peas, asparagus tips, and mushrooms, and a border of saffron rice. Serves 6. *(See illustration, page 242.)*

Crisped Duckling with Peaches, Sauce Cassis

2 4-POUND DUCKLINGS
SALT & PEPPER

While four pounds is not a heavy weight for a duck, it hardly fits the description of a duckling. However, in

3 FRESH PEACHES
2 CUPS SIMPLE SYRUP
(SEE DESSERT BASICS)/
6 TABLESPOONS DRY WHITE WINE
2 TABLESPOONS COGNAC
1 CUP ORANGE JUICE
½ CUP LEMON JUICE
2 CUPS BROWN SAUCE

———————

Gastrite: ⅔ CUP SUGAR,
3 TABLESPOONS WATER,
1½ TABLESPOONS RED
WINE VINEGAR/

———————

¼ CUP CRÈME DE CASSIS

many American cookbooks the terms duckling and duck are used fairly interchangeably. The French call a bird of this size a duckling, so just remember when you buy that you are looking for four-pound birds and don't worry about what your butcher calls them. The object of pricking the skin of ducks during the roasting period is to make it crisper, which is the way it ought to be. And we think you will find the combination of the orange-based sauce bigarade with crème de cassis, which is a black-currant liqueur, most intriguing.

Rub skin of ducklings with salt and pepper. Place on a rack in a roasting pan. Roast in 325-degree oven for 1½ hours, pricking the skin with a fork occasionally. Meantime, peel peaches and cut in half. Discard pits. Poach halves in syrup at a simmer until soft, but not mushy (10–15 minutes). Drain. When ducklings are done, remove from pan, and keep warm. Remove fat from pan. De-glaze pan with wine and cognac. To make sauce bigarade, pour into pan orange juice and lemon juice and reduce to almost dry. Add 2 cups brown sauce and stir well. Add gastrite and mix well. Simmer for 10 minutes. Strain sauce and add crème de cassis. Place ducklings on a platter and decorate with poached peach halves. Serve sauce separately. Serves 6.

Beef, Veal & Lamb

Beef in Aspic

3 POUNDS TOP ROUND OF BEEF
3 LARGE CARROTS
1 BAY LEAF

There is a technique to unmolding aspics and gelatin dishes, such as this handsome one. One method is to dip the mold in very hot water very briefly, run a knife around

1 CUP WHITE WINE

2 CUPS CHICKEN STOCK (SEE STOCKS)

1 CUP PORT ASPIC (SEE STOCKS)

2 LARGE BLACK TRUFFLES

3 HARD-COOKED EGG YOLKS,
CHOPPED FINE/

2 TABLESPOONS CHOPPED PARSLEY

½ CUP TINY ONIONS, COOKED (PAGE 131)

1½ CUPS COOKED GREEN PEAS

SALT & PEPPER TO TASTE

18 CHERRY TOMATOES

the edge, then put a chilled serving dish on top of the mold and turn them both over together so that the plate is on the bottom. The mold will then lift easily away from the contents. Or you can soak a tea towel in very hot water, wring it out and place it around the mold, which you have already loosened around the edge with a flat knife and placed, open side down, on a chilled serving dish.

Put meat, carrots, bay leaf, white wine, and chicken stock into a large flame-proof casserole. Simmer together for 35 minutes. Remove vegetables. Continue simmering the meat for 2½ hours longer. Meantime, cut the cooked carrots into julienne about 3 inches long. When meat is done, remove it and slice it thin. Add the aspic to the liquid in which the meat was cooked. Cook for a few minutes more. Skim off fat and strain the liquid through a cloth. It must be clear. Pour ½ inch of aspic into a round mold that is 2½ inches deep and 10 inches in diameter. Chill in refrigerator until firm. Cut a thin slice from the center of a truffle, and chop remainder and other truffle very fine. Place the slice of truffle in the center of the chilled aspic. Alternate small mounds of chopped truffle and chopped egg around the outside edge of the mold. Cover the chopped truffle with the chopped parsley. Surround the slice of truffle with a ring of tiny onions. Place carrot on aspic, radiating pieces out from ring of onions like spokes of a wheel. Connect outside ends of "spokes" with remaining carrot slices. Fill sections between spokes with green peas. Sprinkle cooked meat lightly with salt and pepper. Roll each slice into a small cone. Place a cherry tomato in the open end of each. Place cones of meat on the vegetables, points toward the center, cherry tomatoes at the edge of the mold. Pour remaining liquid into mold and refrigerate at least an hour. To serve, unmold onto a platter. Serves 6. *(See illustration, page 251.)*

238

1. *Fresh-caught rainbow trout.*

2. *Slitting at top to remove spine.*

3. *Pulling out bones.*

7. *Sautéing shallots with butter & lemon juice.*

8. *Peeling . . .*

9. *and slicing mushrooms.*

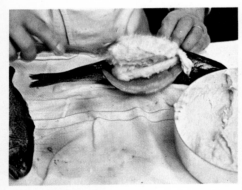

11. *Stuffing trout with mousse.*

14. *Wrapping each fish in parchment paper . . .*

12. *Appearance of completely stuffed fish.*

13. *Dish is ready for final steps.*

16. *Adding wine.*

Mountain Trout Filled with Salmon Mousse

4. *Eviscerating with aid of shears.*

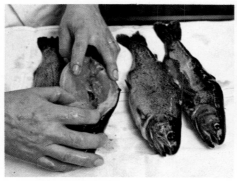

5. *Opening & cleaning cavity.*

6. *Chopping shallots.*

10. *Adding mushrooms to shallots.*

15. *to help keep mousse in place.*

17. *Adding stock.*

18. *Paper removed, cream & stock sauce added. Truffles, too.*

For recipe, see page 233.

Roquefort Steak

6 12-OUNCE SHELL STEAKS,
TRIMMED OF ALL FAT/
SALT & PEPPER
¼ CUP OIL
¼ POUND (½ CUP) BUTTER
¼ POUND ROQUEFORT CHEESE,
CRUMBLED/

Sprinkle steaks very lightly with salt and pepper (remembering that Roquefort is somewhat salty). Put the oil and 2 tablespoons of the butter in a skillet. Sauté steaks over fairly high heat (5 minutes on each side for rare, 7 minutes for medium, and 10 minutes for well done). Remove steaks to serving platter and keep warm. Pour fat from pan and replace pan over heat. Add remaining butter and let it melt. Stir Roquefort thoroughly into melted butter, pour over steaks, and serve. Serves 6.

Entrecôte de Boeuf for Two

1 DOUBLE ENTRECÔTE, 2–3 INCHES
THICK WITH THE BONE IN/
SALT & PEPPER
OIL FOR BRUSHING

This is a double entrecôte cut from the first three or four ribs of beef. The bone is left in and trimmed so that the entrecôte resembles an oversized French lamb chop.

Sprinkle meat with salt and pepper and brush with oil. Broil 10 minutes on each side for rare, 15 minutes for medium, or 20 minutes for well done. Slice and serve as is, or with 1 cup Sauce Bordelaise (see Sauces). Roesti Potatoes are a delicious accompaniment.

Veal Kidneys Flambéed in Armagnac

1 TEASPOON OLIVE OIL
4 TABLESPOONS CLARIFIED BUTTER
(SEE SAUCES)/
½ TEASPOON COARSE SALT
½ TEASPOON FRESHLY GROUND
BLACK PEPPER/
4 VEAL KIDNEYS, SLICED
2 TABLESPOONS CHOPPED SHALLOT
3 TABLESPOONS ARMAGNAC, HEATED

Armagnac is a brandy which comes from Gascony, in southwestern France. It is strong, like the people of the area, and also pungent. It adds vigor and delicious flavor to the kidneys, which are flambéed with it in this recipe.

Heat oil and 2 tablespoons butter in skillet or chafing dish. Sprinkle kidneys with salt and pepper. Place kidneys in pan and heat for 3–4 minutes, turning them continually. They should be rare inside. Remove from pan. Wipe out

243

½ CUP BROWN SAUCE (SEE SAUCES)
CHOPPED PARSLEY

pan and add remaining butter. Sauté shallot until lightly browned. Add kidneys to reheat them. Pour Armagnac over kidneys and ignite. Shake pan until flames die, about 2–3 minutes. Add brown sauce and heat through. Sprinkle with parsley and serve. Serves 6.

Calf Brains in Tomatoes with Hazelnut Butter

3 CALF BRAINS
¼ CUP FLOUR
SALT & PEPPER TO TASTE
¼ CUP CLARIFIED BUTTER (SEE SAUCES)
¼ CUP OIL
6 LARGE TOMATOES
½ CUP (1 STICK) SWEET BUTTER
¼ CUP MINCED HAZELNUTS
4 TABLESPOONS LEMON JUICE

The real fillip to this dish is given by the hazelnuts which go into the butter. Hazelnuts are filberts and one of the sweetest-flavored nuts. They are not used here as much as they should be, but Europeans appreciate them greatly.

Soak the brains in cold water for 2 hours. Pull off as much of filament as possible. Dry brains on paper towels. Dip in flour. Sprinkle with salt and pepper. Heat clarified butter and oil in a skillet. Cook brains 10 minutes on each side over medium heat. Meantime, cut tops off tomatoes and squeeze them to remove seeds. Put tomatoes, cut side up, in a lightly oiled baking pan. Sprinkle with salt and pepper and cook them in a 350-degree oven for 15 minutes. Remove the pan from the oven. Put the tomatoes on a serving dish and top each with half of a calf brain. Remove fat from skillet in which the brains were cooked. Add sweet butter, melt it, and sauté the hazelnuts in it lightly. Add the lemon juice. Pour over the tomatoes. Serve very hot. Serves 6.

Calf Brains en Brioche, Sauce Périgourdine

3 CALF BRAINS, CLEANED, SOAKED
SKINNED & DRAINED (SEE ABOVE)/

The following dish makes a handsome one to serve at luncheon or supper. The crusty brioche is most appetizing,

244

½ RECIPE PÂTE
BRIOCHE (SEE PASTRIES & BATTERS)/
2 EGG YOLKS
½ CUP WATER
1 CUP SAUCE PÉRIGOURDINE
(SEE SAUCES)/
_____
PREHEAT OVEN TO 375 DEGREES

and the sauce sparks the whole beautifully.

Blanch brains in simmering salted water for 20 minutes. Drain. Cut in half. Divide dough into 6 parts. Roll out each part into a ¼-inch-thick oval. Place half a brain at one end of each oval, fold other end of dough over and press edges together tightly. Beat egg yolks and water together well. Seal pressed-together edges of brioche with half the egg wash. Let stand to rise in warm, draft-free place for 20 minutes. Brush remaining egg wash over surface of dough and bake in a 375-degree oven for 10–12 minutes, or until brioche is brown and glazed on top. Serve sauce Périgourdine separately. Serves 6.

Vitello Tonnato

3 POUNDS BONED LEG OF VEAL
½ CUP OLIVE OIL
½ CUP CHOPPED CELERY
½ CUP CHOPPED ONION
1 TEASPOON FLOUR
2 CUPS CHICKEN STOCK (SEE STOCKS)
1½ CUPS DRY WHITE WINE
1 7-OUNCE CAN TUNAFISH
8 ANCHOVY FILLETS
1 CUP MAYONNAISE (SEE SAUCES)
3 TABLESPOONS LEMON JUICE
SALT & PEPPER TO TASTE
CAPERS
COLD BOILED RICE

Pat the veal dry as possible with absorbent paper. Brown lightly in the oil with celery, onion, and flour. Add stock, wine, tuna, and anchovies. Simmer until tender (about 1½ hours). Remove meat and strain the sauce. Cool meat and sauce. Mix sauce with mayonnaise and lemon juice. Season. Slice meat and place it on a platter. Pour sauce over and decorate with capers. Chill thoroughly at least 12 hours before serving. Serve with cold boiled rice. Serves 8.

Stuffed Sweetbreads

3 POUNDS SWEETBREADS,
CLEANED & TRIMMED/
1 POUND MUSHROOMS

This is a very typical French dish, particularly in its use of caul to wrap the sweetbreads. Caul is the white, veil-like membrane of a pig's stomach. It is worthwhile to

245

1 TEASPOON LEMON JUICE
1 TABLESPOON BUTTER
3 TABLESPOONS SAUCE BÉCHAMEL
(SEE SAUCES)/
¼ CUP PÂTÉ DE FOIE GRAS,
CUT IN SMALL DICE/
½ POUND CAUL
¼ CUP OIL
———————

Mirepoix:
1 CARROT, CHOPPED
1 ONION, CHOPPED
1 STALK CELERY, CHOPPED
1 BAY LEAF
1 4-INCH STALK THYME (OR
¼ TEASPOON DRIED)/
———————

½ CUP MEDIUM-DRY MADEIRA WINE
½ CUP DRY WHITE WINE
1 CUP BROWN SAUCE (SEE SAUCES)
1 CUP HEAVY CREAM
SALT & PEPPER TO TASTE
LEMON JUICE

make a search for it, or to persuade your butcher to order it for you, as it adds considerably to the flavor of the sweetbreads. If you can't get caul, wrap the sweetbreads in cheesecloth. Remove it before placing them on the serving platter.

It is not necessary to skin sweetbreads, as one does brains. Soak them in cold water for 30 minutes. Blanch in 2 quarts boiling water for 10 minutes and drain. Place under cold running water to cool. Drain. Mince mushrooms as finely as possible; they should almost be a purée. Mix with lemon juice. Melt butter in a saucepan, add mushrooms. Cook, stirring, until dry (about 5 minutes). Mix in Béchamel, remove from heat and cool. Lightly and carefully mix in diced pâté. Slice sweetbreads lengthwise, ⅔ through. Open and fill with stuffing. Close sweetbreads and wrap with pieces of caul. Heat oil in a heavy flame- and oven-proof casserole. Add mirepoix and brown it. Place wrapped sweetbreads carefully on top. Pour in Madeira, white wine, and brown sauce. Cover and cook 45 minutes in a 350-degree oven. Remove from oven. Arrange sweetbreads in circle on round platter and keep warm. Place casserole over heat and add cream. Reduce by ⅓. Sauce will be light brown. Correct seasoning, if necessary, with salt, pepper, and lemon juice. Strain sauce over sweetbreads and serve. Serves 6.

NOTE: Instead of brown sauce, you may use Sauce Soubise (see Sauces). The rest of the procedure is identical, but the final sauce will be pale yellow.

Mignonnettes of Lamb with Chanterelles

3 RACKS OF LAMB
12 SLICES BACON

Have your meat market bone the racks, keeping only the fillets. Cut each fillet into four 1-inch-thick slices—what the

SALT & PEPPER TO TASTE
¼ CUP OIL
½ CUP (1 STICK) BUTTER
2 POUNDS FRESH CHANTERELLES
(OR 8 OUNCES DRIED, SOAKED 1 HOUR)/
½ CUP BROWN SAUCE (SEE SAUCES)
2 TABLESPOONS FRESH MINCED PARSLEY

French call noisettes, or mignonnettes. Wrap each around the edge with a slice of bacon and secure with toothpicks. Sprinkle with salt and pepper. Heat the oil in a skillet. Put in the mignonnettes. Cook 5 minutes on each side over brisk heat. Put the mignonnettes on a platter and keep them warm. Remove grease from skillet. Put in butter. Add the chanterelles and sauté over medium heat until dry. Add the brown sauce and cook for 5 minutes more. Pour the mixture around the mignonnettes. Sprinkle with the parsley. Serves 6.

Deviled Lamb Chops

12 RIB LAMB CHOPS, TRIMMED
SALT & PEPPER TO TASTE
½ CUP FLOUR
ENGLISH MIXTURE (SEE BELOW)
1 CUP BREAD CRUMBS
¼ CUP OIL
¼ CUP BUTTER

———

English Mixture:
2 EGGS
3 TABLESPOONS OIL
SALT & PEPPER TO TASTE
¼ CUP WATER

Sprinkle chops with salt and pepper. Dip them in flour, then in the English mixture, and then in the bread crumbs. Heat oil and butter in a large skillet. Add chops and cook over medium heat for 4 minutes on each side. Arrange the chops on a serving dish. Put a paper frill on each rib, if desired. Serves 6.

NOTE: Buttered green beans or buttered asparagus and sautéed potatoes are good accompaniments for these chops.

Artichoke Bottoms

12 FRESH ARTICHOKES
2 TABLESPOONS SALT
¼ CUP LEMON JUICE
3 TABLESPOONS FLOUR

Artichokes may be prepared in many ways (see Index.) This recipe requires that everything except the bottom, or *fond,* of the vegetable be discarded.

247

Cut off the leaves to within an inch of the bottom. Cut off the stems flush with the bottom. With a teaspoon scrape out the choke, the feathery filaments at the heart of the vegetable. Put 3 quarts of water into a pot. Add salt, lemon juice, and flour, and mix well. Bring to a boil, put in the prepared bottoms and cook at a low boil until tender (20–30 minutes). Drain well. Serves 6.

Sautéed Artichoke Bottoms, Périgourdine

12 COOKED ARTICHOKE BOTTOMS
4 TABLESPOONS BUTTER
2 TABLESPOONS OIL
4 OUNCES BLACK TRUFFLE,
SLICED JULIENNE/

Slice the artichoke bottoms in thick julienne. Put them into a skillet with butter and oil, and brown them. Two minutes before serving add truffles. Serves 6.

Corn and Chili Soufflé

6 EGG YOLKS
3 OR 4 CANNED GREEN CHILIES
KERNELS SCRAPED FROM 6
MEDIUM EARS CORN/
¾ TEASPOON SALT
1½ TEASPOONS CHILI POWDER
8 EGG WHITES

PREHEAT OVEN TO 375 DEGREES

This dish has a piquant flavor, thanks to the use of the canned green chilies which, though not roaring hot, have a good bit of zest. We have been asked whether one could use canned corn to make this dish. Our answer is no. If you are determined to try it, remember that it will be a concoction totally different from the original.

Whirl egg yolks, chilies, and corn in the blender. Add seasonings. Beat egg whites until stiff but not dry, and fold them into the corn mixture. Pour into a buttered 2-quart soufflé dish and bake in a 375-degree oven 35 minutes. Serve at once—with pork or veal. Serves 6.

Petits Pois à la Française

3 TABLESPOONS BUTTER
6 LEAVES BOSTON LETTUCE, SHREDDED

This may be the most familiar vegetable dish we have inherited from France. It is especially delicious if you are

6 SMALL WHITE ONIONS
1 TABLESPOON SUGAR
½ TEASPOON SALT
3 SPRIGS PARSLEY
½ TEASPOON DRIED CHERVIL
½ CUP WATER
3 CUPS SHELLED GREEN PEAS
½ TEASPOON FLOUR

lucky enough to grow your own peas and can pick them early when they literally are petits pois. If peas are very tender, cooking time can be reduced.

Place 2 tablespoons butter in pot with lettuce, onions, sugar, and salt. Place parsley and chervil in a small bag of washed cheesecloth. Add to pot. Add water and peas. Mix gently and cover pot. Simmer until peas are tender (about 25 minutes). Remove from heat and discard cheesecloth bag. Blend remaining butter with flour and add to peas. Shaking the pan (don't stir), bring liquid to a boil. Drain and serve. Serves 6.

Potatoes Parisienne

3 POUNDS LARGE POTATOES
¼ CUP OIL
¼ CUP BUTTER
SALT & PEPPER TO TASTE

Peel and wash the potatoes. Cut into little balls with large end of a ball cutter. Blanch for 5 minutes in boiling water to cover. Drain potatoes and cool under cold running water. Dry on paper towels. Get the oil and butter very hot in a skillet. Add potatoes and sprinkle them with salt and pepper. Cook slowly, shaking the skillet from time to time, until potatoes are brown and soft. Serves 6.

VARIATIONS:
To shape *Hazelnut Potatoes* use the smaller end of the ball cutter. To shape *Olive Potatoes* use a special French oval cutter.

Sautéed Potatoes

3 POUNDS POTATOES
⅓ CUP OIL
SALT & PEPPER TO TASTE
4 TABLESPOONS CHOPPED PARSLEY

Peel and wash potatoes, and slice them ⅛-inch thick. Get the oil very hot in a skillet. Add potatoes. Sprinkle with salt and pepper. Cook for 25 minutes, shaking skillet from time to time. Sprinkle with parsley. Serves 6.

VARIATIONS:

Sauté 7 or 8 cups thinly sliced onion in ¼ cup oil until soft and light golden brown. Mix with potatoes at serving time for *Sautéed Potatoes Lyonnaise.* For *Sautéed Potatoes à la Provençale,* mince 4 cloves of garlic, mix with 4 tablespoons minced parsley and 2 tablespoons bread crumbs and add to potatoes for last 3 or 4 minutes of cooking time. For *Pommes Sablées,* cut potatoes in small dice instead of slices. At the very last moment of cooking, mix in ¼ cup bread crumbs. ("Sablée" means "sandy," and that's the texture these potatoes should have.) For *Potatoes Sarlandaise,* mix in 1 thinly sliced black truffle just before serving. For *Potatoes Murat,* add 4 sliced artichoke bottoms to the skillet at the same time as the potatoes.

Ratatouille Niçoise

2 MEDIUM EGGPLANTS
3 SWEET RED PEPPERS
3 GREEN PEPPERS
3 ZUCCHINI
1 MEDIUM ONION
3 CLOVES GARLIC
¾ CUP OLIVE OIL
1 4-INCH STALK THYME
(OR ½ TEASPOON DRIED)/
1 BAY LEAF
8 TOMATOES
SALT & PEPPER TO TASTE

Peel eggplant and cut in 1-inch dice. Remove seeds from peppers and cut in thin strips. Slice zucchini in rounds ¼-inch thick. Chop onion and garlic. Heat 2 tablespoons of the olive oil in a flame-proof casserole. Add onion, garlic, thyme, and bay leaf. Cook without browning for 6–7 minutes. Sauté each of the vegetables separately in skillet in the remaining oil. Add each to the onion as it is done (2–3 minutes for eggplant and zucchini, 10 minutes for the peppers). Peel tomatoes and squeeze out the seeds. Chop coarsely and add to the other vegetables. Add salt and pepper. Simmer the ratatouille for 45 minutes on top of the range. Serves 6. *(See illustration, page 261.)*

Parfait of Spinach

4 POUNDS FRESH SPINACH
8 OUNCES BUTTER, CLARIFIED
(SEE SAUCES)/

One of The Four Seasons' more popular vegetable dishes, Parfait of Spinach is on the menu the year around. It is not hard to make and quite spectacular to serve.

6 EGGS
1 CUP HEAVY CREAM
1 TEASPOON WHITE PEPPER
1 TABLESPOON SALT
1 TEASPOON NUTMEG
1 CUP THIN SAUCE BÉCHAMEL
(SEE SAUCES)/
¼ CUP GRATED PARMESAN CHEESE

Put spinach into boiling, salted water. Bring back to boil, drain, and mince fine. Sauté the spinach in half of the butter until dry. Mix eggs with cream, pepper, salt, and nutmeg. Add spinach. Brown the remaining butter and add to the original mixture. Butter a mold and fill it with the mixture. Put the mold into a pan of hot water and cook in a 350-degree oven 30 minutes. Turn out onto a flame-proof plate and top with Béchamel and cheese. Run under the broiler to glaze. Serves 6.

NOTE: This is good to serve with roast veal, veal chops, veal cutlet, or roast beef.

Spinach Elizabeth

3 POUNDS FRESH SPINACH
3 TABLESPOONS BUTTER
1½ TABLESPOONS IMPORTED SOY SAUCE
¾ CUP CHOPPED TOASTED HAZELNUTS
SALT & PEPPER TO TASTE

Heat butter in a big pot without browning. Add spinach and sauté, stirring constantly. After about 5 minutes add soy sauce and blend in. Cook until soft. Add nuts and do not cook further. Season. Serves 6.

Squash with Walnuts

2 POUNDS YELLOW SQUASH
2 TEASPOONS SALT
½ CUP OIL
1 CUP WALNUTS, CHOPPED VERY COARSE
AND TOASTED IN THE OVEN/

The combination of soft, bland squash with crunchy toasted walnuts is startlingly good.

Slice squash about ¼-inch thick. Sprinkle with salt. Heat oil. Sauté squash until soft, but not brown. Drain off any excess oil. Sprinkle toasted walnuts over squash. Serves 6.

Zucchini Niçoise

3 POUNDS ZUCCHINI
½ CUP OLIVE OIL
½ RECIPE TOMATOES CONCASSÉES
(SEE SAUCES)/

Wash but do not peel zucchini. Slice into thin circles. Heat oil in skillet and sauté zucchini until slightly soft and browned. Heat tomatoes concassées and gently mix with zucchini. Serves 6.

Bouillabaisse Salad, Saffron Sauce

1 2-POUND LOBSTER
1 POUND SHRIMP, SHELLED
AND DE-VEINED/
1 POUND FILLET OF RED SNAPPER
COURT-BOUILLON FOR POACHING
(SEE STOCKS)/
1 POUND CRABMEAT
6 LARGE LETTUCE LEAVES
3 LEMONS, QUARTERED
3 TOMATOES, QUARTERED
SAFFRON SAUCE (SEE BELOW)

———————

Saffron Sauce:
1 CUP MAYONNAISE (SEE SAUCES)
½ TEASPOON SAFFRON POWDER
½ TEASPOON TABASCO

The traditional hot bouillabaisse is described earlier in the section on sea foods for summer. Here is a cold salad on the same theme, a superb dish for a summer luncheon. The recipe has been improvised by Chef Chantreau from a title that appeared on an early Four Seasons menu. To the basic mélange of fish and crustaceans, he has added a saffron sauce—precisely the right touch to confirm the "bouillabaisse" character of this salad.

Cook the lobster in boiling salted water to cover for 8 minutes. Cool. Cook the shrimp in boiling salted water until they turn pink (3–5 minutes). Cool. Poach the red snapper in simmering court-bouillon for 3–5 minutes, or until it flakes easily with a fork. Cool. Split the lobster and remove stomach and intestinal vein. Cut the meat in dice. Cut the shrimp in half lengthwise. Cut the red snapper in dice. Mix lobster, shrimp, and snapper with crabmeat. Line a salad bowl with the lettuce leaves. Put the fish mixture in the middle. Decorate with tomato and lemon quarters. Serve sauce separately. Serves 8–10.

Avocado with Sliced White Radish

24 SMALL WHITE RADISHES
¾ TEASPOON SALT
3 AVOCADOS
1½ TABLESPOONS MINCED ONION
¾ TEASPOON CHOPPED CHIVES
¼ TEASPOON FRESHLY GROUND
WHITE PEPPER/
3 TABLESPOONS LEMON JUICE

White radishes are not nearly so common in our markets as the round red ones, but they are grown in the United States and they do make good eating. They are elongated in shape and perhaps a little more delicate in flavor than the red ones. However, if you can't obtain white, use red in this salad. Either way, radish makes a refreshing contrast in flavor to the richness of the avocado.

Peel the radishes and slice thinly. Sprinkle with salt and

place in the refrigerator for half an hour. Drain off excess water. Peel and halve avocados. Combine radishes with remaining ingredients and mound into avocado hollows. Serves 6.

Avocado Shrimp Louis

1 QUART COURT-BOUILLON
(SEE STOCKS)/
30 LARGE PEELED SHRIMP
3 LARGE AVOCADOS
LEMON JUICE
1 CUP DRESSING

This makes an exceptionally pretty salad which may be served as a main luncheon dish, or even as an appetizer, if you prefer.

Bring court-bouillon to a boil, add shrimp, and cook for 4 minutes, or until they turn pink. Drain, cool, shell, and de-vein shrimp. Chill them. Halve and pit avocados. Cut into wedges the thickness of the shrimp and sprinkle lightly with lemon juice. On individual salad plates, alternate shrimp and avocado wedges in a row (using 5 shrimp and ½ avocado for each plate). Spoon dressing down the center. Serves 6.

NOTE: Any dressing you prefer may be used. Very good with this salad are French Dressing, Mayonnaise, and Green Mayonnaise (see Sauces).

Lobster in Shell with Spiced Mushrooms

¾ CUP WHITE WINE VINEGAR
4 TEASPOONS LEMON JUICE
¼ CUP DRY WHITE WINE
2 TEASPOONS SALT
1 TEASPOON WHITE PEPPER
4 TEASPOONS SUGAR
12 LARGE MUSHROOMS
6 1½-POUND POACHED
LOBSTERS (PAGE 35), COOLED/
2 HEADS BIBB LETTUCE
(OR 1 HEAD BOSTON)/

This is a light summer luncheon salad enhanced by the tangy flavor of the mushrooms.

Mix vinegar, lemon juice, wine, salt, pepper, and sugar. Add mushrooms and marinate for 24 hours. Drain. Split lobsters in half from end to end starting at the head. Discard intestinal vein and stomach. Crack claws and slice body meat so that meat may easily be removed. Arrange lettuce leaves on individual salad plates. Place one lobster on each, with a mushroom on each side. Serves 6.

Julienne of Turkey Breast

3 CUPS JULIENNE-SLICED COOKED
TURKEY BREAST/
2¼ CUPS JULIENNE-SLICED PINEAPPLE
18 WHOLE, HULLED STRAWBERRIES
1½ CUPS ORANGE SECTIONS
1½ CUPS GRAPEFRUIT SECTIONS
1½ CUPS MAYONNAISE (SEE SAUCES)

This salad looks most attractive served on an oval platter. At one end, heap the turkey, with the julienne slices neatly horizontal. Do the same with the pineapple at the other end. Arrange the strawberries in a row just in front of the pineapple. Arrange the orange and grapefruit sections in the center of the platter, alternating them. Serve mayonnaise separately. Serves 6.

Raw Mushrooms, Malabar Dressing

1 MEDIUM ONION, FINELY DICED
¼ CUP DICED RED RADISH
1 CUP DICED CELERY
1 TABLESPOON MINCED PARSLEY
1 TABLESPOON MINCED TRUFFLE
2 TABLESPOONS LEMON JUICE
6 TABLESPOONS OLIVE OIL
1 TEASPOON CRACKED
PEPPER, OR TO TASTE/
2 TEASPOONS COARSE SALT,
OR TO TASTE/
18–24 MEDIUM MUSHROOMS
LEAVES OF BOSTON LETTUCE

The name of this salad is taken from the fact that originally it required a coarsely cracked pepper that came from Malabar, on the southwestern coast of India. It is no longer obtainable in the United States, but do not miss this refreshing dish on that account. Just substitute the best cracked pepper you can find. Taste is more important here than authenticity. The salad makes an interesting dish for a host or hostess to prepare before guests.

Combine all ingredients except mushrooms and lettuce in a bowl. Toss well and allow to marinate 5 minutes. Slice mushrooms very thin and add to the marinated ingredients. Toss well again. Serve on a bed of the lettuce leaves. Serves 6.

Salad Mimosa

2 HEADS BIBB LETTUCE
½ HEAD ROMAINE LETTUCE
6 TABLESPOONS FRENCH DRESSING
(SEE SAUCES)/
2 HARD-COOKED EGG YOLKS, GRATED

This is a simple, delicious salad which can be served with almost any entrée you can name. The use of the grated egg yolk lends the essential appeal.

Wash and crisp greens. When ready to serve, tear the

greens into pieces of even size. Toss well with the French dressing. Sprinkle grated egg yolk over all. Serves 6.

Wilted Spinach and Bacon Salad

6 STRIPS BACON
6 TABLESPOONS FRENCH DRESSING
(SEE SAUCES)/
1½ POUNDS FRESH, SMALL
SPINACH LEAVES/

This salad, which is particularly enjoyed by men, makes an excellent accompaniment to a rare steak.

Cut slices of bacon into 1-inch squares and sauté until very crisp. Remove bacon from pan. Strain the bacon fat into the French dressing. Pour the very hot dressing and the bacon over the spinach leaves in order to wilt them. The spinach leaves should be young; if not, be sure to remove veins and stems. Serves 6.

Crabmeat in Sweet Peperoni

3 TABLESPOONS WHITE WINE VINEGAR
1 TEASPOON LEMON JUICE
2 TABLESPOONS DRY WHITE WINE
½ TEASPOON SALT
¼ TEASPOON PEPPER
2 TEASPOONS SUGAR
1 TABLESPOON FINELY CHOPPED FRESH
DILL (OR ¾ TEASPOON DRIED)/
1 POUND LUMP CRABMEAT
6 LARGE YELLOW SWEET PEPERONI,
HALVED LENGTHWISE/
6 CUPS FINELY SHREDDED
BOSTON LETTUCE/
3 FINELY CHOPPED RED RADISHES

The "peperoni" required in this recipe are not the hard, spicy little Italian sausages of that name, but sweet yellow vegetable peppers, which grow six or seven inches long. Cut in half lengthwise and spread over the crabmeat on each individual salad plate, the peperoni give the illusion of being stuffed. The combination of flavors in this dish is marvelous. It can be served as a luncheon salad or, cutting the quantity for each person in half, as a cold appetizer.

Mix vinegar, lemon juice, wine, salt, pepper, sugar, and dill. Mix with crabmeat, being careful not to break the lumps. Place crabmeat on 6 individual salad plates. Completely cover each portion with two peperoni halves. Arrange lettuce on sides and between points of peperoni. Sprinkle lettuce with radish. Serves 6.

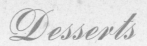

Frozen Anise Soufflé

5 WHOLE EGGS
6 EGG YOLKS
1 CUP PLUS 2 TABLESPOONS SUGAR
1½ PINTS HEAVY CREAM,
WHIPPED (UNSWEETENED)/
2 TABLESPOONS ANISETTE
½ TEASPOON ANISE SEEDS

The Four Seasons is noted for frozen soufflés, three of which appear in this section, with suggestions for variations which may lead you into all kinds of experimentation and invention. An interesting fact about soufflés is that, though they contain a goodly amount of rich whipped cream, they taste like the lightest sweet course you could imagine.

Warm eggs, yolks, and sugar in a double boiler, stirring well to mix. Remove from heat and beat with rotary beater until stiff. Stir in anisette and anise seeds. Fold in whipped cream. Place a collar of paper around an 8-cup soufflé dish so that it stands 2 inches above the edge of the dish. Pour in the mixture and place in freezer for at least 6 hours. Remove collar for serving. Serves 10.

VARIATIONS:
Substitute any liqueur of your choice for the anisette: Grand Marnier, Swedish Punch, Chartreuse, Cherry Heering—what you will. In these cases, omit anise seeds.

Frozen Raspberry Soufflé

1 CUP EGG WHITES
1 CUP PLUS 2 TABLESPOONS SUGAR
2½ PINTS RASPBERRIES, WASHED
3 CUPS HEAVY CREAM, WHIPPED

Warm egg whites and sugar in a bowl over hot water. Remove from heat and beat with a rotary beater until stiff. Force the raspberries through a sieve and fold the purée into the egg whites. Fold in whipped cream. Freeze at least 6 hours. Serves 6.

Frozen Lemon Zest Soufflé

1 CUP EGG WHITES
1 CUP PLUS 2 TABLESPOONS SUGAR
¾ CUP CRÈME PÂTISSIÈRE

The requirement of one cup of egg whites in this recipe is the most accurate way to tell you exactly how much egg white is needed. Never mind how many whites. As any

(SEE DESSERT BASICS)/
GRATED PEEL (ZEST) OF 4 LEMONS
JUICE OF 4 LEMONS
1½ PINTS HEAVY CREAM,
WHIPPED (UNSWEETENED)/

cook is aware, the sizes of eggs, and thus of their yolks and whites, varies greatly.

Warm egg whites and sugar in a bowl over hot water. Remove from heat and beat with a rotary beater until stiff. Mix the crème pâtissière with lemon peel and juice. Fold into egg whites. Fold in whipped cream. Pour into soufflé dish. Freeze at least 6 hours. Serves 6.

Fruit Tart

9-INCH TART OF SWEET DOUGH
(SEE PASTRIES & BATTERS), BAKED/
¾ CUP CRÈME PÂTISSIÈRE
(SEE DESSERT BASICS)/
2 THIN LAYERS OF SPONGE CAKE
(SEE DESSERT BASICS)/
SIMPLE SYRUP (SEE DESSERT BASICS),
FLAVORED WITH RUM/
3 ORANGES, PEELED & SECTIONED
10 STRAWBERRIES, HULLED
& CUT IN HALF/
8–10 MELON BALLS
1 POACHED PEAR
WARM APRICOT GLAZE
(SEE DESSERT BASICS)/

Spread ½ cup of the crème pâtissière on the bottom of the tart. Cut one layer of the sponge cake into 1-inch squares and pile in the tart. Cover with the second layer of sponge cake. Brush with rum-flavored syrup. Spread with remaining crème pâtissière. Place a ring of orange sections around the edge of the tart. Within it make a ring of the halved strawberries. Inside that make a ring of melon balls, then another ring of orange sections. Make thin slices of the poached pear and place in the center of the tart, curling them like petals so that they form an open rose. Put tiny slices of strawberries between the melon balls. Brush the whole with apricot glaze.

NOTE: Depending upon the season, you can use any fruits you like for this tart: various types of melon, raspberries, blueberries, grapes, whatever will be most colorful and contrasting.

Palmiers

1 RECIPE PUFF PASTRY (SEE
PASTRIES & BATTERS)/
GRANULATED SUGAR

Palmiers are one of the easiest things to make out of puff pastry and one of the most delicious pastries in the world —perfect to nibble with an ice cream or sherbet.

Ratatouille Niçoise (page 250).
Following pages: Desserts (from left): Fresh pineapple, apricot parfait,
layered sherbet, fresh berries, cantaloupe & lime, fruit salad,
Hudson Valley Cake (page 68), fresh fruit bowl, Fruit Tart (page 259),
Zabaglione (page 141), Apricot & Strawberry Sherbet
(pages 265-266), Palmiers (page 259), Chocolate Velvet (page 76),
Hacienda Cake (page 138), Hungarian Cheese Cake (page 202).

PREHEAT OVEN TO 425 DEGREES

Sprinkle your pastry board or cloth with sugar. Put the pastry on it and sprinkle the top generously with sugar. Roll out to ⅛-inch thickness in a long strip 10 inches wide. Trim edges of strip. Each long half of the strip is folded over twice so that the inside edges of the folds meet in the center. If strip is 10 inches wide, make first fold about 1½ inches in from the edge; fold over again. Repeat with other half of the strip. Then fold the 2 long halves together. You now have a long roll, with 6 thicknesses of pastry. Sprinkle liberally with sugar again. Chill or freeze. Cut into ¼-inch-thick pieces and place on a baking sheet 2 inches apart. Bake in a 425-degree oven until golden and caramelized (15–20 minutes), watching them carefully to see that they do not burn, and turning them over once. Makes about 25.

NOTE: The Palmiers served at The Four Seasons are tiny ones. If you would like to make yours very small, roll out the long strip 6½ inches wide and make narrower folds. Continue the same procedure as described above.

French Rice Pudding

¼ CUP RICE
1 QUART MILK
½ CUP SUGAR
¼ TEASPOON SALT
½ TEASPOON VANILLA EXTRACT
4 EGG YOLKS, BEATEN

PREHEAT OVEN TO 325 DEGREES

The addition of egg yolks to this recipe makes it rich, and pouring it into a mold makes it look more elegant than the homely rice pudding most of us are used to. French rice pudding may be used as the basis for many desserts. For example, try serving it with peaches in raspberry syrup.

Mix rice, milk, sugar, salt, and vanilla extract and place in a baking dish. Cook in a 325-degree oven 2 hours, stirring frequently. Bake 30 minutes more without stirring, or until rice is very tender. Add a little of the hot pudding to the egg yolks, beating hard. Add to the pudding, beating continuously. Put into a mold and chill. Serves 6.

1.

3.

2.

5.

4.

Peaches Flamed in Bourbon

6 PEACHES, PEELED & HALVED
1 CUP BOURBON
¼ CUP BUTTER
¾ CUP SUGAR
½ CUP PEACH NECTAR
CRUSHED MACAROONS

Soak peaches in bourbon for 24 hours. Drain and reserve bourbon. Melt the butter in a large skillet, add the sugar and cook until caramelized. Add the peaches, flat side down. Cook until lightly browned, turn and repeat. Heat ¼ cup of the bourbon and pour over peaches. Ignite. Shake pan until flames die. Pour in peach nectar and heat for a few moments. Place flat side up on serving dish or dishes. Sprinkle with crushed macaroons and serve. Serves 6.

Strawberry Sherbet

1 PINT STRAWBERRY PURÉE,
MADE FROM 3 PINTS STRAWBERRIES/
1½ PINTS SIMPLE SYRUP
(SEE DESSERT BASICS)/
JUICE OF 2 WHOLE LEMONS
(OR TO TASTE)/

The Four Seasons is celebrated for its fresh fruit and vegetable sherbets. They are really the world's greatest fresh fruit or vegetable ices, as anyone who has tasted them will agree. The fruit ones are, of course, desserts. The vegetable ones are for presentation between the heartier courses of a dinner—to clear the mouth—or as an accompaniment to rich meats. Despite the sugar used, they are not too sweet to the taste.

Hull fruit and purée. (A blender, sieve, or food mill may be used to purée fruit.) Beat the purée with the simple syrup and the lemon juice. The mixture should not be too tart, or too sweet. Freeze a test sample to make sure the mixture is right. If the sample turns out to be icy, add a little simple syrup; if it is too soft, add a little water. Pour the mixture into the container of an electric ice-cream freezer and let it turn for 20 minutes. Makes 1 quart.
VARIATIONS:
In making any of the following sherbets, simply substitute the particular fruit or vegetable, in the amount shown,

for the 3 pints strawberries called for in the Strawberry Sherbet recipe. (Amounts are approximate; you may need more or less, depending on size and juiciness of fruits.) In each case, 1 pint purée (or juice) is required to make 1 quart sherbet. Note that some of the fruits must be poached before they are puréed. Otherwise proceed as in recipe for Strawberry Sherbet, above.

Raspberry Sherbet: 3 pints raspberries
Blueberry Sherbet: 3½ pints blueberries
Pineapple Sherbet: 2½ very ripe pineapples, put through a sieve
Nectarine Sherbet: 10 nectarines, peeled and poached
Pear Sherbet: 8 pears, peeled and poached
Peach Sherbet: 10 peaches, peeled and poached
Apricot Sherbet: 18 apricots, peeled and poached
Rhubarb Sherbet: 12–13 stalks rhubarb, peeled and poached
Tomato Sherbet: 10 tomatoes, peeled and seeded
Asparagus Sherbet: 12–13 stalks asparagus, cooked soft but not mushy

In the following sherbets, substitute 1 pint fruit juice for the 1 pint of purée used in the Strawberry Sherbet recipe. Amounts given are approximately what is needed for 1 pint of juice.
Orange Sherbet: 10–12 juice oranges
Lime Sherbet: 27 limes
Lemon Sherbet: 14 lemons, but omit juice of 2 lemons called for in Strawberry Sherbet recipe

Sherbet Parfait: A parfait can be made simply by layering sherbet and whipped cream in a tall glass, and decorating with bits of whatever fruit you have used in making the sherbet.

Tea and Lemon Granita

6 CUPS BOILING WATER
3 TABLESPOONS TEA
3 CUPS SIMPLE SYRUP
(SEE DESSERT BASICS)/
9 TABLESPOONS LEMON JUICE
(ABOUT 3 LEMONS)/

A "granita" is an Italian ice. The combination of the tea ice with the lemon is about as light and refreshing a dessert as you could want on a hot summer's day.

Pour 3 cups of the boiling water over the tea and let it steep for 5 minutes. Strain through a cheesecloth. Sweeten with half of the syrup. Add 3 cups of boiling water to the lemon juice and the remaining syrup. Freeze each mixture separately in 2 ice trays in the freezing compartment. When ready to serve, spoon a layer of each flavor into 6 parfait glasses. Top with whipped cream, if desired. Serves 6.

Strawberry Charlotte

1 JELLY ROLL, 1½ INCHES IN DIAMETER
(SEE DESSERT BASICS)/
1⅓ PINTS STRAWBERRIES
1 CUP CRÈME PÂTISSIÈRE
(SEE DESSERT BASICS)/
1 TABLESPOON (1 ENVELOPE) GELATIN,
DISSOLVED IN ¼ CUP HOT WATER/
⅔ QUART (2⅔ CUPS) HEAVY CREAM,
WHIPPED & FLAVORED
WITH ½ CUP POWDERED SUGAR/
KIRSCH
RED FOOD COLORING, IF DESIRED
SPONGE CAKE (SEE DESSERT
BASICS) TO FIT TOP OF MOLD/
APRICOT GLAZE (SEE DESSERT BASICS)
½ CUP SWEETENED WHIPPED CREAM FOR
DECORATION/

Note that at The Four Seasons the Charlotte mold is lined with jelly roll cake. If you prefer, you may line it with lady fingers, which is the more conventional way, and the method employed to make Charlotte Russe.

Cut jelly roll into slices ¼-inch thick. Line a round mold 4 inches high and 7 inches in diameter with these slices, pressing the pieces together and against the mold so they stay in place. Hull the strawberries. Put half of the berries through a food mill, or purée in the blender. Beat the crème pâtissière well with a whip. Add puréed berries and mix well. Add dissolved gelatin and mix well. Slice the remainder of the berries. Add whipped cream and sliced berries to original mixture. Flavor with a dash of kirsch and add food coloring if desired. Fill the lined mold. Cover with a slice of sponge cake ½-inch thick. Chill at least 2 hours (overnight is best). Unmold onto a plate, neatly trim sponge cake, which is now on the bottom, and paint Charlotte with apricot glaze. Put the ½ cup of sweetened whipped cream into a pastry bag and mark off the Charlotte into portions with thin stripes of the cream. Make tiny triangular decorations of the cream all around the bottom of the Charlotte. Put a handsome strawberry, dipped into the glaze, in the center on top of the Charlotte. Serves 6–8.

Crème Heart

3 CUPS CRÈME PÂTISSIÈRE (SEE DESSERT BASICS)/ 5 EGG WHITES ½ CUP SUGAR

Warm the crème pâtissière in a double boiler. (It must be warm or it will not absorb egg whites properly.) Beat egg whites until they form soft peaks. Gradually add the sugar and continue beating until they form stiff peaks. Fold into the warm crème pâtissière and put into a heart-shaped mold. Chill until cold (2 to 3 hours). Do not make this dish too far ahead or it will separate. Much more than 3 hours is risky. Unmold onto a serving plate. Serves 6. NOTE: To give this pure white dessert a more handsome appearance, burn it on top in a lattice pattern in accordance with directions for decorative burning of powdered sugar on cakes (page 298).

The Four Seasons Fancy Cake

This cake, which is pictured on page 264, is a "signature" of The Four Seasons. It has been an offering on the dessert cart ever since the restaurant opened. You cannot exactly duplicate it in your home kitchen, but you can come very close. In the restaurant kitchen, for example, special machines are used to roll out the chocolate coating. For the home cook, who has no such facilities, we have devised a different chocolate coating which closely resembles the original.

Allow two days to make Fancy Cake. Make the Bavarian cream the day before you intend to serve the cake. Next day make the cake layer and the chocolate coating and assemble the whole.

Bavarian Cream:
3 ENVELOPES UNFLAVORED GELATIN/
3¾ CUPS MILK
6 EGGS, SEPARATED
¼ TEASPOON SALT
1¼ CUPS SUGAR
¼ CUP DARK RUM
1 CUP HEAVY CREAM, WHIPPED
¾ CUP CRUSHED ALMOND MACAROONS, OR CRUSHED VANILLA WAFERS/
⅓ CUP FINELY CHOPPED WALNUTS OR PECANS/

Sprinkle gelatin over 1 cup of the milk to soften. Heat remaining milk in top part of double boiler placed directly over heat, until tiny bubbles appear around the edge. In a bowl, beat egg yolks with salt and ½ cup of the sugar just until blended. Add the cup of milk with softened gelatin. Gradually add the 2¾ cups hot milk, stirring rapidly. Place mixture in top of double boiler and cook over simmering water, stirring constantly, until mixture coats a metal spoon (about 15 minutes). Remove from heat. Cool slightly. Add rum. Refrigerate, covered, until mixture mounds slightly when lifted with a spoon (about 3 hours). Or hasten chilling by placing pan over ice water, stirring occasionally; this method takes about 30 minutes. Meanwhile, line a 2½ quart bowl with plastic wrap or foil. Diameter of bowl should not be wider than 9 inches. Set aside. In a large bowl or electric mixer, beat egg whites until they form soft peaks. Gradually beat in remaining ¾ cup sugar and continue beating until stiff peaks form. Add whipped cream and gelatin mixture. Beat at low speed until just combined (about 1 minute). Turn into prepared bowl. In a small bowl combine macaroon or wafer crumbs and nuts. Mix well. Sprinkle over mixture in bowl. Press down gently. Refrigerate overnight.

Orange Chiffon Layer:
½ CUP EGG WHITES (3–4)
1 CUP PLUS 2 TABLESPOONS SIFTED CAKE FLOUR/

In the large bowl of your electric mixer, warm egg whites to room temperature (about 1 hour). Sift flour with sugar, baking powder, and salt into another large bowl. Make well in center. Add, in order: oil, egg yolks,

¾ CUP SUGAR
1½ TEASPOONS BAKING POWDER
½ TEASPOON SALT
¼ CUP VEGETABLE OIL
2 EGG YOLKS
6 TABLESPOONS ORANGE JUICE
1½ TABLESPOONS FINELY
CHOPPED ORANGE PEEL/
¼ TEASPOON CREAM OF TARTAR
———————————————
PREHEAT OVEN TO 350 DEGREES

orange juice, and orange peel. Beat with spoon until smooth. With electric mixer at high speed, beat egg whites with cream of tartar until they form very stiff peaks. With wire whisk or rubber scraper, using under-and-over motion, gradually fold orange batter into egg whites until just blended. Do not stir. Pour into ungreased 9 x 1½-inch round layer-cake pan. Bake in a preheated 350-degree oven 30–35 minutes or until cake tester inserted in center comes out clean. Invert cake by hanging pan between 2 other pans. Cool completely (about 1 hour). With spatula, carefully loosen cake from pan. Hit pan sharply on table. Remove cake. Place on serving plate.

½ CUP HEAVY CREAM, WHIPPED

Spread whipped cream on top of orange chiffon layer. Invert Bavarian cream over whipped cream. Remove bowl and peel off plastic wrap. Refrigerate.

Chocolate Almond Cream Coating:
2 POUNDS ALMOND PASTE
1 CUP COCOA

Mix almond paste thoroughly with the cocoa, kneading well to soften the paste for easy rolling. Divide the mixture into 5 portions, 4 of equal size and 1 smaller (for the topknot). On a board sprinkled with powdered sugar roll out the 4 uniform pieces, one at a time, in 8 x 7-inch sheets about ⅛-inch thick. As each sheet is rolled out, place it on the Bavarian, working from the bottom up and pinching the top to make gathers in it. Break off any excess that sticks up at the top. The whole cake should be covered by the 4 sheets. Now roll out the remaining portion of chocolate almond cream, adding to it any excess bits broken off the top of the covering. Roll into an oblong about ⅛-inch thick. Gather this into a topknot, as nearly like the one in the picture on page 264 as you can make it. Place on top of the Fancy Cake. Refrigerate until ready to serve. For ease in slicing, let cake stand at room temperature about 20 minutes before serving. Serves at least 16.

The hot months are rendered happily tolerable by cold white wine. This is the time for delicate country wines, for the light, fresh, and youthful vintages which seldom stray far from home, but revive the spirits of the traveler fortunate enough to encounter them. When the sun is high, a carafe of *vin du pays,* suitably chilled, will enliven the simplest of open-air lunches. Or, after dark, in the hum of a summer night, a stylish patio dinner may be complemented with a dashing Vouvray or an elegant Moselle. A few red wines survive: Beaujolais, the Italian Valpolicella, and some of the lighter California vintages—Zinfandel, Folle Blanche, Gamay, Mountain Red—add pleasure to summer eating. It is entirely proper to cool or chill them. Such strenuous treatment would dim the flavor and bouquet of an important red wine. But it will enhance these lesser breeds.

Summer is the voluptuous season for vegetables and fruits. Everything abounds. Be expansive, festive, and inventive in your dining and drinking. Some examples of good summer dishes, and a list of seasonal wines, follow.

ESCABÈCHE: A cool bottle of Pouilly-Blanc-Fumé, a superbly summery wine made from the Cabernet Sauvignon grape, is a standard for hors d'oeuvres. So is Italian Verdicchio, pale, gossamer light, and deliciously fruity. Either will go well with such dishes as the Escabèche of Scallops, or the Seviche à la Four Seasons.

MOUSSE OF HAM IN WHOLE PEACHES: A relatively recent and completely American creation, this mousse is beautifully accompanied by a soft wine, such as an Alsatian Sylvaner.

MOREL SOUFFLÉ IN CRUST: While hot first courses are not so popular as cold ones in summer, this creation of Chef Chantreau is delectable. A Sancerre rosé would be appropriate.

BAKED WHITEFISH WITH CRABMEAT, GRATINÉE: One fears that the crabmeat might subordinate the delicacy of the whitefish, but not at all. The wine for such a dish might be a white Châteauneuf-du-Pape, an interesting diversion and one of the truly little-known wines of France.

SQUAB CHICKEN CRAPAUDINE: Delightfully light and good summer fare. Drink a Swiss Fendant du Valais with it, or, if you prefer something more traditional, a light Fleurie—cooled, if you will.

CALF BRAINS: Whether in tomatoes or *en brioche,* this dish will be responsive to a good, gay white, cooled and served in precisely cooled glasses. A French Pouilly-Blanc-Fumé, or an Austrian Gumpoldskirchner, would be both summery and good.

VITELLO TONNATO: Despite its Italian origins, Vitello Tonnato has become a completely American summer specialty. It calls for an Italian white, perhaps a Soave or a Verdicchio, well chilled and kept that way.

BEEF IN ASPIC: A classic cold dish that could very well take a very light red wine: a Bouzy from the Champagne district (although not easy to find in the United States), or the old faithful Zinfandel from Louis Martini in the Napa Valley.

BOUILLABAISSE SALAD: A glorious mélange of fish and seafood magnificently dressed and presented, it should have a sparkling wine, such as a Bollinger brut, N.V., or an Almadén Blanc de Blancs.

White:
Châteauneuf-du-Pape blanc—The white version of a famous Rhône Valley name.
Château Grillet—A rare Rhône of great quality.
Condrieu—Another Rhône white, heavily aromatic, served at the Pyramide in Vienne.
Pouilly-Blanc-Fumé—A summer standard.
Sancerre—From the Loire Valley.
Vouvray—From the Loire, may be still or sparkling, a light, fruity wine.
Vinhos Verdes—From northwest Portugal. Light greenish in color, bright, prickly in taste. Perfect for summer.
Blanc de Blancs, California, Wente Brothers, Livermore Valley.
Mountain White, California, Almadén.
Neuchâtel (Swiss).
Fendant du Valais—A lovely light mountain wine from Switzerland.
Moselblümchen—A pleasing wine for regular and large consumption.
Graacher Himmelreich—A fine dry Moselle.
Ockfenner Bockstein Spätlese—Light, flinty, and elegant.
Schloss Johannisberger Rotlack, von Metternich—Dry, moderate.
Gumpoldskirchner Eichberg—Austria's most famous wine.
Grinzinger Auslese—Auslese is wine that has been pressed from specially selected, late-gathered grapes.
Crépy—From the Haute-Savoie.

Champagne:
Blanc de Blancs, California, Almadén.
Ayala Gold Label, brut.
Mesnil Blanc de Blancs.

Rosé:
Pinot Noir—From Alsace.
Sciatino—From Corsica.
Sancerre—From the Loire Valley.

Red:
Moulin-à-Vent—No Beaujolais is more full-bodied than this; drink it as young as possible.
Fleurie—A typical Beaujolais: fresh and fruity, and best drunk young.
Beaujolais Villages—Should be young; very nice when cooled.
Bouzy—A rare red wine from Champagne. Not sparkling.
Corbières—A pleasant wine from around Carcassonne, usually a *vin ordinaire*, but occasionally of good quality and value.
Gigondas—A Rhône Valley *vin du pays*. Also obtainable locally in a distinctive, dark-yellow white wine.
Dole du Valais—A most interesting Swiss red.
Zinfandel, California, Louis Martini, Napa Valley.

—JB

Some Fundamentals

Some Fundamentals

The first quality of wine used for cooking is that it should be palatable enough to drink. Nothing else can be considered ''cooking wine.'' Generally, the wines you use in making dishes will be dry whites or reds. If your recipe calls for a relatively small amount of wine, you may use the wine you're going to serve with the dish. If, on the other hand, a considerable quantity is called for, and you do not wish to use that much of your table wine, you can use one of the less expensive reds or whites that you know to be adequate and flavorful.

In using wine remember that it has to ''cook off.'' The alcoholic content usually is almost entirely evaporated in cooking, so that only the concentrated flavor remains. Therefore, you should use exactly the quantity asked for in the recipe, not a ''dosage'' which will probably overwhelm other flavors in the dish. In cooking with wine never take the point of view that you can't have too much of a good thing.

When using sherry and Madeira keep in mind that there are sweet and dry of each. You never use sweet sherry in soup or in an entrée sauce. Dessert sauces and desserts can take a medium or sweet sherry. The same is true of Madeira. If a recipe asks for port, try to find as brisk and dry a port as you can. For poaching pears and the like you can use a sweeter port.

The alcoholic content of such fortified wines is high and it must be cooked off, except, of course, when the wines are used in cold dishes. Desserts and the like usually require only a small amount of wine. As for quality, again it is wisest to use a wine you would drink. Recipes rarely call for much, so that even though your choice may be expensive, you are unlikely to deplete it seriously.

Cognac is often called for in cooking. If it is to be flambéed it should always be warmed first, which makes it much easier to ignite. There are less expensive brandies which one would perhaps not use for drinking, but which are extremely flavorful for cooking. Many very good cooks have been known to use something less than a very old cognac in the kitchen.

As for liqueurs, again so little is required in most recipes that most people use whatever they have for drinking. In some states you can buy miniature bottles of liqueur which hold about two ounces and fill the bill very nicely for dishes you don't make very often.

Be sparing when you add white wines or liqueurs to fruits. These wines are used to enhance the flavor of fresh fruit, not mask it. Experiment with whatever liqueurs you have to see which you like best with fruits. The possibilities are many.

A kitchen which produces outstanding food must be well supplied with herbs and spices. Provide yourself with ample shelf space for such flavorings. They give a memorable taste to the things you cook, inspire new recipe inventions, and add variety to your menus. If you have a really green thumb, you may be successful at growing a number of the more useful herbs at home, and you may then dry or freeze them for later use.

A word of caution, however. When you first start using herbs and spices, add smaller quantities than you might at first think appropriate. It's easy to overwhelm a dish by the use of too much seasoning, and you can always add more, if necessary. Keep this in mind especially when increasing quantities to serve more people than a recipe provides for. You may safely multiply the main ingredient and any sauce material required, but when adding the seasonings you must taste as you go and make additions tentatively, until you achieve the exact flavor you want.

While fresh herbs are preferable to dried, it is not always possible to find them in the market, and you may have to use the commercially prepared dried herbs. These have much stronger flavor than that of fresh herbs. A ½ teaspoon dried or ¼ teaspoon powdered is the equivalent of 2 scant teaspoons of minced fresh herbs.

We wish to make a strong plea for your owning and using two pepper mills—one for black peppercorns, and another for white peppercorns to use in delicate sauces whose appearance would be spoiled by the coloring of black pepper. The flavor of freshly ground pepper and nutmeg is so superior to that of the equivalent tinned and ready-ground spices that, once you are accustomed to using them in your cooking, you will never succumb to the tinned variety again. Your pepper mill can probably be regulated to grind finer or coarser. Coarsely ground black pepper is what the French call "mignonnette." Coarse salt can be ground in its own type of mill, as can sea salt, which gives a splendid flavor.

Don't put herbs or spices into too many dishes in your menu. The result can be utterly confusing to the palate. Use them well in one, or perhaps two, of your dishes, and you can be sure of pleasing results.

Buy herbs and spices in a shop which sells them by the ounce, if you can. Buy them in very small quantities, renewing them frequently. Keep them in air-tight and, if possible, lightproof jars, and store them in a dark, cool place. Even with these precautions, a spice kept too long will lose its flavor and change its appearance. You can tell that a spice is beginning to go stale when its aroma diminishes and its color fades.

275

"Correct the Seasoning"

This instruction refers to one of the most important processes of cooking. It means that you must taste the sauce or soup or dish you are making to see whether it is properly seasoned. Tasting is absolutely essential to producing good food, even when you have followed a recipe to the letter. As one restaurant director explained: "The carrot you use today may not taste like the one you used yesterday. It may need more salt — or less — or a dash of sugar. How can you possibly tell if you don't taste it?" The simple answer is, you can't tell. So be sure to taste everything you cook and *correct the seasoning* before you serve it.

Stocks

Clarifying Stocks

5 CUPS COLD STOCK
2 EGG WHITES

Completely de-grease the stock. Whip in egg whites. Place in a saucepan over moderate heat and stir constantly until egg whites rise to the surface. Do not boil. Strain through several layers of cheesecloth. Makes about 4 cups.

Beef Stock

8 QUARTS WATER
1 BEEF SHANK
1 OLD STEWING CHICKEN
2 POUNDS BEEF OR VEAL BONES
2 LARGE CARROTS
1 LARGE ONION, STUCK WITH 3 CLOVES
1 STALK CELERY
1 BAY LEAF
FEW PARSLEY STEMS
PINCH OF THYME
5 TABLESPOONS SALT

Bring 4 quarts water to a boil and add beef shank, chicken, and bones. Let water return to a boil and boil 5 minutes. Remove from heat and pour water from pot. To the same pot add 4 quarts fresh water and remaining ingredients. Cook slowly 3 hours, uncovered. Strain. Makes a little more than 2 quarts.

Beef Consommé

1 POUND LEAN GROUND BEEF
1 MEDIUM ONION, CHOPPED
2 LEEKS, CHOPPED
2 CARROTS, CHOPPED
2 LARGE, RIPE TOMATOES, CHOPPED
2 CELERY STALKS, CHOPPED
4 EGG WHITES
3 QUARTS BEEF STOCK (ABOVE), BOILING/

Mix thoroughly all ingredients except stock. Pour stock into vegetable mixture and cook over low heat, uncovered, for 15 minutes. Strain through cheesecloth. Makes about 3 quarts.

276

Chicken Stock

3 POUNDS CHICKEN PIECES, INCLUDING
BONES, WINGS, FAT, NECKS, HEARTS/
3 QUARTS COLD WATER
1 CUP CHOPPED CELERY
1 CUP CHOPPED CARROTS
2 LARGE ONIONS, STUCK WITH CLOVES
1 CUP CHOPPED LEEKS
4 SPRIGS PARSLEY
½ POUND MUSHROOMS,
CUT INTO CHUNKS/
SALT & PEPPER TO TASTE

Put chicken pieces into a pot and add the water. Bring to boil and skim. Lower heat, cover, and simmer for 2 hours. Add vegetables and simmer, covered, for another hour. Strain and season to taste. Clarify (page 276) if desired. Makes about 6 cups.

NOTE: This stock may be frozen.

Chicken Consommé

1 QUART CHICKEN STOCK (ABOVE)
1 QUART BEEF STOCK (PAGE 276)
1 OLD STEWING CHICKEN
1 ONION
1 CARROT
1 STALK CELERY
1 BAY LEAF
FEW STEMS PARSLEY
PINCH OF THYME
SALT TO TASTE
2 EGG WHITES

Combine all ingredients except egg whites in a large pot and cook 2 hours, covered. Strain and clarify with the egg whites according to directions on page 276. Makes about 2 quarts.

Court-Bouillon

4 CARROTS, SLICED
2 MEDIUM ONIONS, SLICED
1 BAY LEAF
1½ CUPS DRY WHITE WINE
3 CUPS WATER
1 TEASPOON SALT

Place all ingredients in a pot and simmer for 30 minutes. Makes about 4 cups.

Fish Stock
Fumet de Poisson

3 TABLESPOONS OIL
⅓ CUP COARSELY CHOPPED ONIONS
⅓ CUP SLICED CARROTS
⅓ CUP SLICED CELERY
SALT & PEPPER TO TASTE
1 QUART DRY WHITE WINE
1 QUART WATER
2 POUNDS FISH HEADS AND BONES
PINCH OF DRIED FENNEL
4 SPRIGS PARSLEY
1 BAY LEAF

Heat oil. Cook vegetables in oil until they just begin to color. Add salt and pepper. Add wine, water, and fish bones. Bring to boil. Skim. Add fennel, parsley, and bay leaf. Simmer 2 hours. Clarify (page 276). Strain through cheesecloth. Makes about 3 cups.

Game Stock

1 OLD PHEASANT
5 POUNDS VENISON BONES
¼ CUP OIL
1 LARGE CARROT, CHOPPED
1 MEDIUM ONION, CHOPPED
1 STALK CELERY, CHOPPED
1 BAY LEAF
1 4-INCH STALK THYME (OR
½ TEASPOON DRIED)/
¼ CUP RED WINE VINEGAR
4 QUARTS MARINADE (BELOW)

Chop pheasant (including bones) and venison bones coarsely with cleaver. Put oil in a baking pan. Add pheasant and bones and place in a 450-degree oven for about 15 minutes, until browned. Add carrot, onion, celery, bay leaf, and thyme. Cook for an additional 10 minutes, or until the vegetables brown. Remove from oven and place bones, pheasant, and vegetables in a large pot. Place vinegar in a saucepan and reduce until almost dry. Add marinade and cook for 10 minutes. Pour this over bones and simmer for 2 hours. Strain through cheesecloth. Cool and refrigerate. Makes 2 quarts.

Glace de Viande

Meat glaze (glace de viande) is a staple of fine cookery. It is made by boiling down 3 quarts of veal, chicken, or beef stock until it becomes a syrup, which turns to a stiff jelly when it cools. This will make about 1½ cups. Since it is so concentrated in flavor, a very little goes a long way and the flavor is far better than any bottled meat extract or bouillon cube. It keeps well, covered, in the refrigerator for weeks and it may be frozen.

Marinade

1 MEDIUM ONION, SLICED
2 CARROTS, SLICED
2 CLOVES GARLIC
2 BAY LEAVES
1 TEASPOON THYME
2 TABLESPOONS VINEGAR
½ CUP OLIVE OIL
2 TABLESPOONS SALT
1 TEASPOON BLACK PEPPER
1 BOTTLE RED BURGUNDY WINE

A marinade gains flavor from the meat it marinates and often becomes a component of the sauce served with the meat. This recipe makes sufficient marinade for 6 pounds of venison, boar, rabbit, beef, etc. Cut the meat as instructed in the particular recipe, removing all fat and connecting tissues. Mix all ingredients and pour over meat. Marinate for as long as the recipe requires.

Port Aspic

1 LEEK
½ MEDIUM ONION
1 CARROT
1 RIPE TOMATO
3 EGG WHITES
3 OUNCES CHOPPED BEEF

Port Aspic is a jellied and flavored stock used for cold platters, for sauce chaud-froid, and, when chopped or cut into various fancy shapes, as decoration.

Slice leek, onion, carrot, and tomato as fine as possible. Put into a pot and mix with egg whites and chopped beef. Soak gelatin in the

4 ENVELOPES UNFLAVORED GELATIN
½ CUP COLD WATER
1 QUART CHICKEN STOCK (PAGE 277)
¼ CUP WHITE PORT

cold water for 5 minutes and add to pot, mixing again. Add the stock. Bring to a boil. Reduce heat and cook very slowly for 20 minutes. It should be clear. Strain through several thicknesses of cheesecloth. Add port. Cool and chill. Makes 4 cups.

Veal Stock

2 POUNDS CRACKED VEAL BONES
1½ POUNDS VEAL SHANK CUT IN
CHUNKS, OR VEAL TRIMMINGS/

————

Mirepoix:
3 MEDIUM CARROTS, CHOPPED;
2 MEDIUM ONIONS, CHOPPED;
1 4-INCH STALK OF THYME
(OR ½ TEASPOON DRIED);
2 BAY LEAVES;
1 STALK CELERY, CHOPPED;
1 CLOVE GARLIC, CHOPPED/

————

1 TEASPOON SALT
PEPPER TO TASTE
WATER TO COVER

Place bones and meat in a large baking pan. Place in a 400-degree oven to brown the meat and bones. Add mirepoix and brown it also. Remove pan from oven, and transfer contents into a large pot. Add water and salt and pepper. Cook stock slowly for 4–6 hours on top of range, skimming off scum occasionally. Makes 1½ quarts.

Soup Garnitures

3 CUPS SPINACH LEAVES,
VERY COARSELY TORN/
1 CUP BOSTON LETTUCE LEAVES,
VERY COARSELY TORN/
1 STALK CELERY, COARSELY CHOPPED
SALT & PEPPER TO TASTE
18 2-INCH WHITE BREAD CIRCLES
FAT FOR DEEP FRYING
¼ CUP SOFTENED BUTTER

Green Spinach Croustades

The ubiquitous crouton is not, by any means, the only garniture for soup. This is a delicious variation, here used with beef broth.

Place vegetables in boiling water to cover for 5 minutes and drain well, squeezing out excess water. Whirl in blender or purée in food mill and season. Deep fry bread until golden brown and drain. Spread with butter and place under broiler for a few minutes, until crisp and brown. Mound purée on croustades, and float in beef broth. Serves 6.

Rosemary Quenelles

1 POUND BREAST OF CHICKEN,
BONED & SKINNED/
2 EGG WHITES
1 TEASPOON SALT
1 TABLESPOON MINCED FRESH
ROSEMARY (OR 1 TEASPOON DRIED)/
DASH WHITE PEPPER
DASH NUTMEG
2 CUPS HEAVY CREAM

These little dumplings are a great adornment to consommé. With the addition of a sauce, they may also be served as an appetizer.

Grind the breast of chicken twice. Put egg whites, salt, rosemary, pepper, nutmeg, and chicken in a bowl. Place in a larger bowl filled with cracked ice. Mix the ingredients together and slowly pour in the heavy cream, beating with the electric mixer. Refrigerate for 24 hours to chill thoroughly. When ready to cook, make a test quenelle, a little cylindrical puff about ½ inch long. Poach it in a little water; if the quenelle mixture is too soft, it will fall apart. In that case, add another egg white to quenelle mixture. Then proceed to shape remainder of mixture into quenelles, and poach them in the consommé in which they are to be served.

Basic Royale

1 PINT CONSOMMÉ
5 EGGS
DASH NUTMEG
ANY ONE OF THE FOLLOWING
AS MAIN INGREDIENT:
TURKEY CUT IN SMALL DICE
GRATED CARROTS
CHOPPED CELERY
GAME OR POULTRY IN SMALL DICE
PURÉE OF PEAS OR CHESTNUTS
FISH OR LOBSTER IN SMALL DICE

This is a classic garniture for soups.

Mix eggs, consommé, and nutmeg well. Strain. Add to the mixture ½ cup of main ingredient. Pour into a shallow mold and poach in a pan of water in a 350-degree oven 30 minutes. Cut into desired small shapes and serve in a clear consommé. This makes enough for 10–12 servings of consommé.

Sauces

Reduction of Sauces

This is the process of reducing the volume of a liquid — usually a sauce — by evaporation. The liquid is boiled with the pan uncovered. Reducing makes a sauce thicker and, by concentrating its essences, more flavorful. A brown sauce which has been reduced becomes more brilliant in appearance. When an instruction tells you to "reduce by ½," it is not necessary to measure the sauce before and after reducing. If you reduce it to approximately half of its former volume you will have accomplished your objective. You will also quite often be instructed to "reduce by ⅔" which means you will have about one-third the amount of sauce you started with. Another fairly common instruction is "reduce to dry," which means exactly what it says — to eliminate all liquid and leave a concentrate on the bottom of the pan for mixing with something else. Reducing to dry must be watched carefully to be sure that neither the pan nor its contents burns.

When you are asked in a recipe to use a "thin" (or "light") sauce of any kind, use less of the thickening agent required in the basic recipe, or thin the sauce with stock or wine, or whatever basic liquid is called for.

Sauce Aïoli

8–10 CLOVES GARLIC
2 EGG YOLKS
1 TEASPOON SALT
DASH WHITE PEPPER
1 PINT OLIVE OIL

Put garlic cloves through garlic press. Put resulting purée in blender with egg yolks and salt and pepper. Blend at lowest speed for a few moments. Drop by drop, slowly add olive oil. Sauce will be very thick. Makes about 2 cups.

Sauce Allemande

5 EGG YOLKS
¼ TEASPOON PEPPER
¼ TEASPOON NUTMEG
2 TABLESPOONS LEMON JUICE
½ CUP PLUS 2 TABLESPOONS
CHICKEN STOCK (SEE STOCKS)/
1 QUART SAUCE VELOUTÉ (PAGE 290)
½ CUP CHOPPED MUSHROOMS
6 TABLESPOONS BUTTER

Beat egg yolks, seasonings, lemon juice, and chicken stock together. Add velouté and mushrooms, and cook about 10 minutes. Strain. Off heat, "finish" by stirring in the butter a little at a time. Makes about 4 cups.

Sauce Américaine

1 1-POUND LIVE LOBSTER
SALT & PEPPER
¼ CUP OIL
1 SMALL ONION, CHOPPED
1 CLOVE GARLIC, MINCED
1 TEASPOON MINCED FRESH TARRAGON
(OR A DASH DRIED)/
1 RIPE TOMATO, PEELED & DICED
1 CARROT, PEELED & SLICED
2 TABLESPOONS COGNAC, WARMED
½ CUP DRY WHITE WINE
½ CUP WHITE WINE SAUCE (PAGE 290)

Sever spinal cord at base of lobster's head. Split lobster lengthwise. Reserve the coral. Sprinkle lobster meat with salt and pepper. Bring the oil to high heat in a flame-proof casserole. Put in the lobster and cook, turning until the shell turns red and the meat is seared. Remove lobster. Add onion, garlic, tarragon, tomato, and carrot, and cook over moderate heat until brown. Place lobster on top of the vegetables, pour in the warm cognac and flame it. Pour in the white wine and reduce by ⅓. Add the white wine sauce or brown sauce; if white wine sauce, add also tomato purée. Add salt and pepper to taste. Cook in a 300-degree oven for 20 minutes.

Remove lobster from casserole. Take out the meat and cut it in very fine dice. Keep warm. Add the heavy cream to the

OR BROWN SAUCE (PAGE 283)/
1 TABLESPOON TOMATO PURÉE
(IF YOU USE WHITE WINE SAUCE)/
¼ CUP HEAVY CREAM
3 TABLESPOONS SWEET BUTTER
DROP OF TABASCO
½ TEASPOON LEMON JUICE

sauce and reduce by ⅓. Strain. Add the sweet butter and mix well. Add Tabasco, lemon juice, and lobster coral, and mix well again. The sauce should be light and delicate. Add the diced lobster meat. Makes about 1¼ cups.

Anchovy Sauce

2 CUPS LIGHT BÉCHAMEL
(BELOW)/
3 TABLESPOONS SHELLFISH BUTTER
(PAGE 284)/
8 ANCHOVY FILLETS, WASHED
HEAVY CREAM, WARMED
(IF NECESSARY)/

Mix all ingredients except cream and cook 5 minutes. Strain sauce well. Anchovy Sauce should be thick but still pour easily. If too thick, add a little cream. Makes about 2 cups.

Sauce Béarnaise

¼ CUP WHITE WINE VINEGAR
¼ CUP DRY WHITE WINE
1 TABLESPOON MINCED SHALLOTS
1 TABLESPOON MINCED FRESH
TARRAGON, OR 1 TABLESPOON MINCED
TARRAGON IN VINEGAR (FROM JAR)/
DASH PEPPER
PINCH OF SALT
3 EGG YOLKS
½ CUP MELTED CLARIFIED BUTTER
(PAGE 283)/

Reduce the vinegar, wine, shallots, tarragon, and salt and pepper over moderate heat until dry. Watch very carefully to see that the mixture does not burn. Cool. In the top of a double boiler, over hot but not boiling water, beat the egg yolks with the cooled mixture until thick. Beat in the clarified butter by droplets. Continue beating until thickened to the degree you desire. Correct seasonings. Makes 1½ cups.
NOTE: This sauce is best served lukewarm. If you try to make it too hot, it is likely to "crack," or curdle.

Sauce Béchamel

¼ CUP (½ STICK) BUTTER
½ CUP FLOUR
1 QUART MILK, HEATED
1 CARROT, SLICED
½ ONION, STUCK WITH 4 CLOVES
BOUQUET GARNI: PARSLEY,
BAY LEAF, AND CELERY/

This recipe will make a medium Béchamel. If you wish to make a thin Béchamel substitute ¼ cup flour for the amount called for in the recipe; if you want a thick Béchamel, substitute 1 cup flour.

Melt butter and stir in flour until smooth. Cook over low heat a few minutes and add milk. Stir until thickened. Add carrot, onion, and bouquet garni. Simmer 10 minutes and strain. Makes about 4 cups.

Sauce Bordelaise

1 CUP FULL-BODIED RED WINE
2 TABLESPOONS CHOPPED SHALLOTS
1 TEASPOON FRESHLY GROUND
BLACK PEPPER/
DASH THYME
½ BAY LEAF
4 CUPS BROWN SAUCE (BELOW)
SALT TO TASTE
4 TABLESPOONS MARROW

Bordelaise is served with broiled steak, côte de boeuf, and some venison dishes.

Reduce wine, shallots, pepper, thyme, and bay leaf by ¾. Add brown sauce and salt and cook over low heat for 10 minutes. Skim off fat and scum. Strain sauce into a casserole. Add marrow, diced or sliced, and poach about 2 minutes. Makes 4 cups.

Bread Sauce

1 ONION, STUCK WITH A CLOVE
2 BAY LEAVES
1 PINT HEAVY CREAM
2 CUPS SOFT, FRESH BREAD CRUMBS
1 TEASPOON NUTMEG
SALT & PEPPER TO TASTE

This sauce is excellent with game.

Cook onion, bay leaves, cream, and bread crumbs together over low heat for 10 minutes. Strain. Cook another 10 minutes. Strain again. Season with salt and pepper and nutmeg. Makes 2 cups.

Brown Sauce
(Sauce Espagnole)

½ CUP SLICED CARROTS
¼ CUP CHOPPED ONION
1 TEASPOON DRIED THYME
1 BAY LEAF
2 TABLESPOONS DICED FATBACK
1 TABLESPOON SALT
1 TEASPOON PEPPER
1¼ CUPS FLOUR
⅓ CUP BUTTER
1½ QUARTS BEEF STOCK
(SEE STOCKS)/
1 POUND FRESH TOMATOES,
PEELED AND CHOPPED/
1 CUP WHITE WINE

Put carrots, onion, thyme, bay leaf, and fatback into a pot, and brown. Add salt and pepper. Mix flour with butter to form a roux and add, mixing well. Add a quart of the beef stock. Simmer over low heat for 3 hours. Strain. Let stand overnight. Put into a pot with remaining beef stock, tomatoes, and white wine. Simmer 2 hours, skimming off fat and scum with a spoon. Strain. Cool. Makes about 4 cups. This sauce will keep in the refrigerator for a few days and may be frozen.

Clarified Butter

This is used for sautéing delicate foods, and for making brown butter. It burns less readily than ordinary butter, and because of its clarity it leaves no residue in the dish in which it is used.

To obtain clarified butter, melt ordinary butter over low heat. Skim off the foam which rises to the top. The remainder will be separated into 2 parts: a clear yellow liquid and a white residue which sinks to the bottom of the pan. Strain off the clear yellow butter into a bowl; this is the clarified butter. Discard the white residue.

Maître d'Hôtel Butter

½ CUP (1 STICK) SWEET BUTTER
1 TABLESPOON CHOPPED
FRESH PARSLEY/
1 TEASPOON CHOPPED FRESH CHERVIL
SALT & PEPPER TO TASTE
6 DROPS WORCESTERSHIRE SAUCE
3 DROPS LEMON JUICE

A curl of this will enhance the flavor of many dishes, including broiled beef fillet or steak, veal kidneys, and mixed grill.

Mix all together very well. Form into a roll in waxed paper or foil. Refrigerate for at least 30 minutes.

Shellfish Butters

1 CUP SHELLFISH SHELLS,
LEGS, AND CORAL IF ANY
(OR SHELLFISH MEAT)/
½ CUP (1 STICK) BUTTER
2 TABLESPOONS BOILING WATER
SALT & FRESHLY GROUND
WHITE PEPPER/

Using shellfish meat in this sauce gives you less delicate color than when shells are used. When using meat, you may add a tablespoon of tomato paste to color the butter and for slight additional flavor.

Put shells and legs into a 375-degree oven 8 minutes to dry them. Whirl in blender to crush completely. If using shellfish meat put it through the grinder. Melt butter in the top of a double boiler. Add shells and coral or meat, and cook over hot water 10 minutes. Strain through cheesecloth. Add the boiling water to the shells and let stand 5 minutes. Strain the water into the previously strained butter. Season to taste with salt and white pepper. Pour into a dish or crock, and refrigerate at least 2 to 3 hours. The butter will harden and can easily be removed from the liquid underneath, which can be discarded. Makes about ⅔ cup. NOTE: This butter may be frozen.

Sauce Choron

Mix ⅔ cup Tomatoes Concassées (page 290) with 1 recipe for Sauce Béarnaise (page 282).

Sauce Diable

12 SMALL SHALLOTS, CHOPPED
6 TABLESPOONS WHITE VINEGAR

Place shallots, vinegar, wine, and pepper in a saucepan. Reduce over low heat until all the liquid evaporates. Add brown sauce

284

6 TABLESPOONS DRY WHITE WINE
DASH COARSELY GROUND
BLACK PEPPER/
¾ CUP BROWN SAUCE (PAGE 283)
¼ CUP BUTTER
SALT TO TASTE

and bring to a boil. Add butter and beat well. Add salt to taste and serve. Makes about 1 cup.

Duxelles

2 POUNDS MUSHROOMS, STEMS AND
CAPS, CHOPPED VERY FINE/
½ CUP (1 STICK) BUTTER, MELTED
2 SHALLOTS OR 1 SMALL ONION,
FINELY CHOPPED/
SALT TO TASTE

Duxelles is a great addition to many sauces and to egg and vegetable dishes. It will keep for a couple of weeks in the refrigerator and it freezes well.

Cook mushrooms in melted butter in a heavy skillet with the shallots or onion. Cook over low heat, stirring occasionally, until all the liquid has evaporated and the mushrooms are quite black in color. Add more butter if necessary. Salt to taste and store in a covered jar in the refrigerator. Makes about 4 cups.

Italian Duxelles

¼ CUP MINCED SHALLOTS
¼ CUP CLARIFIED BUTTER
(PAGE 283)/
1½ CUPS CHOPPED MUSHROOMS
1 TEASPOON LEMON JUICE
3 OUNCES BOILED HAM, DICED
¼ CUP DRY MADEIRA

Sauté the shallots in the clarified butter over moderate heat for 2 minutes. Add mushrooms and lemon juice, and sauté 4–5 minutes. Add ham and sauté 5 minutes more. Pour in Madeira, heat through, and set aside. Makes about 1½ cups.

French Dressing
(Sauce Vinaigrette)

6 TABLESPOONS OIL (VEGETABLE
OR OLIVE)/
2 TABLESPOONS VINEGAR
(ANY KIND YOU PREFER, OR YOU
MAY SUBSTITUTE LEMON JUICE)/
SALT & FRESHLY GROUND PEPPER
TO TASTE/

Beat all ingredients together. Makes ½ cup (enough for 6 servings).

Game Sauce

1 LARGE ONION (ABOUT
½ POUND), MINCED/

Sauté onion and ham in oil. Add vinegar and bouquet garni. Reduce until dry. Add flour to make roux. Add game stock and

285

3 OUNCES RAW HAM, MINCED
½ CUP OIL
1 CUP VINEGAR
BOUQUET GARNI: PARSLEY,
CELERY, AND BAY LEAF/
½ CUP FLOUR
3 CUPS GAME STOCK (SEE STOCKS)
½ CUP PORT WINE
2 TABLESPOONS BAR-LE-DUC

cook, stirring occasionally, for 20–25 minutes. Remove bouquet garni. Add wine and Bar-le-Duc and stir to mix well. Makes about 2 quarts.

Garniture Grand'mère

2 CUPS BOILING WATER
1 POUND PORK BACK BELLY,
IN SMALL DICE/
2 TABLESPOONS BUTTER
2 TABLESPOONS OIL
1 POUND SMALL ONIONS, COOKED
(PAGE 131)/
1 POUND MUSHROOMS, QUARTERED

Blanch back belly in water for 10 minutes, drain. Heat butter and oil in skillet and sauté onions until lightly browned. Remove onions from pan. Sauté mushrooms in the same fat for 5 minutes. Remove from pan and mix with back belly and onions. Serves 6.
NOTE: As a garniture for veal chops and chicken, add sautéed small round potatoes. For *Garniture Cévenole,* follow the procedure above, but substitute cèpes for mushrooms, and smoked ham for back belly.

Hollandaise Sauce

4 TABLESPOONS WATER
2 TABLESPOONS WHITE VINEGAR
1 TEASPOON WHITE PEPPER
1 TEASPOON SALT
5 EGG YOLKS
1 CUP MELTED CLARIFIED BUTTER
(PAGE 283)/
1 TABLESPOON LEMON JUICE

Put water, vinegar, pepper, and salt into the top part of a double boiler and reduce by ½ over direct heat. Add the egg yolks and place pan over hot but not boiling water in the bottom of the double boiler. Whip energetically with a wire whisk until the eggs are well mixed and slightly thickened. Remove the pan from the heat and, adding a little at a time, beat in the clarified butter. Continue beating until the sauce reaches the degree of thickness you like. Correct seasoning with salt and lemon juice. Makes about 1½ cups.
NOTE: If your Hollandaise separates, beat in about a tablespoonful of hot water to smooth it again.
VARIATION:
Minted Hollandaise: To ¼ cup Hollandaise, add 2 tablespoons very finely minced parsley, ¼ teaspoon white mint liqueur, 1 teaspoon dry white wine, ½ teaspoon lemon juice, and salt to taste. Mix all ingredients together. Makes about ½ cup.

Sauce Nantua

2 CUPS SAUCE BÉCHAMEL (PAGE 282)
1 CUP HEAVY CREAM
2 TABLESPOONS CREAM
6 TABLESPOONS SHELLFISH BUTTER
(PAGE 284) MADE WITH CRAYFISH/
1 TABLESPOON SHELLED AND
CHOPPED CRAYFISH TAILS/

Bring Béchamel to a boil, add the cup of cream, and reduce by ⅓. Force through a fine sieve. Add the 2 tablespoons cream, shellfish butter, and crayfish tails. Mix well. Makes about 2 cups.

Sauce Périgourdine

To 1 cup of Madeira Sauce (below) add 1 or 2 coarsely chopped black truffles.

Lobster Sauce
(Sauce Cardinal)

1 CUP WHITE WINE SAUCE
(PAGE 290), OR 1 CUP SAUCE/
BÉCHAMEL (PAGE 282)
⅓ CUP HEAVY CREAM
10 TABLESPOONS SHELLFISH BUTTER
(PAGE 284), MADE WITH LOBSTER/
½ TEASPOON TABASCO

Mix white wine sauce (or Béchamel) with cream. Cook gently for 5–6 minutes in saucepan. Add the shellfish butter and Tabasco. Mix well over heat and strain. Makes about 1½ cups.

Madeira Sauce

1 CUP BROWN SAUCE (PAGE 283)
⅓ TO ½ CUP MEDIUM-DRY
MADEIRA WINE/

Reduce brown sauce by ⅓. Add enough Madeira wine to make sauce the same thickness as before reduction. Correct seasoning if necessary. Makes about 1 cup.

Sauce Maltaise

½ CUP ORANGE JUICE
1 CUP SAUCE HOLLANDAISE
(PAGE 286)/
¼ CUP MINCED ORANGE PEEL

Reduce the orange juice by ½ over moderate heat and add to Hollandaise. Stir well. Mix in orange peel. Makes about 1½ cups.

Mayonnaise

4 EGG YOLKS
½ TEASPOON SALT
1 TEASPOON DRY MUSTARD

Have all ingredients (except water) at room temperature. Into a warm bowl put egg yolks, salt, mustard, and vinegar or lemon juice. Beat until thick, either by hand with a wire whisk, or with

4 TEASPOONS WHITE WINE VINEGAR
OR LEMON JUICE/
1 PINT OLIVE OIL, SALAD OIL,
OR A MIXTURE OF BOTH/
2 TABLESPOONS BOILING WATER

the electric mixer. Add oil, drop by drop, and never stop beating until the mixture thickens. After that, the oil may be added 1 or 2 tablespoons at a time — again, with continuous beating. Add the boiling water to insure that the mayonnaise will not "crack," or curdle. Makes about 2½ cups.

Mayonnaise for Chaud-froid: Mix ⅓ cup liquid Port Aspic (see Stocks) with ⅔ cup mayonnaise. Increase quantities in the same proportions if more is needed.

Curry Mayonnaise: To a cup of mayonnaise add curry powder to taste.

Green Mayonnaise (Sauce Verte): To a cup of mayonnaise add ½ cup mixed finely minced parsley, chervil, and spinach. If you like, you may also add capers.

Sauce Mignonnette

¼ CUP FINELY CHOPPED SHALLOTS
3 TABLESPOONS COARSELY GROUND
BLACK PEPPER/
1 CUP MALT VINEGAR
2 TEASPOONS OIL
SMALL PINCH OF SALT
SMALL PINCH OF WHITE PEPPER

This is traditionally served on clams and oysters.

Mix all ingredients well and serve. Makes a little more than a cup.

Sauce Mornay

1 CUP MEDIUM SAUCE BÉCHAMEL
(PAGE 282)/
2 EGG YOLKS, LIGHTLY BEATEN
¼ CUP GRATED SWISS CHEESE

Mix the ingredients in a saucepan and heat over low heat until the cheese melts and is incorporated, beating continuously with a wire whisk. Makes about 1¼ cups.

Sauce Mousseline

This is a combination of Sauce Hollandaise (page 286) and chilled whipped cream in the proportion of 1½ cups Hollandaise to ½ cup heavy cream, whipped: the chilled cream is blended with the warm Hollandaise just before serving.

Mustard Dressing

¼ CUP WHITE VINEGAR
½ CUP WATER
1 TABLESPOON SUGAR
1 TEASPOON SALT
½ TEASPOON PEPPER
1 CUP PREPARED MUSTARD
2 CUPS OLIVE OIL

Mix vinegar, water, sugar, salt, pepper, and mustard together well. Beat in the olive oil slowly, using a wire whisk or an electric mixer. Makes about 2½ cups.

Oyster Sauce

1 PINT OYSTERS
1 PINT RICH BEEF STOCK
(SEE STOCKS)/
3 TABLESPOONS CHOPPED SHALLOTS
¼ CUP BUTTER
¼ CUP FLOUR
1 TABLESPOON LEMON JUICE
1 TABLESPOON ANCHOVY PASTE
(OR TO TASTE)/
DASH CAYENNE

Cook oysters in beef stock for 10 minutes. Remove oysters, chop them very fine, and return to the liquid (there should be about 3 cups). Force through a sieve or whirl in the blender. Brown shallots in butter. Add flour, stir, and cook 1 minute. Add oyster mixture and stir. Add lemon juice, anchovy paste, and cayenne. Continue cooking, stirring occasionally, until thickened. Makes about 3 cups.

Sauce Soubise

2 CUPS SLICED YELLOW ONIONS
3 TABLESPOONS BUTTER
2 TABLESPOONS FLOUR
1 CUP BOILING MILK
SALT & PEPPER TO TASTE
DASH NUTMEG
2–4 TABLESPOONS HEAVY CREAM

Sauté onions in butter over low heat, covered, until soft but not brown (20–30 minutes). Stir in flour. Remove pan from heat and stir in milk. Return to heat and simmer 10 minutes, stirring occasionally. Press through a sieve or purée in the blender. Add seasonings and thin to desired consistency with cream. Makes 1¼ cups.

Sauce Suprême

10 TABLESPOONS BUTTER
½ CUP FLOUR
2 CUPS BOILING CHICKEN STOCK
(SEE STOCKS)/
DASH FRESHLY GRATED NUTMEG
SALT & WHITE PEPPER TO TASTE
2 CUPS HEAVY CREAM
LEMON JUICE TO TASTE

Melt the butter in a saucepan, add flour, and mix with a wire whisk. Add chicken stock and nutmeg. Cook the sauce slowly, being careful not to let it burn, until reduced by ⅓. Season with salt and pepper. Stir in cream gradually over heat. Add lemon juice. Makes 3 cups.

Tomato Sauce

¼ CUP OIL
1 CARROT
1 ONION
4 OUNCES RIND OF FAT SALT PORK,
COARSELY CHOPPED/
BOUQUET GARNI: CELERY, PARSLEY,
BAY LEAF, AND THYME/
4 CUPS PURÉED TOMATOES
¾ CUP FLOUR
2 QUARTS CHICKEN STOCK
(SEE STOCKS)/
2 TEASPOONS SALT
2 TEASPOONS SUGAR
1½ TEASPOONS WHITE PEPPER

Put oil, carrot, onion, pork, bouquet garni, and puréed tomatoes in a saucepan and cook 5 minutes. Add flour, mix in well. Add chicken stock, salt, sugar, and white pepper. Cook 1½ hours. Strain. Makes about 2 quarts.
NOTE: To make light (or thin) tomato sauce use only ¼ cup of flour, instead of the ¾ cup required above.

Tomatoes Concassées

4 POUNDS VERY RIPE TOMATOES
2 TABLESPOONS BUTTER
2 TABLESPOONS CHOPPED ONION
2 BAY LEAVES
1 TEASPOON MINCED GARLIC
1 4-INCH STALK THYME (OR
¼ TEASPOON DRIED)/
1 4-INCH STALK MARJORAM (OR
¼ TEASPOON DRIED)/
1 TEASPOON SUGAR
1 TABLESPOON SALT
1 TEASPOON PEPPER

Tomatoes "concassées" are peeled, seeded, juiced, and chopped tomatoes. In this version, tomatoes "concassées au four," they are also seasoned and dried in the oven. Reducing the water content in this way concentrates the flavor.

Blanch tomatoes in boiling water for a few seconds to loosen skin. Cut out stems and peel. Cut horizontally and squeeze out seeds. Chop coarsely. In a flame-proof casserole, sauté the onions in butter until soft but not browned. Add bay leaves, garlic, thyme, and marjoram, and cook for 1 minute longer. Remove from heat and add the tomatoes, sugar, salt, and pepper. Place in a 300-degree oven and cook, uncovered, for at least 30 minutes, until quite dry. Remove bay leaves, thyme, and marjoram. Makes about 3 cups.

Sauce Velouté

½ CUP CLARIFIED BUTTER
(PAGE 283)/
1 CUP FLOUR
1½ QUARTS HOT CHICKEN STOCK
(SEE STOCKS)/

Make a roux of the butter and flour. Add chicken stock and cook, stirring, until smooth. Simmer 20–25 minutes. Makes about 5 cups.

Victoria Sauce

1 TABLESPOON CHOPPED SHALLOTS
1 TABLESPOON LEMON JUICE
2 TABLESPOONS CHOPPED MUSHROOMS
10 TABLESPOONS SOFT BUTTER
2 TABLESPOONS CHOPPED PICKLES
DASH VINEGAR
1 TABLESPOON SUGAR
1 TEASPOON CHOPPED TARRAGON

This sauce is excellent with fried oysters, broiled fillet of sole, and other fish.

Place shallots, lemon juice, and mushrooms in a small skillet and reduce to dry. Add butter and mix well. The sauce should be creamy. Add pickles, vinegar, sugar, and tarragon and stir. Makes less than a cup.

White Wine Sauce

1 TABLESPOON CHOPPED SHALLOTS
½ CUP CHOPPED MUSHROOMS
(INCLUDING STEMS)/
7 TABLESPOONS BUTTER
2 TABLESPOONS LEMON JUICE
1 CUP DRY WHITE WINE

Put shallots, mushrooms, and 1 tablespoon each of the butter and lemon juice into a saucepan. Add the wine. Cook until dry. Add clarified butter and flour. Mix well. Add fish stock and cook, stirring constantly, until thickened and smooth. Add 1 cup of the cream. Reduce by ⅓. Add remaining cream and again reduce by ⅓. Strain. Correct seasoning with remaining butter (6 table-

½ CUP CLARIFIED BUTTER
(PAGE 283)/
1 CUP FLOUR
6 CUPS FISH STOCK (SEE STOCKS)
2 CUPS CREAM
SALT TO TASTE

spoons) and lemon juice (1 tablespoon) and salt to taste. Makes about 6 cups.

Yogurt Dressing

1 CUP YOGURT
4 TEASPOONS LEMON JUICE
4 TABLESPOONS OLIVE OIL
SALT & PEPPER TO TASTE

Mix all together well.

Sweet Sauces

Chocolate Sauce

6 SQUARES (6 OUNCES)
SEMI-SWEET CHOCOLATE/
1 SQUARE (1 OUNCE)
UNSWEETENED CHOCOLATE/
¾ CUP HEAVY CREAM

Melt both chocolates in top of double boiler. Stir in cream and continue stirring until smooth. Makes a generous cup of sauce.

Crème Anglaise
(Soft Custard)

4 EGG YOLKS
¼ CUP SUGAR
2 CUPS MILK
1 TEASPOON VANILLA EXTRACT

Beat egg yolks and gradually add the sugar, beating until the mixture forms a ribbon when lifted above the bowl. Bring milk to boil. While beating egg yolk mixture, very slowly pour the boiling milk into it. Place in a double boiler. Over hot water beat constantly with a wooden spoon until mixture coats the spoon. Be careful not to overcook or the custard will separate. Cool. Flavor with vanilla extract. Chill, unless the custard is to be used in a hot dish. Makes 2 generous cups.

Melba Sauce

1 PINT RASPBERRIES
1 CUP WATER
½ CUP SUGAR

Crush raspberries or whirl in blender. Put into small saucepan. Add water and sugar and mix. Cook over low heat until reduced by ⅓. Makes about 1½ cups.

Beignet Batter
(Pâte Beignet)

4 CUPS FLOUR
¼ TEASPOON SALT
1 TEASPOON SUGAR
2 TEASPOONS OIL
1 CUP BEER
½ CUP WATER
2 EGGS, SEPARATED

Mix all ingredients except egg whites into a smooth batter. Beat egg whites until stiff and fold into batter. Makes about 2 quarts.
BEIGNET VARIATIONS:
Fiddlehead ferns (put 6 on a wooden skewer for 1 serving); eggplant (chunks); zucchini (sliced fairly thick); cauliflower (cooked flowerets); sweetbreads; brains; scallops; lobster pieces; apple slices (thick and cored); apricot halves; bananas (thick slices).

Salt and pepper your vegetable and meat choices. Dip pieces into beignet batter and fry to golden brown in 375-degree deep fat. For the sweet fruit beignets, fry the same way and sprinkle with sugar before serving.

Bouchées

½ RECIPE FOR PUFF PASTRY
(PAGE 296) /
2 EGGS, LIGHTLY BEATEN
PREHEAT OVEN TO 350 DEGREES

Roll out puff pastry ⅛-inch thick. Trim off edges. Cut 6 ovals, 4 inches long. Put together scraps from cutting the ovals and roll them out ½-inch thick. Cut into strips ½-inch wide and make borders on the ovals with them. Place on cookie sheet and chill well. Prick bottoms of bouchées well with a fork. Brush rims with beaten egg. Bake in a 350-degree oven until golden brown (about 45 minutes), pricking the bottoms of the bouchées several times during the first 20 minutes of baking. Fill as directed. Makes 6 bouchées.

Cream Puffs

1 RECIPE PÂTE À CHOUX
(PAGE 295)
1 WHOLE EGG, BEATEN
PREHEAT OVEN TO 400 DEGREES

Spoon pâte à choux into a pastry tube with a medium-size opening. You may use either a plain or star tube. On a buttered baking sheet, squeeze out cream puffs the size of a ping-pong ball. Brush with egg and bake in a 400-degree oven 15–20 minutes, until puffs are lightly browned. Make small slits in the sides of the puffs, turn off oven heat, and leave puffs in the oven 10 minutes to dry out. To fill, puffs may be sliced in half, filling spooned in, and top replaced; or, filling may be squeezed in through the slits. Makes about 3 dozen cream puffs.

Crêpe Batter
Pâte à Crêpes

1 TEASPOON SALT
6 EGGS

Put salt in bowl. Break in eggs and beat with wire whisk. Add flour and mix well. Add milk and butter and beat. Strain. The

2 CUPS FLOUR
3 CUPS MILK
½ CUP CLARIFIED BUTTER
(PAGE 283)/

batter should be the consistency of thick cream. Lightly butter a 4½-inch crêpe pan. Heat to smoking over moderately high heat. Pour in a generous tablespoonful of batter. Tilt pan to spread batter over bottom in a thin film. Return pan to heat for about 1 minute, until the crêpe is lightly browned. Turn the crêpe over and cook for about 30 seconds on the second side. It will brown in a spotty fashion. (Crêpes may be made ahead, refrigerated, and reheated when needed.) Makes about 30 4½-inch crêpes.

Dessert Crêpes: Add to the above mixture 6 tablespoons of sugar and ½ cup of dark rum or liqueur of your choice.

Croissants

2 PACKAGES DRY YEAST
3⅓ CUPS FLOUR
2 TEASPOONS SALT
1½ CUPS (3 STICKS)
SWEET BUTTER/
1 CUP COLD MILK (APPROXIMATE)
2 EGGS, BEATEN

PREHEAT OVEN TO 475 DEGREES

Prepare yeast according to package directions. Mix flour and salt in a bowl. Make a well in the center of the mixture and add yeast. Cut ½ cup of the butter into pieces and add to bowl. Add milk slowly, gradually incorporating all of the flour mixture until dough is just firm but not springy. Refrigerate dough (in bowl) 10 minutes. Meanwhile, form remaining butter into a flat rectangle on a floured board. Place between floured sheets of waxed paper. With a rolling pin, shape butter into a ¼-inch-thick square. Cut square in half and refrigerate, still wrapped in waxed paper. Reflour board and place chilled dough on it. Roll out dough until length is 3 times the width. Remove excess flour from dough and place one of the chilled half-squares of butter crosswise in the center of the dough. Fold ⅓ of the dough over the butter. Place second piece of butter on the folded piece of dough and fold the remaining piece of dough back over it. Press edges of dough together. Reflour board and place dough on it, with one of the narrower edges next to you. Roll out dough into the size of the original rectangle. Remove excess flour. Fold dough into 4 layers, by first bringing the ends of rectangle together in the middle, then folding the 2 halves together. Again press edges together. Refrigerate dough 1 hour, wrapped in aluminum foil or plastic wrap. Repeat procedure of rolling out dough in long rectangle and folding in 4 layers. Rewrap dough and chill 3 hours. Cut dough in 2 parts and roll out each to a thickness of ⅛ inch. Cut 5-inch-wide strips, and cut these into triangles. Roll up each triangle, starting at the long side, into little cigar-shaped rolls. Pull dough out very slightly as you roll it. Place croissants on a buttered cookie sheet. (If you wish to freeze croissants, do it at this point. To bake, bring almost to room temperature, let rise for ½ hour, and proceed with recipe.) If you are planning to bake all the croissants at once, let them rise ½ hour at room temperature. Curve each into crescent shape and brush with beaten egg. Place in 475-degree oven for 5 minutes, reduce heat to 400 degrees for 6–9 minutes, until croissants are golden. Makes about 36 regular-sized croissants.

NOTE: The croissants served at The Four Seasons are unusually small. If you like them that way, cut your long strips of dough only 3 or 4 inches wide.

Croustades

1 RECIPE RICH PASTRY
(PAGE 296)/
½ RECIPE PUFF PASTRY
(PAGE 296)/
——————————————
PREHEAT OVEN TO 350 DEGREES

Roll out the rich pastry about ¼-inch thick. Cut into 6 ovals. Roll out puff pastry ¼-inch thick and cut into strips ½-inch wide. Make a border of this around each of the rich-pastry ovals. Place on cookie sheet and chill thoroughly. Prick the bottoms well. Bake in a 350-degree oven about 25 minutes or until golden brown.

Four Seasons Ice-Cream Shells
(Gaufrettes)

⅔ CUP (7 OUNCES) CANNED
ALMOND PASTE/
¼ CUP SUGAR
2½ TABLESPOONS FLOUR
4 EGG WHITES
——————————————
PREHEAT OVEN TO 300 DEGREES

Mix almond paste with sugar and flour. Add egg whites gradually, beating with electric mixer at low speed. Butter a large piece of parchment paper. Place on a cookie sheet. Spread the batter thinly into circles about 5 inches in diameter. Bake in a 300-degree oven 15 to 20 minutes or until golden. Remove from oven and quickly put the circles into fluted molds, then place another of the molds inside of each and press down to make fluted shells. If you have no fluted molds, turn a water glass upside down and place the circles on it, one at a time, shaping them into shells with your hands. Makes about 18 shells.

Meringue

2 EGG WHITES
DASH SALT
½ CUP SUGAR
¼ TEASPOON VANILLA EXTRACT
——————————————
PREHEAT OVEN TO 275 DEGREES

Beat egg whites until frothy. Sprinkle salt over top and beat until stiff. Gradually beat in half of the sugar, 2 tablespoons at a time. Add vanilla extract, then fold in the remaining sugar. With a pastry bag or spoon, shape meringues in mounds on an ungreased baking sheet, covered with parchment paper. Bake in a 275-degree oven 45 to 60 minutes, or until dry on the surface. Remove from the paper while warm. If the meringues stick to the paper, moisten the paper by placing it on a wet cloth, then remove meringues with a spatula. This makes about 18 large or 30 small meringues.

VARIATIONS:

Meringue Mushrooms: Make fairly flat rounds of meringue about

2 inches in diameter for the "caps." Make "stems" 1 inch high and about ½ inch in diameter at the bottom and pointed at the top. When the meringues have cooled, gently make a hole in the bottom of each cap with a pointed knife. Dip the pointed end of the stem into whipped cream to make it stick and insert it into the hole. Sprinkle very lightly with cocoa.

Pâte Brioche

5 PACKAGES DRY YEAST
1 CUP WARM MILK
7 EGGS
7 CUPS CAKE FLOUR (SEE NOTE)
1 TABLESPOON SALT
¾ CUP SUGAR
1½ CUPS (3 STICKS) BUTTER
1 DROP VANILLA EXTRACT
2 EGGS, LIGHTLY BEATEN
(FOR BRUSHING) /

PREHEAT OVEN TO 375 DEGREES

Prepare yeast as directed on package. Add warm milk and the whole eggs. Stir well. Mix flour, salt, and sugar. Add to original mixture with butter and vanilla. Knead thoroughly, until smooth and elastic (about 10 minutes). Place dough in bowl and dust with flour. Cover with a tea towel and place in warm, draft-free place to rise. When dough has doubled in bulk (30 minutes to an hour), remove from bowl and punch down. Put back in bowl, cover, and let rise again until almost double in bulk. Proceed to use dough as instructed in any particular recipe.

If you simply want to make brioches, grease brioche or muffin tins. Cut off pieces of the dough about the size of an egg. Roll each into an oval. Pinch the dough deeply about ⅓ from the end so that the 2 parts are almost completely separated. Set dough into tins, on the large rounded ends. Shape smaller top portion of each into a ball and press well into the larger portion of the dough. Allow brioche to rise until the dough almost fills the tins. With the kitchen scissors, snip 2 or 3 times around the knob of each brioche. Brush with beaten egg. Bake in a 375-degree oven 30–35 minutes, or until golden brown. Makes about 3 dozen brioches.

When making pâte brioche to enclose meat, use only a dash of sugar instead of the ¾ cup required above.
NOTE: It is even better to use half cake flour and half bread flour, if you can find the latter (see note following recipe for Couronne of Whole Brie).

Pâte à Choux

½ CUP (1 STICK) BUTTER
1 CUP WATER
1 CUP SIFTED FLOUR
¼ TEASPOON SALT
4 EGGS

PREHEAT OVEN TO 375 DEGREES

Stir butter and water together in a saucepan. Cook until mixture boils. Turn heat to low. Combine flour and salt and add all at once. Stir hard until mixture shapes firmly into a ball. Remove saucepan from heat and add 4 eggs, 1 at a time, beating vigorously after each addition. (This is done most easily with an electric mixer, but do not beat any more than is needed for egg to be absorbed.)

Shape pâte according to instructions in the recipe you are following. Bake in a 375-degree oven until golden brown. Make small slits in the sides of the pastries. Turn off the oven heat. Leave small pastries in the oven 10 minutes, larger ones 15 to 20 minutes, to dry them out. Pâte à choux is used for making a variety of hors d'oeuvre, entrée, and dessert shells. This recipe will make approximately what you would need for any recipe serving 6 to 8 people.

Puff Pastry

1½ CUPS SIFTED FLOUR
½ TEASPOON SALT
¼ CUP ICE WATER
1 CUP (2 STICKS)
VERY COLD BUTTER/

Sift flour and salt together. Stir in water with a fork, then knead dough until it is satiny smooth and elastic. On a floured board roll the dough into two neat rectangles each about 6 inches by 11 inches. Slice each stick of butter 2 times lengthwise and put 3 slices on the upper half of each rectangle, laying them across the width and leaving a ½-inch margin. Fold the lower half of the dough up over the butter and press the edges together. Bang the dough with a rolling pin several times to flatten the butter, then roll out 18 inches long and 6 inches wide. Fold dough into thirds, bringing one end over, then folding the other end over that. You now have 2 dough squares of 3 layers. It is important to keep edges of the squares neat and to work quickly so that the butter doesn't get too soft. Wrap each piece in aluminum foil and chill 30 minutes. Take out 1 piece and place on board so that the folded sides are on your left and right. Roll lengthwise, again to 18 inches in length, and fold as before. Repeat with second piece. This is called a "turn." After each turn, the dough is refrigerated again for 30 minutes. Give it at least 5 turns. Keep in the refrigerator until ready to bake, or freeze for long keeping.

Rich Pastry

¾ CUP (1½ STICKS)
BUTTER, SOFTENED/
6 TABLESPOONS VEGETABLE
SHORTENING/
½ CUP ICE WATER
½ TEASPOON SALT
1½ CUPS SIFTED FLOUR

With electric mixer blend butter and shortening until smooth. Add ice water, salt, and flour, and mix well. Roll into a ball, cover with foil or waxed paper, and chill until firm (at least 30 minutes). Roll out on floured pastry cloth. Line pie pan or cut into circles to make individual tarts. If you don't use all of the pastry, it will keep for some time in the refrigerator or it may be frozen. See following recipe for baking instructions.

Tarts, Tartlets & Barquettes

1 RECIPE FOR RICH PASTRY (ABOVE)
PREHEAT OVEN TO 400 DEGREES

Roll out pastry about ⅛-inch thick. Place over tart or barquette pans. Press down gently into the hollow of each pan, being careful

296

not to break the dough. When dough is touching bottoms of pans, run rolling pin over tops to cut away excess dough. Prick the bottoms of the shells with a fork. Line shells with foil. Fill with dry beans and bake in a 400-degree oven 7–8 minutes or until pastry is set. Remove beans and foil. Prick the bottoms of the shells again and return to the oven for 2–3 minutes or until pastry is just beginning to color. Remove shells from pan and cool on rack.

Sweet Dough

2 CUPS FLOUR
½ CUP SUGAR
¼ CUP PLUS 1½ TABLESPOONS BUTTER
1 EGG
DASH SALT
¼ TEASPOON VANILLA EXTRACT
PREHEAT OVEN TO 400 DEGREES

Mix ingredients together lightly, but thoroughly. Wrap in waxed paper or foil, and chill. For tart shells, roll out ¹⁄₁₆- to ⅛-inch thick. For pie crust, roll out ⅛-inch thick. Makes one 12-inch shell. To bake unfilled shells or crusts, line baking tins with dough. Prick bottom of dough well with fork, or line with foil and fill with beans (remove foil and beans a few minutes before baking is finished). Bake in a 400-degree oven 15-20 minutes, until golden.

Vacherin Layers

1 RECIPE FOR MERINGUE
(PAGE 294)
PREHEAT OVEN TO 325 DEGREES

Grease and flour a cookie sheet or sheets. Trace three circles 8 inches in diameter. Fit a pastry bag with a large round tube. Fill with meringue. Within each circle, starting at the center, make concentric circles ¼-inch thick in a continuous strip until circle is completely filled in. Bake in a 325-degree oven 30–35 minutes.

Dessert Basics

Apricot Glaze

½ CUP APRICOT JAM
2 TABLESPOONS WATER

Heat jam and water together, stirring constantly until well blended. While still warm, spread over item to be glazed with a pastry brush.

Butter Cream

5 EGG YOLKS
1 CUP SUGAR
⅛ TEASPOON CREAM OF TARTAR
⅓ CUP WATER
1 CUP SOFTENED BUTTER

Beat egg yolks until thick and fluffy in a mixing bowl. Set aside. Combine sugar, cream of tartar, and water in a saucepan. Stir over low heat until sugar is completely dissolved. Bring to a boil and boil without stirring until candy thermometer reads 240 degrees (soft ball in cold water). Add syrup to the egg yolks in a thin stream, beating constantly. Beat until cool. The mixture will become thick and light. Cool completely. Beat in the butter. Flavor as desired. Makes about 2 cups.

Crème Pâtissière

1 QUART MILK
8 EGG YOLKS
1 CUP PLUS 2 TABLESPOONS SUGAR
¾ CUP FLOUR
½ TEASPOON VANILLA EXTRACT

Scald the milk. Beat egg yolks with sugar until mixture is pale yellow. Beat in the flour. Gradually pour on the hot milk, beating all the while. Pour into a saucepan and cook, beating constantly with a wire whisk, until smooth and thick. Remove from heat and stir in the vanilla extract. Makes about 3 cups.

Decorative Burning of Powdered Sugar on Cakes

A cake sprinkled with powdered sugar can be given character by burning a design on it with hot metal. Pastry chefs have a special iron they use for this, but it can be done with a straightened unpainted metal coat hanger with equally good effect. Heat the metal until it is red. Then, using a mitt or a pot holder, lay the hot metal on the cake to make lines or crisscross designs.

Decorations for Cakes

These may be made from melted semi-sweet chocolate or butter cream. If chocolate is used, it should be allowed to cool but not harden. It is perhaps easiest to draw the decoration you wish to make on waxed paper and then fill it in with the chocolate or butter cream from either a pastry bag or a paper cornucopia. Then refrigerate the decoration to harden. One very simple way to make a flower, for example, is to make four hearts with their points together (the flower), a stem coming down from them, and perhaps a leaf for balance. You can make anything that suits your fancy in this manner.

Frangipane

½ POUND BUTTER
1 CUP PLUS 2 TABLESPOONS SUGAR
2 SCANT CUPS ALMOND FLOUR
5 EGGS
¼ TEASPOON SALT
GRATED RIND OF 2 LEMONS
⅓ CUP CORNSTARCH

To make this filling, blend butter and sugar. Add almond flour and mix on medium speed of beater. Beating continuously, add eggs, one at a time. Add salt and lemon rind. When almost completely blended, add cornstarch and beat a little longer. Makes about 4 cups.
NOTE: If you can't buy almond flour, pulverize ½ pound of blanched and toasted almonds in the blender.

Jelly Roll

⅔ CUP SIFTED FLOUR
1 TEASPOON BAKING POWDER
¼ TEASPOON SALT

Mix and sift flour, baking powder, and salt. Beat egg yolks until thick and lemon-colored. Gradually beat sugar into egg yolks. Add lemon rind and juice. Beat egg whites until stiff but not dry. Fold

3 EGGS, SEPARATED
¾ CUP SUGAR
½ TEASPOON GRATED LEMON RIND
1 TABLESPOON LEMON JUICE
1 CUP JELLY OR JAM

PREHEAT OVEN TO 350 DEGREES

in half of the egg whites. Gradually fold in flour, about 3 table-spoonsful at a time. Fold in remaining egg whites. Grease a 9 x 13½ x 1-inch jelly-roll pan, line it with heavy paper, and grease the paper. Pour in mixture. Bake in a 350-degree oven 20 minutes. Turn from pan onto waxed paper. Remove the heavy paper and cut off any crisp edges on the cake. Spread with jam or jelly and loosely roll up lengthwise.

NOTE: To use in making Strawberry Charlotte, use seedless strawberry jam and roll tightly to about 1½ inches in diameter.

Simple Syrup

1 CUP SUGAR
2 CUPS WATER

Boil sugar and water 5 minutes. Cool. Flavor as desired.

Sponge Cake
(Genoise)

6 EGGS
6 EGG YOLKS
1 CUP SUGAR
1 CUP SIFTED FLOUR
½ CUP CLARIFIED BUTTER
(PAGE 283), COOLED/
1 TEASPOON VANILLA EXTRACT

PREHEAT OVEN TO 350 DEGREES

Stir together eggs, yolks, and sugar in a bowl. Place the bowl in a smaller saucepan containing hot water, but not enough to touch bottom of bowl. Place both over low heat; water should not boil. Beat the mixture continuously as it warms. You can tell when the beaten eggs are warm enough by dipping a finger into them; not more than 1 drop should fall from your finger. Remove from heat and beat with an electric mixer at high speed for about 15 minutes, or until the mixture cools and is very fluffy. The genoise mixture will be triple in volume and have the consistency of whipped cream. Sprinkle flour over mixture. At the same time gradually add clarified butter and vanilla. Fold into mixture very carefully and delicately. Grease and lightly flour pans required by your recipe (layer-cake tins or a jelly-roll pan). Pour in the batter. Bake in a 350-degree oven 25–30 minutes, or until cake is browned lightly and shrinks away from the sides of the pan. Immediately remove cakes from pan or tins and place on rack for cooling.

Vanilla Sugar

For this use a glass jar with a screw top that will provide a tight seal. Fill jar with a pound of sugar and bury 2 or 3 vanilla beans in it. Close the jar tightly. This may be done with granulated, powdered, or confectioner's sugar. The vanilla beans will begin to flavor the sugar within a few hours and the flavor becomes more redolent as time goes by. Vanilla sugar is used more for its aroma than for its taste, usually for dusting cakes before serving.

Entrée Soufflé

4½ TABLESPOONS BUTTER
4½ TABLESPOONS FLOUR
1½ CUPS BOILING MILK
1 TEASPOON SALT
DASH FRESHLY GROUND
WHITE PEPPER/
DASH FRESHLY GROUND NUTMEG
6 EGGS, SEPARATED, PLUS
2 EGG WHITES/
BUTTER FOR SOUFFLÉ DISH

PREHEAT OVEN TO 375 DEGREES

Melt butter over low heat and blend in the flour. Add the milk and mix well. Remove to bowl. Add seasonings and egg yolks. Beat egg whites stiff and fold in gently. Butter a 9-cup soufflé dish. Pour in mixture. Cook for 35 minutes in a 375-degree oven, or until puffed and lightly brown. Serve immediately. Serves 6.

NOTE: Ingredients which may be added to the yolk mixture to vary the soufflé repertoire include:

Fondue Soufflé Four Seasons is made by adding 1½ cups grated Swiss cheese (reserving 3 tablespoons) to the egg yolk mixture. Use the reserved cheese to sprinkle the buttered mold before pouring in soufflé mixture.

White Truffle: Add 1 truffle, slivered.

Lobster: Add 1½ cups cubed lobster.

Crabmeat: Add 1½ cups shredded crabmeat.

Salmon: Add 1½ cups flaked salmon.

Artichoke: Add 1½ cups puréed artichoke bottoms.

Broccoli: Add 1½ cups puréed broccoli.

Spinach: Add 1½ cups puréed spinach.

Dessert Soufflé

4½ TABLESPOONS BUTTER
4½ TABLESPOONS FLOUR
1½ CUPS BOILING MILK
6 EGGS, SEPARATED,
PLUS 2 EGG WHITES/
½ CUP SUGAR

PREHEAT OVEN TO 375 DEGREES

Melt butter and blend in flour smoothly. Add milk and cook, stirring constantly, until thick. Add egg yolks and beat in well. Add your chosen flavoring (see below). Cool mixture slightly. Beat egg whites until they form soft peaks. Add the sugar gradually and continue beating until they form stiff peaks. Fold into the yolk mixture. Grease a 9-cup soufflé dish and dust it with sugar. Pour in mixture and bake in a 375-degree oven 35 minutes, or until puffed and lightly brown. Serves 6. Serve with a sauce of melted ice cream with a little whipped cream added to it.

VARIATIONS:

Minted Chocolate: Add 2 squares of unsweetened chocolate, melted, and a dash of mint liqueur to the yolk mixture.

Vanilla: Add 1 tablespoon vanilla extract.

Lemon: Add ¼ cup lemon juice and 1 tablespoon grated lemon rind.

Liqueur: Add ¼ cup of Grand Marnier, Chartreuse, crème de cacao, or other liqueur of your choice.

BARD	To lay a piece of bacon, or salt or fresh pork fat over any part of meat you wish to protect (such as a delicate breast of poultry or game). Tie the bard in place with white kitchen string. Barding fat usually is removed before serving, except in the case of game, which is customarily served with it.
BASTE	To pour or brush melted fat, water, wine, or other liquid over food. A bulb baster is most handy for this operation.
BEAT	To mix briskly with a spoon, whisk, rotary beater, or electric beater, so that the ingredients beaten will be thoroughly combined.
BEAT LIGHTLY	A term usually applied to eggs, meaning to beat gently with a fork to mix yolks and whites completely, but not to beat them so much that they become frothy.
BEAT STIFF	As applied to egg whites, this means to beat with an electric or rotary beater until almost dry, and until peaks will hold their shape when the beater is lifted up through the whites. (The action of most electric blenders is too severe for this process and the whites simply remain liquid.) The term is also applied to heavy cream, which should be watched carefully when it begins to thicken to be sure that it doesn't turn into butter.
BIND	To hold foods together with a liquid or sauce, so that they form a cohesive mass.
BLANCH	In American terminology this means to immerse foods in boiling water briefly, or sometimes to boil for a couple of minutes. The French sometimes speak of blanching a vegetable for as long as 15 minutes (as with cabbage to remove the strong taste); this is what Americans call parboiling. One purpose of blanching is to make it easier to slip off the skins of nuts, tomatoes, and some fruits.
BOUQUET GARNI	A combination of herbs, preferably fresh, tied together in cheesecloth and immersed in a dish during the preparation. It is always removed at the end of the cooking. The basic components are a sprig of parsley, a stalk of thyme, a stalk of celery, and a bay leaf. Other herbs sometimes added are basil, chervil, tarragon, rosemary, savory, and garlic. In this book, the additions are always given when the recipes have specific requirements.
BRAISE	Cooking meat or vegetables in hot fat to brown them. A small amount of liquid is then added, and the food is cooked, covered, over low heat.
BREADING	Covering in crumbs. Often food is first dredged with flour, then dipped in beaten egg, then in crumbs.
BRUSHING	To coat food with melted fat or liquid. A pastry brush is most satisfactory for accomplishing this job.
CARAMELIZE	To melt sugar over low heat, stirring constantly with a wooden spoon, until sugar turns liquid and browns to the degree desired.

301

CLARIFY	See *Clarifying Stock* (page 276) and *Clarified Butter* (page 283).
CRISPING GREENS	To prepare lettuce or other greens for salad by first washing in cold water, draining, and refrigerating for two or more hours.
DE-GLAZE	To dissolve the browned particles and dried juices left in a pan after food has been browned, by pouring in a liquid and stirring. The flavorful stock that results is used as a base for gravy or sauce.
DE-GREASE	To remove fat from the surface of hot liquid. This can be done with a skimming spoon or with paper towels. If you have time to let the liquid cool and chill in the refrigerator, the top layer of solidified fat can easily be removed with a knife or spatula.
DICE	To cut food into cubes.
DREDGE	To cover food completely with a dry ingredient, such as flour or crumbs. It can be done by shaking the food in a paper bag with the dry ingredients (and seasonings, if desired), or by using a shaker designed for the purpose.
FILLET	A boneless piece of fish or meat. Filleting is the process of de-boning and cutting.
FINISH	To add butter to a hot sauce just before serving. It is added a little at a time off heat. The sauce should not be reheated.
FLAMBÉ	When warmed liquor is poured over food and set ablaze. Sometimes known in the United States as "blazing," or "flaming."
FOLD	To combine gently two or more ingredients, using a spoon, a spatula, or the hand. This usually is called for when a mixture is too delicate for hard beating. Whatever implement you use for folding, put it down through the mixture to the bottom of the bowl, across, and up to the top. This is continued until the ingredients are well mixed but still retain air.
FRY	To cook food in fat. In pan frying, food is cooked in shallow fat over moderate heat. In deep-fat frying, food is completely immersed in very hot fat.
GARNITURE	In the United States this refers to a decoration on a dish; in France it refers to anything added to a dish after it is cooked.
GASTRITE	A glaze composed of dark caramelized sugar and red wine vinegar which also adds flavor. It is often used in the preparation of duck.
GLAZE	This term has several meanings. First, ham and pork and some other meats may be glazed by brushing over them, during the last half hour of cooking, jam or honey or just sugar, which will become shiny and sometimes a little caramelized. Vegetables may be glazed in butter, often with a little sugar. Then, the French also use the term to indicate running a dish covered with a sauce (frequently containing a bit of whipped cream) under the broiler to brown and "glaze." The French call this a "glaçage."
JULIENNE	Food cut into match-like strips.
KNEAD	To work dough (folding, turning, and pressing with the heels of

the hands) until it becomes smooth and elastic, or whatever way the particular recipe requires. There are dough hook attachments for some mixers which take all the work out of this job.

LARDING   To insert thin strips of fat into lean meat. Fat for larding (usually salt pork or bacon) should be cut into rectangular slabs, then cut in thin strips (lardoons) of whatever length is required by the thickness of the meat to be larded. It should be kept cold until you are ready to use it. A larding needle is required for this process. It is threaded with fat, inserted into the meat and pulled through, leaving the fat in place inside the meat. Trim the ends flush with the meat, unless the recipe instructs otherwise.

MARINADE   Usually a mixture of oil, acid (wine or vinegar), and seasonings in which food is soaked (marinated) prior to cooking to season it and sometimes to tenderize it. The marinade, or some of it, is often used in the cooking or saucing of the dish.

MASKING   Covering food completely with aspic or a thick sauce such as mayonnaise.

MEAT GRADES   Beef, veal, and lamb are all graded by the Government and the grades stamped in purple on the entire length of the carcass. "Prime," the highest grade, is marbled and encased with fat, which is a sign of tenderness. True Prime meat is scarce and is bought mostly by clubs and restaurants. "Choice" is the next grade and the best available in most retail markets. It is less fatty and thus more economical than Prime. The next grade is "Good," which is suitable for pot roasts and other braised-meat dishes, but not for roasting or sautéing.

Make use of the great variety of meats available. Veal and lamb, for some reason, are little appreciated by Americans. Both are delicious if properly cooked, which is to say, *not* overcooked. Lamb, roasted until just pink, is magnificent and highly underrated.

A good butcher should be sought out by anyone who is serious about cooking. Sadly, the small, independently-owned butcher shops are disappearing from the scene. However, when you see that a supermarket meat section is well run, offering good, fresh cuts of meat, ask the chief butcher to advise you on your meat requirements.

MIREPOIX   A mixture of herbs, diced vegetables, and sometimes ham, cooked gently in butter, and used in the preparation of many sauces and sauced dishes.

OIL   When a recipe in this cookbook calls for oil in which to sauté or fry foods, it means vegetable oil of any kind you like. These oils are almost tasteless and odorless and do not burn as readily as does butter. Peanut oil has perhaps the least flavor and odor of any such oil. Frequently, you will be asked to use part oil (to

303

prevent burning) and part butter (for flavor). The French are also inclined to use vegetable oil for salad dressing.

PARBOIL   To cook food in boiling water until partially done. The French call this blanching.

POACH   To simmer food gently in a hot liquid.

QUATRE ÉPICES, OR ''FOUR SPICES''   A combination of spices much used in France. Years ago each purveyor of spices had his own formula. Today the usual mixture is about 1 cup ground white pepper, 1½ tablespoons powdered cloves, 3½ tablespoons powdered ginger, and 4 tablespoons freshly grated nutmeg. A similar mixture is available prepared, as Spice Parisienne, under the Spice Islands label.

REDUCE   See Reduction of Sauces at beginning of Sauces section.

RENDER   To melt down animal fat so that the liquefied fat can be separated from connective tissue.

ROUX   A mixture of flour and butter cooked together for a few minutes before addition of liquid. For a white sauce, this is done over low heat so that the roux will not brown. For a brown sauce, the mixture is browned before liquid is added.

SAUTÉ   Cooking or browning food on top of the range in a small amount of fat. Foods to be sautéed should be dry on the surface and there should be no crowding of pieces in the skillet.

SCALD   To heat a liquid (such as milk) just to the boiling point, but not letting it boil. When the scalding point is reached, tiny bubbles will appear around the edge of the pot.

SCORE   To make slashes in food with a sharp knife. Can apply to meat and to bread or cakes before baking.

SEAR   To brown food fast over high heat or in a hot oven. Usually refers to meat. The process seals in the juices and adds flavor.

SIMMER   To cook gently in liquid below the boiling point. Bubbles coming to the top of the liquid should be only barely observable.

SKIM   To remove scum, fat, or other floating substances from a liquid. It is usually done with a spoon, or a type of slotted spoon called a ''skimmer.'' To remove fat, it is often best to lay a paper towel over the surface, then lift it off when it is saturated.

SLIVERING   Cutting food into thin pieces, as with nuts.

STEAMING   Cooking food over boiling water which does not touch it. There are specially constructed pots for steaming, also racks which can be put into pots to lift the food above the water. Steaming is sometimes used also with reference to food cooked in a very little liquid or fat, as with onions to make them ''soft, but not brown.''

STEWING   Cooking long and slowly in liquid.

TRUSS   To tie the wings and legs of a bird to the body so that shape is not lost in cooking. A ball of white string in the kitchen for such purposes (and many others) is indispensable.

Equivalent Weights & Measures

	WEIGHT OF 1 CUP	CUPS IN 1 POUND	MISCELLANEOUS
MEAT, COOKED, DICED	5 oz.	3⅛	1 lb. lean boneless meat makes 1 lb. cooked
ALMONDS, WHOLE SHELLED, SLIVERED, OR CRUSHED	5½ oz.	3	
BUTTER & OILS	½ lb.	2	1 stick=8 tablespoons=½ cup
BREAD CRUMBS, DRY	¼ lb.	4	1 slice=⅓ cup
BREAD CRUMBS, FRESH AND SOFT	1 oz.	16	1 slice=¾ cup
CHEESE, GRATED	¼ lb.	4	
CHOCOLATE			1 square=1 oz. (Does not always apply to chocolate packaged in oblong pieces.)
FLOUR: ALL PURPOSE, SIFTED	¼ lb.	4	
FLOUR: ALL PURPOSE, UNSIFTED	4⅓ oz.	3⅔	
FLOUR: BREAD, SIFTED	¼ lb.	4	
FLOUR: CAKE, SIFTED	3⅓ oz.	4¾	
GELATIN			1 envelope=1 tablespoon =¼ oz.
MACARONI, 1-INCH PIECES, UNCOOKED	¼ lb.	4	1 lb. after cooking measures 9 cups
RICE, LONG-GRAIN, UNCOOKED	6½ oz.	2½	Rice about triples in volume while cooking.
SUGAR, BROWN, PACKED	7 oz.	2¼	
SUGAR, GRANULATED	8 oz.	2	
SUGAR, CONFECTIONER'S, PACKED	4⅝ oz.	3½	

Liquid Measure Equivalents

LESS THAN ⅛ TEASPOON	Dash
3 TEASPOONS	1 tablespoon
2 TABLESPOONS	1 fluid ounce
3 TABLESPOONS	1 jigger
4 TABLESPOONS	¼ cup
5 TABLESPOONS PLUS 1 TEASPOON	⅓ cup
8 TABLESPOONS	½ cup
12 TABLESPOONS	¾ cup
16 TABLESPOONS	1 cup
2 CUPS (16 FLUID OUNCES)	1 pint
2 PINTS	1 quart
4 QUARTS	1 gallon

Sources of Ingredients   Some of our recipes call for ingredients which are common to the cookery of other nations and which may be difficult to obtain in your own locality. There follows here a selected list of stores in the New York City area that we have found to be reliable sources for such exotic items. Almost all of these stores fill mail orders.

Bazaar de la Cuisine, Inc., 160 East 55th Street, New York, N.Y. 10022
*Every kind of cookware, mostly imported.**

Cheese of All Nations, Inc., 153 Chambers Street, New York, N.Y. 10007
Cheeses from all over the world.*

Mrs. de Wildt, 4B Lakeview Drive, Kinnelon, New Jersey 07405
*Oriental ingredients, especially Indonesian.**

Eastern Trading Company, 2801 Broadway, New York, N.Y. 10025
Ingredients from all Oriental countries.

House of Yemen East, 370 Third Avenue, New York, N.Y. 10016
Middle East specialties. Fine selection of coffees.

Java-India Condiment Co., 438 Hudson Street, New York, N.Y. 10014
Indian specialties.*

Katagiri and Company, Inc., 224 East 59th Street, New York, N.Y. 10022
*Japanese and Chinese specialties, many in cans. Soy sauce. Fresh gingerroot.**

Manganaro Foods, 488 Ninth Avenue, New York, N.Y. 10018
Every Italian specialty and delicacy.*

Maryland Gourmet Mart, Inc., 412 Amsterdam Avenue, New York, N.Y. 10024
*Specialties and game.**

Nyborg & Nelson, Inc., 937 Second Avenue, New York, N.Y. 10022
Scandinavian specialties, including anchovies in oyster sauce and many other canned fish.

H. Roth & Son Paprika Co., 1577 First Avenue, New York, N.Y. 10028
Wide selection of spices and herbs, dried beans and legumes.
*Almond paste. Wheat (Bulgur). Tarhonya noodles. Strudel dough. Cooking accessories, including spätzle makers.**

Sahadi Importing Co., 187 Atlantic Avenue, Brooklyn, N.Y. 11201
Many ingredients for Middle Eastern cookery, including
Bulgur wheat and feta cheese.*

Trinacria Importing Co., 415 Third Avenue, New York, N.Y. 10016
Imported foods from all over the world, with special emphasis on India and Italy.

* Catalog or price list available

Acknowledgments

Rosenthal Studio-Haus
Lord & Taylor | B. Altman & Co. | Bonniers | Georg Jensen
Bloomingdale's | Gimbels | Alexander's | Tablerie | D/R International
Boutique Margot | Cardel, Ltd. | I. D. Fabrics, Inc.
John Matouk & Co. | Nettle Creek Industries | Desley Fabrics, Inc.
Kirk Brummel Associates | Karl Mann Associates
Belgian Linen Associates | The Wallpaper Council | Raymor
Hopbrook Farm, Holmdel, New Jersey
Meiselman Imports, Inc. | H. E. Lauffer Co., Inc. | Arthur M. Miller Associates
Jean's Silversmiths, Inc. | Wallace Silversmiths, Wallingford, Conn.
Waterford Glass, Inc. | R. F. Brodegaard & Co., Inc. | Etco Industries, Inc.
Dorothy C. Thorpe Creations, Inc. | Peter Breck Corp.
Decorative Crafts, Inc. | Royal Crown Derby, Boston, Mass. | Lough & Amsterdam
Georges Briard Designs | Herman C. Kupper, Inc.
La Rosa Bakery | Zampieri Bakery | Baird Farm, Sugarloaf, New York
Department of Marine & Aviation, New York City

All are located in New York City except where address is given.

Index

Picture references in italics

A

Aïoli sauce, 281
Alaskan salmon trout, 42
Allemande sauce, 281
Alsatian apple tart, 67
Amaretti, zabaglione with, 141
Américaine sauce, 281–282
Anchovy
  butter, 48
  sauce, 282
Anise
  fig tarts, 68
  frozen soufflé, 258
Appetizers, 20–26, 84–90, 148–152,
    210–215
  barquettes of lamb, 24, *27*
  beignets of artichoke bottoms, 150
  caviar
    Malossol Beluga, with blinis,
      85–86
    smoked salmon with, 211
    steak Tartare canapés with, 22
    sturgeon and, 87
  celery with brandied Roquefort,
    148
  couronne of whole Brie, 84–85
  crabmeat Imperial, 19
  crêpes
    avocado, 212–213
    green spinach, 23–24
  deviled clams fried in shell, 213
  eggs
    Maintenon, 26
    omelette grand'mère,
      214–215, *220*
    poached Armenonville, 214
    Tartare, 210
  escabèche of scallops, 210–211
  fish milt in shell, 150–151
  galantine of pheasant, 21–22
  lamb in lettuce leaves, 148
  mousse
    chicken liver, 23
    ham in whole peaches, 211, *217*

  of trout, Four Seasons, 149–150
  mussels
    chilled stuffed, 20–21
    in pink sauce, 148–149
    stuffed, 88–89
  oyster(s)
    baked, fines herbes, 89
    fried, in horseradish
      sauce, 89–90
    and mushroom tartlets, 25–26
  quiche aux endives, 24
  salmon
    smoked, with caviar, 211
    smoked, cornets of, 149
  seviche à la Four Seasons, 212
  shrimp
    crisped with mustard fruit, 151
    Kiev, 151–152
  smoked eel, sauce verte, 87
  snails, ramekins of, 19
  soufflés
    marrow, in crust, 90
    morel, in crust, 213–214
  steak Tartare canapés, 22, *27*
  sturgeon and caviar, 87
  talmouse with sweetbreads and
    brains, 25, *27*
  terrine
    of hare with pistachios,
      20–26, *27*
    Winter Farmhouse, 88
  trout
    mousse, Four Seasons, 149–150
    smoked native, 22
Apple(s)
  Alsatian tart, 67
  honey-glazed with applejack
    cream, 67
  Hudson Valley cake, 68–73,
    262–263
  loin of pork stuffed with, 56–57
  vichyssoise, 90–95
Applejack

  chicken baked in, 170
  cream, 67
Apricot(s)
  glaze, 297
  glazed, loin of pork with,
    113, 119
  sherbet, 266
  soup with sour cream, 26
Artichoke bottoms, 247–248
  beignets of, 150
  gratinés, 62
  sautéed, Périgourdine, 248
  stuffed with foie gras, choron, 62
  stuffed with spinach, 192
Asparagus, 192–193
  Mornay, 193
  Parmesan, 193
  Polonaise, 194
  sherbet, 266
  soup, 152
  wild, Chinoise, 194
Aspic
  beef in, 237–238, *251*
  port, 278–279
Avocado
  crêpes filled with crabmeat,
    212–213
  sautéed calf liver with, 111
  and shrimp Louis, 255
  with sliced white radish, 254–255
  soup, cream of, *217*, 221

B

Bacon, wilted spinach with, 257
Barquettes, 296–297
  of lamb, Lebanese, 24, *27*
Basic royale (soup garniture), 280
Basque chicken, 42–43
Bass
  sea
    baked stuffed, *30*, 34–35
  striped
    bourride, 159

cold, 223–224
Batters, 292–294
   See also names of batters
Béarnaise sauce, 282
Béchamel sauce, 282
Beef, 46–53, 105–110, 174–175,
      237–243
   in aspic, 237–238, *251*
   Bourguignon, 106
   carbonnade of, Flamande, 107
   consommé, 276
   English mixed grill, *104,* 105–106
   entrecôte for two, 243
   filet mignon
      poivre flambé, *39,* 47
      Stroganoff, 48–52
      twin tournedos with woodland
         mushrooms, *167,* 174
   pot-au-feu ménagère, 107–108
   steak
      with anchovy butter, 48
      double, stuffed with
         oysters, 47–48
      Gypsy, sauce Bordelaise, 107
      Occitane, 46–47
      Roquefort, 243
      sirloin Bercy, 174–175
      sirloin Niçoise, 175
      Tartare, 108–109
   steak Tartare, canapés with
      caviar, 22, *27*
   stock, 276
   tripes à la mode de Caen, 109–110
Beets, jellied consommé with
      onions, 215–216
Beignets
   batter, 292
   red caviar, 41
Bisque
   caraway squash, 31
   lobster, 33–34
Black Forest cake, 202–203
Blinis, 86

Blueberry sherbet, 266
Bluefish à la Grenobloise, 35
Boeuf Bourguignon, 106
Bordelaise sauce, 283
Boston sole Four Seasons, 100
Bouchée(s), 292
   à la Toulousaine, 182
Bouillabaisse, 231–232
   salad, saffron sauce, 254
Bourride, 159
Brains, calf
   en brioche, sauce Périgourdine,
      244–245
   deviled, 183–184
   talmouse with, 25, *27*
   in tomatoes, 244
Bread, 84–85
   sauce, 283
Brioche, stuffed legs of
      baby lamb en, 185–186
Broccoli Mornay with smoked
      salmon and shrimp, *156–157,*
      163–164
Brown sauce, 283
Bûche de Noël, 135
Buckwheat blinis, 86
Butter(s)
   anchovy, 48
   clarified, 283–284
   cream, 297
   hazelnut, 244
   lemon, 183
   maître d'hotel, 284
   shellfish, 284
   tarragon, 226

C

Cabbage
   chukar partridge in cognac with,
      60–61
   red, au caramel, 62–63
   stuffed, à la menagère, 129
Café Santos parfait, 140

Cakes
   Black Forest, 202–203
   decorations for, 298
   decorative burning on, 298
   Four Seasons Fancy, *264,*
      268–270
   Genoise, 299
   Hacienda, 138–139, *262–263*
   Hudson Valley, 68–73, *262–263*
   Hungarian cheese, 202, *262–263*
   sponge, 299
Calf brains, *See* Brains
Capon à la Sainte Ménéhould,
      102–105
Caramel
   filigree, 77–78
   red cabbage au, 62–63
Caraway squash bisque, 31
Carbonnade of beef, Flamande, 107
Cardinal sauce, 287
Carp, baked, 37
Carré of lamb Bretonne, 55–56
Carrot(s)
   blinis, 86
   purée of, 129
   spiced vichyssoise, 216
Cassoulet de Toulouse, 112–117
Caviar
   beignets, 41
   Malossol Beluga, with blinis,
      85–86
   smoked salmon with, 211
   steak Tartare canapés with, 22, *27*
   sturgeon and, 87
Celery with brandied Roquefort,
      148
Cévenole, 286
Champagne
   breast of chicken paprikás in, 43
   sauerkraut with, 63
   truffled chicken in, 170–171
   turbot braised in, 38–41
Chartreuse of vegetables, 124,

126–127
Chaud-froid, mayonnaise for, 288
Chausson of strawberries, 141–142, *145*
Cheddar cheese soup, 95
Cheese
  breast of chicken with, 236, *242*
  Brie, couronne of, 84–85
  Cheddar, soup, 95
  Gruyère, baked chicken with, 169
  Parmesan
    asparagus with, 193
    baked chicken with, 169
  Roquefort
    brandied, celery with, 148
    steak with, 243
Cheese cake, Hungarian, 202
Chestnuts
  brace of quail with purée of, 61
  purée, 130
Chicken, 42–46, 102–105, 169–171, 233–236
  in applejack and cream, 170
  Basque, 42–43
  breast of
    baked with two cheeses, 169
    with cheese and tongue, 236, *242*
    guinea hen with dariole of noodles, 45–46
    with herbed mushrooms, 235–236
    Monte Carlo, 169
    paprikás in champagne, 43
    Polignac, 233–234
    quenelles with creamed mushrooms, 44–45
    scallops, 234
    suprême, with oysters in cream, 43–44
    truffled, in champagne, 170–171
  consommé, 277

livers, hot mousse of, 23
poularde, stuffed, 102
poule-au-pot, 234–235
poulet à la Sainte Ménéhould, 102–105
poulet sauté Beaulieu, 171
squab
  Crapaudine, 235
  in casserole, *158*, 173
stock, 277
See also Turkey
Chilies, green, and corn soufflé, 248
Chinese snow peas, *see* Mange-touts
Chipolata sausages, 32–33
Chocolate
  icing, 77
  nut crêpes, 74–75
  sauce, 291
  Velvet Four Seasons, 76–77, *262–263*
  white, ice cream, 204
Choron sauce, 284
Chukar partridge in cognac with cabbage, 60–61
Clams
  curried soup, 152–153
  deviled, fried in shell, 213
Coffee cup soufflé, 136
Confit d'oie, 112, 117
Consommé
  beef, 276
  Bellevue, 153
  chicken, 277
  of game with quenelles, 32
  jellied beet and onion, 215–216
Corn and chili soufflé, 248
Coupe filigree, 77–78
Couronne of whole Brie, 84–85
Court-bouillon, 277
Crabmeat
  avocado crêpes filled with, 212–213

baked flounder stuffed with, 161
baked whitefish with, gratinée, 231
  Casanova, 160
  Imperial, 19
  soufflé Neptune, 97
  in sweet peperoni, 257
Crabs, soft-shell, amandine, 159–160
Crayfish, gratin of, 36
Cream puffs, 292
Crème Anglaise, 291
Crème Heart, 268
Crème pâtissière, 298
Crêpes
  Aurora, 137
  avocado, filled with crabmeat, 212–213
  batter, 292–293
  chocolate nut, 74–75
  green spinach, 23–24
  Harlequin, 200
  Scotch, Four Seasons, 37–38
  toasted strawberry, 201
Croissants, 293–294
Croquembouche Bruno, 203–204
Croustades, 294
Cucumber salad Ilona, 199
Curry (ied)
  clam soup, 152–153
  loin of pork, 118–119
  mayonnaise, 288
Custard, soft, 291

D

Dandelion and egg salad, 198
Désir de roi, 137
Desserts, 67–78, 135–145, 200–204, 258–270
  apple
    Alsatian tart, 67
    honey-glazed with applejack cream, 67
  apricot sherbet, 266

basics, 297–299
blueberry sherbet, 266
Bûche de Noël, 135
cakes
    Black Forest, 202–203
    Four Seasons Fancy, *264,*
        268–270
    Hacienda, 138–139, *262–263*
    Hudson Valley, 68–73,
        262–263
    Hungarian cheese, 202,
        262–263
Chocolate Velvet Four Seasons,
    76–77, *262–263*
coupe filigree, 77–78
Crème Heart, 268
crêpes
    Aurora, 137
    chocolate nut, 74–75
    Harlequin, 200
    toasted strawberry, 201
croquembouche Bruno, 203–204
désir de roi, 137
diplomat pudding, 137
figs, anise tart, 68
French rice pudding, 260
gâteau progrès, 138
lemon
    sherbet, 266
    and tea granita, 267
lime sherbet, 266
nectarine sherbet, 266
orange sherbet, 266
pain perdu banane, 135–136
palmiers, 259–260, *262–263*
parfait
    café Santos, 140
    Kabuki, 78
    sherbet, 266
Paris brest, 140
peach(es)
    flamed in bourbon, 265
    sherbet, 266

pear(s)
    in meringue, 68
    sherbet, 266
pineapple
    bourdaloue, 139–140
    sherbet, 266
raspberry sherbet, 266
rhubarb
    mousse, 201–202
    sherbet, 266
Riz à l'impératrice, 75–76
semolina pudding, 201
sherbets, 265–266
soufflés
    anise, frozen, 258
    basic, 300
    coffee cup, 136
    lemon zest, frozen, 258–259
    raspberry, frozen, 258
strawberry(ies)
    Charlotte, 267–268
    chausson of, 141–142, *145*
    fresh, in cassis, 200
    sherbet, 265–266
    sugar-glazed, 78
    toasted crêpes, 201
    vacherin, 200
tarts
    Alsatian apple, 67
    anise fig, 68
    fruit, 259, *262–263*
tea and lemon granita, 267
Torte Sorrano, *70–71,* 73–74
white chocolate ice cream, 204
zabaglione with amaretti, 141,
    262–263
Diable sauce, 284–285
Diplomat pudding, 137
Dover sole, turban of, 100
Dressings, *see* Salad dressings
Duck, 101, 236–237
    crisped, with peaches and
        sauce cassis, 236–237

Farmhouse au poivre, 42
roast
    mallard, with olives, 58
    sauce bigarade, 101
Duxelles, 285
    Italian, 285

E
Eel, fillet of smoked,
    sauce verte, 87
Egg(s)
    and dandelion salad, 198
    Maintenon, 26
    omelettes
        grand'mère, 214–215, *220*
        poached, Armenonville, 214
        with sweetbreads, sauce
            Béarnaise, 184
    Tartare, 210
Endive
    and grapefruit salad, 65, *69*
    quiche, 24
English mixed grill, *104,* 105–106
Entrecôte de boeuf for two, 243
Escabèche of scallops, 210–211
Espagnole sauce, 283

F
Fall, 20–78
    appetizers, 20–26
    beef, 46–53
    desserts, 67–78
    duck, 42
    fish, 34–42
    game, 58–61
    lamb, 55–56
    pork, 56–57
    salads, 65–66
    seafood, 34–42
    soups, 26–34
    veal, 53–55
    vegetables, 62–63
Fancy cake, *264,* 268–270

Fiddlehead ferns, 194–195
  gratinées, 195
Figs
  anise tart, 68
  candied, pigeon with, 172
Filet mignon
  poivre flambé, *39*, 47
  Stroganoff, 48–52
  twin tournedos with woodland
      mushrooms, 167, 174
Fish, 34–42, 97–100, 159–166,
    223–233
  Alaskan salmon trout, 42
  bluefish à la Grenobloise, 35
  bouillabaisse, 231–232
    salad, saffron sauce, 254
  bourride, 159
  carp, baked, 37
  fillet of sole
    Béarnaise, 228
    Boston, Four Seasons, 100
    Caprice, 228
    Dover, turban of, 100
    Four Seasons, 227–228
    Orly, 228–231
    sautéed with shrimp, 160–161
  flounder
    baked, stuffed with
        crabmeat, 161
    barquette of, 224
    frogs' legs Provençale, 37
  halibut, bourride, 159
  milt, in shell, 150–151
  pike quenelles, 162–163
  red snapper
    baked, 99
    bourride, 159
  salmon
    chaud-froid, 164
    mousse, mountain trout
        filled with, 233, *240–241*
    poached, with sauce
        Hollandaise, 41

Scotch crêpes Four Seasons,
    37–38
  smoked
    broccoli Mornay with, 163–164
    with caviar, 211
    cornets of, 149
    steaks en papillote, 226–227
  sea bass, baked stuffed, *30*, 34–35
  shad roe, 164–165
  smoked eel with sauce verte, 87
  stock, 277
  striped bass
    bourride, 159
    cold, 223–224
  sturgeon and caviar, 87
  trout
    amandine, 160
    boned, à la point, 165
    mountain, filled with salmon
        mousse, 233, *240–241*
    mousse, Four Seasons, 149–150
    salmon, Alaskan, 42
    smoked native, lemon
        mayonnaise, 22
    whole, in soufflé, 166
  turbot
    bourride, 159
    braised in champagne, 38–41
  whitefish
    baked with crabmeat,
        gratinée, 231
    bourride, 159
  See also Frogs' legs;
      Seafood; Snails
Flageolets
  minted, 195–196
  purée, 63
Flounder
  baked, stuffed with crabmeat, 161
  barquette of, 224
Foie gras
  artichoke bottoms stuffed with, 62
  veal chops stuffed with, 181

Fondue soufflé Four Seasons, 300
Frangipane, 298
French dressing, 285
French rice pudding, 260
Frogs' legs
  Provençale, 37
  in vermouth with truffles, 161
Fruit tart, 259, *262–263*

G

Galantine of pheasant, 21–22
Game, 58–61, 120–123
  chukar partridge in cognac with
      cabbage, 60–61
  consommé with quenelles, 32
  duck, mallard, roasted with
      olives, 58
  hare
    saddle of, Chantreau, 122
    terrine with pistachios,
        20–26, *27*
  pheasant
    galantine of, 21–22
    with juniper berries
        and gin, 120
    roast, *50–51*, 59
    salmis of, 59–60
    with fresh tarragon, 120
  quail
    brace, purée of chestnuts, 61
    stuffed with game pâté, 120–121
  sauce, 285–286
  stock, 278
  venison
    cutlet, grand veneur, 58
    estouffade of, 122–123
    saddle of, sauce poivrade, 123
  wild turkey, salmis of, 121–122
Garniture
  cévenole, 286
  grand'mère, 286
Gâteau Progrès, 138
Gaufrettes, 294

Gazpacho, green tomato, 31
Genoise cake, 299
Gin, pheasant with, 120
Glace de viande, 278
Glossary of cooking terms, 301–304
Goose
    cassoulet de Toulouse, 112–117
    preserved, 117
    wine-braised, *94*, 101–102
Granita, tea and lemon, 267
Grapefruit and endive salad, 65, *69*
Green mayonnaise, 288
Green tomato gazpacho, 31
Gruyère cheese, baked chicken
        with, 169
Guinea hen, breast of, with dariole
        of noodles, sauce Smitane,
        45–46
Gypsy beefsteak, sauce
        Bordelaise, 107

H

Hacienda cake, 138–139, *262–263*
Halibut, bourride, 159
Ham, mousse, in whole
        peaches, 211, *217*
Hare
    saddle of, Chantreau, 122
    terrine with pistachios, 20
Harlequin crêpes, 200
Hazelnut butter, 244
Hearts of palm and zucchini
        salad, 199
Herbs and spices, 275
Hollandaise sauce, 286
Horseradish sauce, 89–90
Hudson Valley cake, 68–73, *262–263*
Hungarian cheese cake, 202,
        262–263

I

Ice cream
    shells, 294

white chocolate, 204
Italian duxelles, 285

J

Jelly roll, 298–299
Juniper berries, pheasant with, 120

K

Kabuki parfait, 78
Kidney(s)
    veal
        flambéed in Armagnac,
            243–244
        in mustard cream, 111
        with rosemary, 55
Knob celery soup, 95–96

L

Lamb, 55–56, 105–106, 112, 117,
        185–192, 246–247
    carré of, Bretonne, 55–56
    cassoulet de Toulouse, 112
    chops
        braised in lettuce, 191
        deviled, 247
    English mixed grill, *104*, 105–106
    Lebanese barquettes of, 24, *27*
    in lettuce leaves, sweet and
            sour, 148
    mignonnettes, with chanterelles,
            246–247
    moussaka, 117
    noisette of, 188–191
    rack of
        boned, in crust, *178–179*
            186–188
        roast persillée, *180*, 188
    roast epaulets with rosemary,
            191–192
    roussette of, 185
    stuffed leg of, en brioche,
            185–186
Lebanese barquettes of lamb, 24, *27*

Leeks
    à la Grecque, 65–66
    cleaning, 66
    in cream, 130
Lemon
    butter, 164–165, 183
    frozen zest soufflé, 258-259
    mayonnaise, 22
    sherbet, 266
    and tea granita, 267
Lentil soup with sausages, 32–33
Lettuce
    lamb chops braised in, 191
    lamb in, sweet and sour, 148
    soup, cream of, 33
Lime sherbet, 266
Liver
    calf, sautéed with avocado, 111
    chicken, hot mousse with
            sauce suprême, 23
Lobster
    Américain in croustade, 225–226
    aromatique, 97
    bisque, 33–34
    broiled, with tarragon butter, 226
    croustade, 97–98
    gratin of, 36
    à la nage, 35–36
    quiche, 98
    sauce, 287
    in shell with spiced
            mushrooms, 255
    soufflé Neptune, 97
    Thermidor, 162

M

Madeira sauce, 287
Maître d'hotel butter, 284
Malabar dressing, 256
Mallard duck with olives, 58
Malossol Beluga caviar with
        buckwheat, potato, and carrot
        blinis, 85–86

Maltaise sauce, 287
Mange-touts(s) *180*, 197
  and pickled veal salad, 199
Mango rice, 132
Marinade, 278
Marrow soufflé in crust, 90
Mayonnaise, 287–288
  for chaud-froid, 288
  curry, 288
  green, 288
  lemon, 22
Melba sauce, 291
Meringue, 294–295
Mignonnette sauce, 288
Mimosa salad, 256–257
Minted flageolets, 195–196
Morel(s)
  soufflé in crust, 213–214
  soup, 153
  veal cutlets, meadow, with,
    181–182
Mornay sauce, 288
Moussaka, 117
Mousse
  chicken liver with sauce
    suprême, 23
  of ham in whole peaches,
    211, *217*
  of rhubarb, 201–202
  salmon, mountain trout filled
    with, 233, *240–241*
  of trout, Four Seasons, 149–150
Mousseline sauce, 288
Mulligatawny, 222–223
Mushrooms
  herbed, breast of chicken with,
    235–236
  and oyster tartlets, 25–26
  quenelles of chicken breast
    with, 44–45
  salad
    raw, 66
    raw, Malabar dressing, 256

scallops with shrimp and, 165
soup, cream of, 153–154
spiced, lobster in shell with, 255
wild, rack of veal with, 175–176
woodland, twin tournedos with,
  167, 174
Mussels
  chilled stuffed, 20–21
  cleaning, 21
  marinière, 98–99
  in pink sauce, 148–149
  stuffed, 88–89
Mustard
  crumbs, 184–185
  dressing, 288
Mutton, *see* Lamb

N
Nantua sauce, 287
Nectarine sherbet, 266
Noodles
  breast of guinea hen with
    dariole of, 45–46
  Charlotte, 64
  tarhonya, 64
Nuts, chocolate crêpes, 74–75

O
Olive(s)
  and onion salad, 198
  roast mallard duck with, 58
Omelette, grand'mère, 214–215, *220*
Onion(s)
  boiled tiny white, 131
  in onions, 130–131
  and ripe olive salad, 198
  soup
    golden jellied, 154
    gratinée, 96
Orange sherbet, 266
Oyster(s)
  baked, fines herbes, 89
  double steak stuffed with, 47–48

fried, in horseradish sauce,
  89–90
and mushroom tartlets, 25–26
sauce, 289

P
Pain perdu banane, 135–136
Palmiers, 259–260, *262–263*
Parfait
  café Santos, 140
  Kabuki, 78
  sherbet, 266
Paris brest, 140
Parmesan cheese
  asparagus with, 193
  baked chicken with, 169
Parsley, fried, 196
Partridge in cognac with cabbage,
  60–61
Pastries, 292–294
  See also names of pastries
Pâté, Winter farmhouse, 88
Pâte à choux, 295–296
Pâte à crêpes, 292–293
Pâte beignet, 292
Pâte brioche, 295
Peach(es)
  crisped duck with, sauce
    cassis, 236–237
  flamed in bourbon, 265
  mousse of ham in, 211, *217*
  sherbet, 266
Pear(s)
  glazed, deviled pork chops
    with, 57
  in meringue, 68
  and potato salad, *128*, 134
  sherbet, 266
Peas
  petits pois à la Française,
    248–249
  See also Mange-touts
Périgourdine sauce, 287

Petits pois à la Française, 248–249
Pheasant
    galantine of, 21–22
    roast, *50–51*, 59
    salmis of, 59–60
Pigeon, 171–173
    with candied figs, 172
    potted, with wild rice, 171–172
Pike, quenelles of, 162–163
Pimientos, purée of, 196
Pineapple
    bourdaloue, 139–140
    sherbet, 266
Pistachio nuts, terrine of
    hare with, 20–26, *27*
Pork, 56–57, 105–106, 112, 113,
    118–119
    cassoulet de Toulouse, 112
    chipolatas, 32–33
    chops, deviled, with pears, 57
    double rack of, smoked, 56
    English mixed grill, *104*, 105–106
    loin of
        braised, 119
        curried, 118–119
        with glazed apricots, *113*, 119
        stuffed with apples, 56–57
    roast suckling pig, boned, 118
    sausages, lentil soup with, 32–33
Port wine sauce, 34–35
Potato(es)
    blinis, 86
    julienne of, 197
    Parisienne, 249
    and pear salad, *128*, 134
    roesti, 131–132
    sautéed, 249
        Lyonnaise, 250
        Murat, 250
        à la Provençale, 250
        sablées, 250
        Sarlandaise, 250
    sweet

    glazed, 196
    tangerine, 132
    vichyssoise, 96
    vichyssoise, 154
Pot-au-feu ménagère, 107–108
Poule-au-pot, 234–235
Poulet
    à la Sainte Ménéhould,
        102–105
    sauté Beaulieu, 171
Pudding
    diplomat, 137
    rice, French, 260
    semolina, 201
Puff pastry, 296

Q

Quail
    brace of, with purée of
        chestnuts, 61
    stuffed with game pâté, 120–121
Quenelles
    of chicken breast with creamed
        mushrooms, 44–45
    consommé of game with, 32
    of pike, 162–163
    rosemary, 280
Quiche
    aux endives, 24
    lobster, 98

R

Radishes, white, avocado with,
    254-255
Ragoût of veal Niçoise, *40*, 54
Ramekins of Snails, 19
Raspberry(ies)
    frozen soufflé, 258
    sherbet, 266
Ratatouille Niçoise, 250, *261*
Red cabbage, au caramel, 62–63
Red snapper
    baked, 99

    bourride, 159
Rhubarb
    mousse of, 201–202
    sherbet, 266
Rice
    à l'impératrice, 75–76
    with mangos, 132
    pudding, French, 260
    risotto con pignole, 195
    with saffron, 132–133
    wild
        nutted, 198
        potted pigeon with,
            171–172
Rich pastry, 296
Ris de veau, 182
Risotto con pignole, 195
Riz à l'impératrice, 75–76
Roquefort cheese
    brandied, celery with, 148
    steak with, 243
Rouille, 232

S

Saffron
    rice, 132–133
    sauce, 254
Salad(s), 65–66, 134, 198–199,
    254–257
    avocado
        and shrimp Louis, 255
        with sliced white radish,
            254–255
    bouillabaisse, saffron sauce, 254
    crabmeat, in sweet peperoni, 257
    cucumber Ilona, 199
    dandelion and egg, 198
    endive and grapefruit, 65, *69*
    leeks à la Grecque, 65–66
    lobster, in shell with
        spiced mushrooms, 255
    marinated turnip, dill dressing,
        134

mimosa, 256–257
mushroom
　raw, 66
　raw, Malabar dressing, 256
onion and ripe olive, 198
pear and potato, *128*, 134
pickled veal and mange-tout, 199
spinach, wilted, with bacon, 257
tomato, 134
turkey, julienne of, 256
zucchini and hearts of palm, 199
Salad dressings
　French, 285
　Malabar, 256
Salmon
　chaud-froid, 164
　mousse, mountain trout filled
　　　with, 233, *240–241*
　poached, with sauce
　　　Hollandaise, 41
　Scotch crêpes Four Seasons,
　　　37–38
　smoked
　　broccoli Mornay with shrimp
　　　and, *156–157*, 163–164
　　with caviar, 211
　　cornets of, 149
　steaks en papillote, 226–227
　trout, Alaskan, 42
Sauces, 280–291
　aïoli, 281
　Allemande, 281
　Américaine, 281–282
　anchovy, 282
　Béarnaise, 282
　Béchamel, 282
　Bercy, 174–175
　bigarade, 101
　Bordelaise, 283
　bread, 283
　brown, 283
　cardinal, 287
　cassis, 236–237

chocolate, 291
choron, 284
crème Anglaise, 291
diable, 284–285
duxelles, 285
Espagnole, 283
game, 285–286
Hollandaise, 286
horseradish, 89–90
Italian duxelles, 285
lobster, 287
Madeira, 287
Maltaise, 287
Melba, 291
mignonnette, 288
Mornay, 288
mousseline, 288
mustard dressing, 288
Nantua, 287
Niçoise, 175
oyster, 289
Périgourdine, 244–245
poivrade, 123
port wine, 34–35
reduction of, 280–281
saffron, 254
salmis, 121–122
Smitane, 46
soubise, 289
suprême, 102, 289
sweet, 291
tomato, 289
velouté, 290
verte, 288
Victoria, 290
vinaigrette, 285
white wine, 290–291
yogurt dressing, 291
Sauerkraut with champagne, 63
Sausages
　chipolatas, 32–33
　lentil soup with, 32–33
Scallops

escabèche of, 210–211
with mushrooms and shrimp, 165
seviche à la Four Seasons, 212
in shell, 41
Sea bass
　baked stuffed, with port wine
　　　sauce, *30*, 34–35
Seafood, 34–42, 97–100, 159–166,
　　　223–233
　bouillabaisse, 231–232
　　salad, saffron sauce, 254
　clams
　　curried soup, 152–153
　　deviled, fried in shell, 213
　crab, soft-shell amandine,
　　　159–160
　crabmeat
　　avocado crêpes filled with,
　　　212–213
　　baked flounder stuffed
　　　with, 161
　　Casanova, 160
　　soufflé Neptune, 97
　crayfish, gratin of, 36
　lobster
　　Américain in croustade,
　　　225–226
　　aromatique, 97
　　bisque, 33–34
　　broiled with tarragon
　　　butter, 226
　　croustade, 97–98
　　gratin of, 36
　　à la nage, 35–36
　　quiche, 98
　　Thermidor, 162
　mussels
　　chilled stuffed, 20–21
　　marinière, 98–99
　　in pink sauce, 148–149
　　stuffed, 88–89
　oysters
　　baked, fines herbes, 89

316

double steak stuffed with,
47–48
fried, in horseradish
sauce, 89–90
and mushroom tartlets, 25–26
scallops
escabèche of, 210–211
with mushrooms and shrimp,
165
seviche à la Four Seasons, 212
shrimp
and avocado Louis, 255
broccoli Mornay with smoked
salmon and, *156–157*,
163–164
crisped, with mustard
fruit, 151
fillet of sole sautéed
with, 160–161
gratin of, 36
Kiev, 151–152
soufflé Neptune, 97
See also Frogs' legs; Snails
Seasoning, correcting, 276
See also Herbs and spices, 275
Semolina pudding, 201
Senegalese soup, 223
Seviche à la Four Seasons, 212
Shad roe in lemon butter, 164–165
Shallot soufflé, 133
Shellfish
butters, 284
See also names of shellfish;
Seafood
Sherbet, *262–263*
apricot, 266
asparagus, 266
blueberry, 266
lemon, 266
lime, 266
nectarine, 266
orange, 266
parfait, 266

peach, 266
pear, 266
pineapple, 266
raspberry, 266
rhubarb, 266
strawberry, 265–266
tomato, 266
Shrimp
and avocado Louis, 255
broccoli Mornay with smoked
salmon and, *156–157*,
163–164
crisped, with mustard
fruit, 151
fillet of sole with, 160–161
gratin of, 36
Kiev, 151–152
scallops with mushrooms and, 165
Snails
à la Mistral, 166
ramekins of, 19
Soft-shell crabs amandine, 159–160
Sole, fillet of
Béarnaise, 228
Boston, Four Seasons, 100
Caprice, 228
Dover, turban of, 100
Four Seasons, 227–228
Orly, 228–231
sautéed with shrimp, 160–161
Sorbet, *See* Sherbet
Sorrel, soup, cream of, 221
Soubise sauce, 289
Soufflés
anise, frozen, 258
basic, 300
coffee cup, 136
corn and chili, 248
dessert, 300
entrée, 300
fondue Four Seasons, 300
lemon zest, frozen, 258–259
marrow, in crust, 90

morel, in crust, 213–214
Neptune, 97
raspberry, frozen, 258
shallot, 133
whole trout in, 166
Soup, 26–34, 90–96, 152–154,
215–223
apricot with sour cream, 26
caraway squash bisque, 31
Cheddar cheese, 95
consommé
Bellevue, 153
of game with quenelles, 32
jellied beet and onion, 215–216
cream
of avocado, *217*, 221
of lettuce, 33
of sorrel, 221
of squash, 222
curried clam, 152–153
garnitures, 279–280
basic royale, 280
green spinach croustades, 279
rosemary quenelles, 280
gazpacho, green tomato, 31
knob celery, cream of, 95–96
lentil, with sausages, 32–33
lobster bisque, 33–34
morel, 153
Mulligatawny, 222–223
mushroom, cream of, 153–154
onion
golden jellied, 154
gratinée, 96
Senegalese, 223
vichyssoise, 154
apple, 90–95
spiced carrot, 216
sweet potato, 96
watercress, 216
wild asparagus, cream of, 152
Spätzle, 64–65
Spinach

artichoke bottoms stuffed
with, 192
crêpes, 23–24
croustades, 279
Elizabeth, 253
parfait of, 250–253
salad, with bacon, 257
Sponge cake, 299
Spring, 148–204
appetizers, 148–152
beef, 174–175
chicken, 169–171
desserts, 200–204
fish, 150–151, 159–166
lamb, 185–192
pigeon, 171–173
salads, 198–199
seafood, 159–166
soups, 152–154
veal, 175–185
vegetables, 192–197
Squab chicken
in casserole, *158*, 173
Crapaudine, 235
Squash
and caraway bisque, 31
soup, cream of, 222
with walnuts, 253
Steak
with anchovy butter, 48
double, stuffed with
oysters, 47–48
filet mignon
poivre flambé, *39*, 47
Stroganoff, 48–52
twin tournedos with woodland
mushrooms, *167*, 174
Gypsy, sauce Bordelaise, 107
Occitane, 46–47
Roquefort, 243
Tartare canapés with caviar, 22
Stock, 276–279
beef, 276

chicken, 277
clarifying, 276
court-bouillon, 277
fish, 277
game, 278
veal, 279
Strawberry (ies)
Charlotte, 267–268
chausson of, 141–142, *145*
fresh, in cassis, 200
sherbet, 265–266
sugar-glazed, 78
vacherin, 200
Stroganoff, rare fillets of
beef, 48–52
Sturgeon and caviar, 87
Summer, 210–270
appetizers, 210–215
beef, 237–243
chicken, 233–236
desserts, 258–270
duck, 236–237
fish, 223–233
lamb, 246–247
salads, 254–257
seafood, 223–233
soups, 215–223
veal, 243–246
vegetables, 247–253
Suprême sauce, 289
Sweet dough, 297
Sweet potato (es)
glazed, 196
tangerine, 132
vichyssoise, 96
Sweetbreads
bouchée à la Toulousaine, 182
eggs with, sauce Béarnaise, 184
medallions of, sautéed with
mustard crumbs, 184–185
stuffed, 245–246
talmouse with, 25, *27*
Syrup, simple, 299

T

Tangerine, sweet potatoes with, 132
Tarhonya noodles, 64
Tarragon
butter, 226
pheasant with, 120
Tartlets, 296–297
oyster and mushroom, 25–26
Tarts, 296–297
Alsatian apple, 67
anise fig, 68
fruit, 259, *262–263*
Tea and lemon granita, 267
Terrine
of hare with pistachios, 20–26, *27*
Winter Farmhouse, 88
Tomato (es)
calf brains in, with hazelnut
butter, 244
concassées, 290
gazpacho, green tomato, 31
salad, 134
sauce, 289
sherbet, 266
Tongue, breast of chicken with,
236, *242*
Torte Sorrano, *70–71*, 73–74
Tournedos with woodland
mushrooms, *167*, 174
Tripes à la mode de Caen, 109–110
Trout
amandine, 160
boned, à la point, 165
mountain, filled with salmon
mousse, 233, *240–241*
mousse, Four Seasons, 149–150
smoked, with lemon mayonnaise,
22
whole, in soufflé, 166
Truffles
chicken in champagne with,
170–171
frogs' legs in vermouth with, 161
Turbot

bourride, 159
braised in champagne, 38–41
Turkey
breast of
julienne of, 256
Xeres, 105
wild, salmis of, 121–122
Turnips marinated with dill
dressing, 134

V

Vacherin layers, 297
Vanilla sugar, 299
Veal, 53–55, 104–106, 110–111,
175–185, 243–246
bouchée à la Toulousaine, 182
calf brains
en brioche, sauce
Périgourdine, 244–245
deviled, 183–184
sautéed with avocado, 111
in tomatoes with hazelnut
butter, 244
chops
sautéed Zingara, 54
stuffed with foie gras, 181
cutlets
grand'mère, 110–111
meadow, with morels, 181–182
Parisienne, 183
with primeurs, 173
English mixed grill, *104*, 105–106
kidneys
flambéed in Armagnac,
243–244
in mustard cream, 111
with rosemary, 55
pickled, and mange-tout
salad, 199
Pojarski, 176
rack of, with creamed wild
mushrooms, 175–176
ragoût of, Niçoise, 54

saddle of, Orloff, 53
scallops, with lemon butter,
168, 183
stock, 279
sweetbreads
bouchée à la Toulousaine, 182
eggs with, sauce Béarnaise, 184
medallions of, sautéed with
mustard crumbs, 184–185
stuffed, 245–246
vitello tonnato, 245
Vegetables, 62–63, 124–133,
192–197, 247–253
See also names of vegetables
Velouté sauce, 290
Venison
cutlet of, grand veneur, 58
estouffade, 122–123
saddle of, sauce poivrade, 123
Vermouth, frogs' legs with
truffles in, 161
Verte sauce, 288
Vichyssoise, 154
apple, 90–95
spiced carrot, 216
sweet potato, 96
watercress, 216
Victoria sauce, 290
Vinaigrette sauce, 285
Vitello tonnato, 245

W

Walnuts
squash with, 253
zucchini with, 133
Watercress vichyssoise, 216
Weights and measures,
equivalents, 305
White chocolate ice cream, 204
White wine sauce, 290–291
Whitefish
bourride, 159
with crabmeat, gratinée, 231

Wild asparagus Chinoise, 194
Wild mushrooms, rack of veal
with, 175–176
Wild rice
nutted, 198
potted pigeon with, 171–172
Wild turkey, salmis of, 121–122
Wines
autumn, 78–79
for cooking, 274
spring, 205–206
summer, 271–272
winter, 143–144
Winter
appetizers, 84–90
beef, 105–110
chicken, 102–105
desserts, 135–145
duck, 101
farmhouse terrine, 88
fish, 97–100
game, 120–123
goose, 94, 101–102, 117
lamb, 105–106, 112, 117
pork, 105–106, 112, 113, 118–119
salads, 134
seafood, 97–100
soups, 90–96
veal, 105–106, 110–111
vegetables, 124–133
Woodland mushrooms, twin
tournedos with, 174

Y

Yogurt dressing, 291

Z

Zabaglione with amaretti,
141, *262–263*
Zucchini
and hearts of palm salad, 199
Niçoise, 253
with walnuts, 133